The Oldest Profession

The Oldest Profession

A HISTORY OF PROSTITUTION

Lujo Bassermann

Translated from the German by James Cleugh

NEW ENGLISH LIBRARY
TIMES MIRROR

First published in Great Britain by Arthur Barker Ltd., in 1967
This translation © 1967 by Arthur Barker Ltd.,

© 1965 by Econ-Verlag GmbH, Vienna and Dusseldorf
First published in Germany by Econ-Verlag under the title *DAS ALTESTE GEWERBE*
Eine Kulturgeschichte

*

FIRST NEL EDITION JUNE 1969

*

NEL Books are published by The New English Library Limited from Barnard's Inn, Holborn, London E.C.1. Made and printed in Great Britain by Hunt Barnard & Co. Ltd., Aylesbury, Bucks.

45000234 9

CONTENTS

FOREWORD

It is not exactly a pleasant reflection that the oldest commercial aim of humanity has been the exploitation of partiality to women. Consequently underground gossip about venal love has been prevalent throughout history and any discussion of it begins with an apology. But the present work differs from its important predecessors, above all, in having no need for any such excuses. Dufour's six volumes, for instance, appeared at a time when public morality and the ethical principles of private individuals functioned with relative efficacy in the control of society. Today, however, after two world wars and radical changes in government and social organization, the existence of prostitution may be reasonably and frankly admitted to be only one of the least harmful influences upon mankind. Nowadays no one regards prostitutes as more dangerous than political pressure groups. Even if whole classes of schoolchildren were to be taken on their walks through a red light district the dim little windows might be presumed to have far less effect upon any healthy youngster than the contemplation of a scene of murder acted on the television screen. The peril to public morals does not by any means arise only from sexuality. The undermining of ideals of conduct is much more harmful. Every scandal in which famous personalities are involved deepens the sense of insecurity not only among adolescents but also among the majority of adults. The phenomenon of prostitution, which after all is only occasionally noticed, does comparatively little damage in this way.

Accordingly, the subject of venal love and its place in the history of civilization have been treated in this book from the standpoint that these are historical themes and do not greatly differ from other features of human development. A history of torture, for example, would discuss far more drastic perversions of the nature of man than are dealt with here. A history of diplomacy would be concerned with a great deal more wickedness, venality and fraud than are to be found in the following pages, while if anyone were ever to give an honest and duly documented account of prison conditions, slavery or the marriage market, any public prosecutor would be more justified in ordering the confiscation of such a work than in seizing my own study of the oldest profession in the world.

The fact that gossip about prostitution was clandestine impelled me to undertake the work. For most of the events recorded in this connection took place quite openly. Taboos were imposed only upon consideration of the subject in historical literature. All France knew that Voltaire visited the establishment in the Hôtel du Roule, where Madame Justine Pâris put her girls at his disposal. But no one mentioned the fact. In my view such taboos are senseless, not only in the case of the man who wrote the *Pucelle* or the charming erotic romance of the princess from Babylon. Consequently I have taken the trouble to investigate the relations which have subsisted, ever since the days of Phryne and Praxiteles, between prostitution and art, and those, since the time of Aspasia and Pericles, between prostitution and politics. The attractions of such a journey through the centuries are mainly due to the prizes which it offers. But I also found it pleasurable because it almost always led along the heights. The lowlands of seaport taverns and street-corner brothels have changed astonishingly little between the era of the show-girls of the Piraeus and their modern successors. So I have used this framework merely to round off the central picture. I was also obliged to do so on practical grounds, since the hordes of nameless prostitutes are not only timeless but also have no history and can therefore be understood from their present representatives alone. On the other hand the women who were able to rise from the rank and file owing to their intelligence, beauty, popularity or simply good luck were soon recognized by contemporary observers, so that we too are enabled to cultivate their society.

In the space of a single volume it is of course only possible to notice a few such women, every one of whom enjoyed more varied experiences than a whole collection of respectable housewives. I have, moreover, given preference to those of less fame, since it is relatively easy to obtain information about the best known. The earliest beginnings of prostitution have also been disregarded in the present work, as all trace of their connection with modern times has now been lost. Neither prostitution as a form of hospitality nor religious prostitution can be plausibly related to subsequent practice in the sale of feminine favours. In any case the former customs had little influence during the historical period and their revival on any considerable scale is hardly to be expected.

Instead of assembling a succession of reports of obscene details and exclaiming on every tenth page how dreadful it all is, I have dispensed with both improprieties and moral censure. Prostitution cannot be regarded as even slightly obscure, ambiguous or latent in its working. It accordingly provides a most conspicuous bastion amid the stormy seas of sexuality.

I might also have been worried by the pointing finger of the moralist. For only too many people are anxious to browbeat others and have already invaded, on the most diverse pretexts, the private lives of adults in order to obtain an arena for repressed instincts of domination. Well, we cannot ignore wars, revolutions and epidemics. But there is really no special exertion required for the avoidance of brothels, strolling prostitutes or indecent films. Anyone who can't do so of his own accord or finds the sight of an occasional prostitute or the mere existence of prostitution offensive should indubitably visit a psychiatrist. Neither ordinary advice nor official prohibitions will be any good to him.

For these reasons I may as well state that I consider the sale of sexual satisfactions an integral part of the urban life of mankind. I regard it as one of the many constant and troublesome sources of danger in a tightly-packed community of this sort. Yet history and present experience alike prove that the perpetual mistakes made by civil authorities and administrators in dealing with the phenomenon are more dangerous than prostitution itself. There is no miraculous panacea for it. It is just one of those enigmatic poisons which can not only produce ruinous consequences but can also, if withdrawn from circulation, plunge the social organism into critical infection by other maladies.

Nevertheless, the very close connections which have existed at all historical periods between prostitution and society at large, together with the hidden reciprocal effects operating between the positive nucleus and its dangerous marginal environment, have suggested the need for stocktaking by historians. No such proceeding can solve the many outstanding problems of prostitution. But it can provide the data for solution in the form of a contribution by historians to a very modern debate between medical men, theologians, lawyers and government officials. No historian, however, has yet participated.

History creates distance. It does not have to be studied at close quarters as if it were an antechamber or guardroom full of depraved individuals. I have therefore been able and in fact obliged to refer to a number of surprising features which constantly recur in the collisions of serious, pseudo-serious and frankly non-serious components of society. Such references have been made in no spirit of frivolity but simply because I have not wished to become involved in the vortex of my material but to retain an overall view from a separate standpoint. I rely for my justification on the fine passage in which Lessing, a somewhat unconventional character, once wrote:

'Those who never do anything but lament their vices instead of deriding them have never really seemed to me very comprehensible in their abhorrence of such failings. Perhaps their lamentations are only due to fear of a punishment they do not wish to evade. But those who merely deride vice at the same time prove their contempt for it.'

L.B.

BOOK I

THE PAGAN SEX MARKET

*

Rivalry between Athens and Corinth

'The female heart is an Athenian market under a
gloriously blue sky.' – LUDWIG BÖRNE (1786–1837)

At no time and in no city in the world have prostitutes and their
trade been more active than at Athens and Corinth during the
golden age of Greek civilization. In modern Paris, London and
Tokyo unpaid and paid sexual pleasures have come to be enjoyed
to a certain extent in separate compartments of society. But in
ancient Greece every sphere of urban life was dominated by the
worship of Aphrodite.

Solon inaugurates a State brothel

It is not yet quite clear why the Greeks threw themselves with such
enthusiasm into the cult of prostitution. Possibly they hoped by this
expedient to escape homosexuality. On the other hand they may
simply have regarded the freedom they accorded to the female
devotees of Aphrodite as an incidental feature of the democracy
they held in such affection and guarded so jealously. It is certain,
however, that the philosopher and legislator Solon first prescribed
the brothel for Athenians in order to preserve them from homosexuality. It is equally certain that no medicine was ever so
delightedly swallowed.

The change is too striking to be referred solely to the development of Athens into a metropolis. During the heroic or Homeric
age of Greece women were regarded as items of the spoils of war,
objects of little more than material value. For example, the reputation of Lesbian women for special dexterity in the art of love interested the warriors of the Homeric era chiefly because higher
market-prices could be demanded for them as slaves.

Hesiod, too, in his *Works and Days*, growled out: 'Don't let yourself be beguiled by any woman who makes a show of her hinder parts when she comes to visit you in your humble dwelling with flattering words.' He thus condemns the same charms which once caused Prince Paris, who had obviously been corrupted at an early age, to postpone his decision between the merits of three beauteous goddesses until they had turned their backs on him.

The relative chastity of the Homeric age is to be attributed to the fact that the surplus energy of each sex was expended within its own limits, as was indeed obligatory owing to the strict separation between boys and girls then still in force. The males went to battle, which has at all times exhausted a considerable proportion of specifically masculine passions, and even while in camp practised the homosexuality then so specially important in preserving the solidarity of many military units and indeed the warlike spirit of whole nations.

Erotic cults and pastimes

Women's customs were less bloodthirsty. The number and course of their rites varied as the centuries advanced. Eventually wild popular festivals, called *Dionysia*, took place. Whole families participated in them, but everyone was permitted to let off steam in his own way. According to Thassilo von Scheffer, 'We can scarcely be said to have any very clear notion of what went on at such celebrations. Nor would modern sensibility be anything but repelled by such features of them as the unabashed carrying in procession of gigantic representations of the sexual organs in the guise of fertility symbols.' At a later stage genuine secret rites were introduced, such as the *Aphrodisia*. They were never officially recognized, but they had to be allowed in order to provide an outlet for the ardours of Greek femininity. Only women and girls took part in such festivals. Little is known of their details, but it is certain that at the feast of Aphrodite Anosia in Thessaly, for instance, flagellation was particularly in evidence and the rites terminated in a promiscuous orgy of what today is called 'Lesbianism'.

Pausanias, in his *Description of Greece*, declared: 'Women from Attica meet women from Delphi every year on Mount Parnassus, where they hold revels in honour of Dionysus. It is their custom to perform their dances at a number of places near the highway to

12

Athens. One of these localities is named Panopeus.'

Such outbreaks might occur annually or only once in four years. The Greek housewife, nevertheless, lived mainly in a narrow domestic seclusion. The woman who was least talked about or better still remained practically unknown elicited the most admiration. The streets and markets were frequented mostly by men, boys and the frivolous.

Solon extolled as a benefactor

It was in these social circumstances that Solon is said to have established the first brothel in Athens. The statement cannot be confirmed beyond doubt, for no decree dealing with any such step has survived. The belief rests only on the testimony of contemporaries and their descendants. Nikander of Colophon, a priest in the service of Apollo, categorically affirmed that the event took place. The Syracusan dramatist Philemon (361–263 B C), in his *Delphians*, addressed Solon as follows: "Thus didst thou become the benefactor of thy fellow-citizens, believing that such an establishment would secure their health and peace of mind. The place was unquestionably necessary, too, in a city where the impetuous young could no longer restrain themselves from tempestuously yielding to the most potent of nature's injunctions. Thou didst avert great mischief and inevitable disorder by installing women in certain houses.'

The eulogy proceeds in this style at such length and in so much detail as to render an erroneous tradition most unlikely. Moreover, the evidence of Nikander and Philemon is substantiated by Athenaeus, who recorded in fifteen volumes an immense number of quotations and paraphrases taken from the wise sayings and imaginative literature of ancient Greece.

Unfortunately for many schoolmasters who have misunderstood the truly libertarian spirit of Solon, it must follow that the brothel was domesticated, in Europe at least, not by one of the many voluptuaries of antiquity but by one of its few genuine sages. No doubt he had to defend himself against misinterpretation of his motives in taking such an initiative and hence made enemies. He may well have found his eventual decision very hard to arrive at. But he was not content merely to propose a measure. He himself did what he believed to be right. For in this sort of enterprise it

13

would be particularly dangerous to make a mistake. A false step would not only have ruined him politically but would also have covered him with ridicule.

Slave-traders under contract

Solon therefore acquired, on behalf of the State of Athens, a suitable building and ordered a supply of suitable women and girls from the slave-traders. At that period the training of a competent staff had long ceased to constitute a problem. On the contrary, the vast majority of the slave-traders, who were for the most part Levantines, took special care to instruct their young female charges in the highly esteemed technique of erotic cajolery. For the trader could then expect, in addition to the pleasure he experienced in educating his pupil, a much higher market price for her.

Solon's next step was to fix so low an entrance fee to his establishment that for this reason alone the Athenians made him the subject of their sincerest praise. He may have come to the statesmanlike conclusion that the rich being already well provided with slave-girls and concubines, the city's restlessness and the danger it represented to decent women and well-behaved maidservants arose primarily from the poorer strata of the population. It was alleged, however, that Athens drew considerable profits from this first of its brothels, a circumstance which provoked certain reproaches against Solon.

The *demi-monde*, always active in Athens, had nothing to worry about, for the more exacting of the female votaries of Aphrodite would in any case have scorned visitors to the public brothel. It did not affect the ladies in question if Scythian watchmen and yokels from Attica went to Solon's building to fill the public purse.

But this first brothel was soon followed by others. The merchandise grew more copious, the atmosphere more agreeable. The inmates achieved popularity even in smart society. A change was bound to come and it took the form of a defensive expedient still general in wage-earning groups exposed to aggression. A system of organization began.

Three classes of prostitutes

It naturally resulted in a threefold division, based upon distinctions which had become automatic in the course of time. They comprised the inmates of the brothels, called *deikteriades* (show-girls); the flute-players and dancers (*auletrides*); and finally the *hetairai*. According to Pierre Dufour, 'The first were, so to speak, slaves in the world of prostitutes, the second were their trainers and the third their sovereigns.'

From early history until the American Civil War the female slave served as the concubine of the head of the family and quite often as his sons' first mistress. Egyptian princes had their first erotic relations with young negresses and so did farmers' sons in Alabama, Mississippi and Georgia four thousand years later. But domestic slaves were usually safeguarded by custom and under the Roman Empire actually by law from the dismal fate of the common prostitute. The inmates of the Athenian brothels were therefore generally foreigners or unacknowledged by their parents. It soon became a profitable business to train recruits for such establishments.

A certain woman named Nikareta is related to have purchased seven little girls in the slave-market with a view to training them to become prostitutes. She must have embarked upon more than one of these transactions, for her long experience in the trade was obvious. In fact we know from a speech by Demosthenes that she regarded this work as her profession and made a good living out of it. One of the most famous of Greek hetairai, Neaera, graduated from her school. But usually the road from such 'educational' establishments led to Piraeus, the harbour settlement on a rocky peninsula two hours' journey from Athens, or else to Corinth, described by Pauly-Wissowas in his valuable *Encyclopaedia of Classical Antiquity* as 'perhaps the oldest but certainly the most frequented' city of prostitution in Greece, since hardly any decent people lived on the isthmus.

It was of course possible for many such slaves to purchase their freedom. In fact they could probably do so more easily than the less attractive or more morally straitlaced of those in the same unfortunate position. But promotion of this sort occurred rarely and scarcely ever led to social respectability. Much more often the result would be admission to the ranks of freelance hetairai, an ambition probably cherished by all *deikteriades*. Meanwhile they had to endure a life hardly more enviable than that of their modern successors. Such advantages as they derived from their situation as

State employees were more than counterbalanced by its drawbacks and restrictions.

They were controlled by petty officials, a circumstance which could not have been very agreeable. Their receipts, moreover, wree closely supervised and subject to a certain degree of taxation.

Taxation of prostitutes at Athens

This tax bore the significant name of *pornikotelos* and is alleged to have been in force at a very early period. Nothing is known of its originator, but it is clear that the Athenian Government, like those of modern countries, though eager enough to tax the wages of sin, experienced certain inhibitions about the method of collection. In antiquity the proceeds of certain taxes, tariffs or dues could be farmed out. In return for the payment of a prescribed commutation fee the exclusive right of collection of certain tributes or groups thereof could be awarded. The profits made by the purchaser depended entirely upon his personal energy or lack of scruple. In Rome, in medieval Provence, and above all in France at a later period, those who acquired the right of tax collection became very wealthy. But even in Athens those who paid for the privilege do not seem to have done so badly, if the indignant complaints of the *deikteriades* are to be believed. The lessees also exercised a certain influence on the spread of prostitution, since each new brothel that opened naturally increased their earnings.

The relatively modest State of Athens was obliged to finance ship-building and other armaments out of tax yield. Prostitutes were accordingly of special importance and every diminution in the numbers of *deikteriades* represented a definite loss to the Government. The women had to obtain a formal licence to cross the frontiers and to offer acceptable guarantees of their return. This stipulation did not work so oppressively as the protective custody which was imposed for many years on the inmates of several modern brothels. But the practical object in both cases was the same. The wretched females were not driven from the towns, as was customary in later centuries. But since the evil was recognized to be ineradicable it was resolutely accepted as a part of national life and placed under legal control, so that the State, at any rate, could benefit from its existence.

Strict regulations

One rule forbade the *deikteriades* to go out except in the evenings, at an hour when respectable women would only be abroad in exceptional circumstances. It is true that a different attitude seems to have prevailed in undisguised regions of prostitution, such as the environments of harbours or the city of Corinth. But even in these places prostitutes remained conspicuous. For Solon himself had invented a special form of garment for them and other Greek cities had followed the example of Athens. Certain colours which would attract the attention of the guardians of the law had to be worn by prostitutes. They do not seem to have raised any particular objection, for after all this rule was helpful to the promotion of their professional interests, as a sort of advertisement. The brothels were indicated just as unmistakably. They were not identified by the modern symbols, which are often misleading. Neither red lamps nor house numbers of exceptional size were used. The entrance was merely surmounted by a representation, either painted or carved in low relief, of the familiar Priapic emblem.

Such regulations, imposed by public authority, present an agreeable contrast with modern vacillation. One may take exception, in detail, to the measures adopted or regard them as impracticable nowadays. But they certainly prove that Athens remained consistently uncompromising in its attitude to the problem of prostitution. Once that attitude had been assumed it was neither exaggerated nor allowed to lapse. A double standard was not employed. The whole subject was kept clear of the official hypocrisy that prevails in nearly all capital cities today as soon as the word prostitution appears on municipal agenda.

Flute-players

Control of the flute-players and dancers (*auletrides*) was not quite so rigid as that of the 'show-girls' and brothels. As compared with the lowest class of prostitutes, who were mostly slaves, the *auletrides* had one great advantage. They had learnt a trade. They could dance and also perform on some musical instrument, usually the flute. They were not therefore absolutely compelled to earn their living by prostitution. In one sense, however, they were particularly exposed by the very nature of their profession. While the brothel-whores went about their business in the shadows of evening and

17

could choose any light they pleased to put their personal attractions on show, the flute-players had to act on festal occasions. They danced and made their music at banquets, holiday celebrations and ceremonies of all kinds, before large assemblies, under merciless illumination from every direction, so that no physical shortcoming could escape observation.

Athenaeus describes a wedding feast held at the house of a rich man, with its almost endless procession of courses, consisting mainly of poultry, from pigeons to partridges, and finally, 'just as we had most pleasantly taken leave of sobriety', in came the girl flute-players and vocalists. 'They all looked to me absolutely naked. But some of the guests declared that they wore a single flimsy garment.'

The *auletrides* were therefore clad for their professional displays either with their beauty unadorned, as in ancient Egypt, or else in the famous 'Coan vest', of a cobweblike texture which concealed nothing. In this garb they played the zither or the flute, beat drums, danced, sang and presented a variety of acts now performed at cabarets by men only, such as juggling, feats of gymnastics with drawn swords, fire-swallowing and so on.

Popularity of the auletrides

While the *deikteriades* were despised and the hetairai envied and often hated, the *auletrides* enjoyed considerable popularity. They appeared regularly at festivals and in fact were their principal attraction. Whatever might subsequently happen, with or without the girls' participation, was not regarded as debauchery but as covered by the general licence of behaviour allowed on such occasions. The mood of the revellers, invariably festive, was increased for hour after hour by the presence of the flute-players till this happy state of excitement finally burnt itself out in a climax of satisfaction.

The nicknames applied to most of these female acolytes of Aphrodite prove their general popularity. The familiar appellations by which girl musicians or dancers were known suggest a certain affection wholly lacking the facetious malice which the *deikteriades* and even often the hetairai had to endure. A particularly light-footed dancer was called Pyrallis ('little bird'). Another was compared with a specially sweet scent and a third, who was in the habit of appearing dazzlingly nude at the culmination of a banquet, was named Parene ('sparkler'). Sigea, the 'promontory', was so styled because many parents' hopes were wrecked on her account. She acquired immortality two thousand years later when the lawyer Nicolas Chorier of Grenoble borrowed her name for his *Conversations with Aloisia Sigea*. Certain writers of antiquity mention with compassion the fate of the fair Phormesium, who died in the arms of an ardent feminine admirer.

Banquets given by hetairai

Phormesium's death illustrates the strange relations subsisting between *hetairai* and *auletrides*. Both took part in festivals. Accordingly, just as Athenian ladies sometimes indulged in wild parties where men were not allowed, so the wealthy *hetaira* would occasionally give banquets to which, apart from her equally rich female friends and colleagues, only girl flute-players, dancers and singers were admitted. Such compensations for the company of males could be enjoyed easily enough as a result of the high degree of social independence open to such women.* In the famous letter included in the collection made by Alciphron a certain Megara begins by bitterly reproaching her female friend Bacchis for not turning up because of a husband when even Philumena, who had only just been married, slipped out of the matrimonial chamber to join the party. Megara then proceeds, however, to give Bacchis a confidential account of what actually happened there.

We had a glorious time – you deserve that cut to the heart, I think – singing, jesting and drinking till cockcrow. Perfumes, garlands and sweetmeats abounded. We feasted in the shade of bay-trees. In short, nothing was lacking but yourself. We've often drunk deep before, but seldom enjoyed it so much. The best of all was the competition between Thryallis and Myrrhina to decide which of them possessed the handsomest hindquarters . . . But there were other competitions of this sort too, for instance one about bosoms. When we came to the belly, though, none could compare with Philumena's, for it's never been deformed by childbirth and is as firm as ever. We went on like that all night long, while we cursed our lovers and yet wished ourselves more of them, for nothing is so interesting as a new love-affair. Then, after all this carousing, we

* Modern research among prostitutes in a capital city has shown that seventy-three per cent of the 500 women interviewed maintained lesbian relationships.

rushed out of doors and played all sorts of pranks in the streets, finishing up at the house of Deximachus in Golden Lane, for that boy's only just inherited a load of cash from his father.

Beauty competitions without male spectators

The details reported by Megara (which cannot be reproduced here) reveal a high level of gymnastic ability and skill in dancing among some of her feminine cronies. They were not mere strip-teasers who execute a few dance-steps simply as an excuse to undress. They were fully trained professional dancers or musicians well aware of their privileged status in society. They could accept or decline the blandishments of men just as they pleased or deny any request a lover might make. Sometimes enraged revellers, disappointed in their expectations, fell upon the flute-players with their fists, tore the costly and flimsy robes from their bodies and smashed their instruments.

The effects of the displays by *auletrides* were often too much for the dignity of the spectators. Philosophers and statesmen would forget what they owed to their self-respect and their public reputation. Antigonus, Satrap of Phrygia (382–301), once gave a reception for certain ambassadors from Arcadia at his court. Athenaeus describes most amusingly the exemplary and even modest behaviour of the diplomats throughout the meal provided, up to the moment when Antigonus called in the girl dancers. When the speed and ardour of the dances increased and the girls began to lay aside their clothing, the envoys from the much admired Arcadian countryside could no longer restrain themselves. They forgot where they were and made a rush for the *auletrides*. Antigonus collapsed in a paroxysm of laughter, though he had in fact anticipated some such transformation of his respectable visitors.

Bacchis and Megara

Bacchis appears from epistolary sources to have been a remarkably decent *hetaira*. Megara on the other hand is depicted as a particularly dissolute flute-player. Nevertheless, they were friends. Similar contrasts seem to have been common among both classes of women. But on the whole strikingly favourable accounts are given of the *auletrides*. Epicrates, a writer of comedies who flourished about the middle of the fourth century B C, declared: 'When in

20

search of pleasure avoid the *hetairai*. You'll be more easily contented with a flute-player.'

The rise to wealth and renown, so seldom the reward of *deikteriades*, came with comparative ease to the flute-player. Even if she did not acquire a rich lover, there were always a considerable number of usually well-heeled citizens, who found her a more attractive proposition than her rivals. For the *hetairai* were reputed to be addicted to the use of all sorts of artificial allurements, as well as of love-potions and other sordid expedients. But the *auletrides* could never disguise their faults and shortcomings. Such a musician or dancer could often date the start of an entirely new life from a single evening performance. Phayllus, the ruler of Phocaea, the most northerly of the Ionian cities of Asia Minor, sent the flute-player Bromiade, after being present at one of her displays, a large silver goblet and a gold wreath imitative of ivy-leaves. At the seaport of Alexandria two remarkably fine houses bore the names of the flute-players Mnesis and Pothyne. The Lagid emperor Ptolemy Philadelphus II* had presented the buildings to these girls. He was no indiscriminate libertine, but a monarch of notable energy and discretion.

Two ladies called Lamia

The most successful of all the *auletrides*, however, were Lamia the Elder and Lamia the Younger, both experts in flute-playing and the art of love. The first-named started her career modestly enough as Number Four in the famous team of Themistocles. But in the end she became rich enough to finance from her own resources the restoration of the ruined picture gallery at Sicyon in the Peloponnese, a city once celebrated for its painters. Lami the Younger was first employed at the court of the Lagid rulers of Egypt. She then became the mistress for many years of the Macedonian king Demetrius Poliorcetes (336–283), who had probably inherited the taste of his father Antigonus for flute-players. Demetrius had captured her after a sea-battle in 306, at which he had defeated the Egyptian fleet and seized Cyprus as well as the lady. But that highly-skilled instrumentalist, by this time fairly well on in years, proved a most dangerous acquisition. Her remarkable talents included not only

---

* Belonging to a dynasty of Macedonian kings founded by one Lagus. The family ruled Egypt from 323 to 30 B C. [J.C.]

mastery of the arts of love and music but also a degree of intelligence and education – to which her letters testify – that enabled her to dominate the Macedonian king to an exceptional extent. It was long before any of her younger rivals could supplant her.

Since Lamia was an Athenian by birth and Demetrius the enemy and conquerer of Athens, few liaisons of Greek antiquity were so much discussed and written about as that between the Macedonian monarch and his flute-player. The relationship appears to have been extremely passionate for both so that neither applicants for Lamia's favours not the king's other mistresses had the slightest chance of breaking it up. Whenever the pair were obliged to separate for a while Lamia kept her hold over Demetrius by correspondence.

Tributes to a Prostitute

As her name meant a sort of man-eating female monster and the Greeks were never ashamed of puns they were perpetually teasing her in verse and prose. Demetrius took his revenge by imposing on Athens after his conquest of the city a tribute of 250 talents of silver and making his mistress a present of this vast sum. Funds obtained in this way enabled Lamia, by then forty years of age, to behave like an oriental despot. The splendour of her festive occasions outshone anything that Athens had seen for many years. Eventually, so it was reported, she met her death during one of these fabulous orgies.

It was only then that the Athenians realized that their conquerer and tyrant had been subdued by one of their own countrywomen. She became the subject of legends and a temple dedicated to her as Aphrodite-Lamia was erected. Accordingly, though only after death, she had accomplished the long journey from the status of a humble flute-player to royal and finally divine honours. Nor, in spite of all those who slandered her, can she be denied admission to the Olympus reserved for the great lovers of all times.

The *hetairai*, accorded as much praise and blame as fell to the lot of Helen, have throughout history afforded more matter for debate than their colleagues in other parts of the world. There were unquestionably far fewer of them than there were of the *deikteriades* and *auletrides*. At a certain juncture only 135 *hetairai* could be counted in Athens. Yet individuals in the two lower classes have been forgotten and cannot now be identified. The *hetairai*, on the contrary, are so vividly remembered that even such a standard work of reference as Pauly's *Encyclopaedia of Antiquity*, which in other contexts regularly employs Latin appellations, makes the following reluctant admission in a footnote to its article under HETAIRAI. 'In this case we have deliberately departed from the principleon which we have acted in using only the Roman expression for the title of an entry. For in the present instance modern linguistic usage has been so overwhelmingly in favour of the Greek term that the investigator of the subject in question could hardly be recommended to turn in the first place to the franker Roman words SCORTUM or MERETRIX.

We must leave it to the keener sensibilities of philologists to determine why the Roman *meretrix* should be a 'franker' expression than the Greek *hetaira* ('companion'). It is certain, however, that although the idea remains familiar the 'subject in question' has not survived the course of the centuries. The last *hetairai* seem to have died about the same time as Torquato Tasso and Giordano Bruno. In other words they did not live to see the seventeenth century. They were succeeded by the courtesans.

A creation of the cities

The courtesan presupposes the court of a prince. But the *hetaira* flourished at her best in the temperate, democratic atmosphere of the Mediterranean city-states, from Athens to Venice and from Alexandria to Genoa. The precocious cosmopolitanism of these towns, their sunny markets by the seashore, the wealth of their commercial magnates, the admirable buildings and the exotic attractions of merchandise brought from distant parts of the world, all seemed to derive their special character, in those days, from the presence of *hetairai*. It was in this environment that they felt most at home, for the situation which had arisen through the seclusion of wives and the isolation of men of talent soon became a dominant feature of such cities owing to the unexpected increase in the numbers of *hetairai*, due to the astonishing rapidity with which these women reached positions of influence.

In German school dictionaries the word *hetaira* is translated *Buhlerin* ('mistress'), a perfectly good German word, but not much more intelligible for that reason. The Greeks meant *hetaira* to connote something like 'woman friend' or 'female companion', without trying to disguise its basic significance by such an idea. Surviving letters from *hetairai* and much historical evidence prove the existence of many lasting relationships between Athenian citizens and the women in question, liaisons which were not merely sexual. The *hetaira* was very often regarded by an Athenian as something more than a bed-companion, more also than the wife who shared his bed and board at home. Nor were *hetairai* always at anyone's disposal. They might often remain faithful to a single lover for months and years at a time and were capable of taking the initiative themselves when attracted by a man. In all that the *hetaira* was and did she differed entirely from a legitimate wife. But she also differed considerably from ordinary prostitutes, dancers and musicians.

Deikteriades *and* hetairai

These two classes really belonged to different worlds. The former haunted the shadows along a waterfront and were obliged to wear blonde wigs and distinctive clothing. Or else they waited, naked or scantily dressed, in the brothels or in the courtyards outside their cubicles, for seamen and foreigners. Xenarchus and Eubulus, writers of comedies, described the wretched existences of these slaves of love. When they grew old they hid in corners to entrap drunkards. While they were still young they covered their faces and breasts with transparent veils to allure clients. They enjoyed only one privilege, the inviolability of their brothels, where both they and their visitors were immune from interference. No father could pursue a son and no constable could arrest a criminal inside of these establishments.

The *hetairai*, on the other hand, participated fully in urban life. They strolled in broad daylight through the Ceramicus, a garden suburb between the Academy at Athens and a cemetery. It was very pleasant to go walking there or lounge in the shade of trees, in the privacy afforded by bushes or on comfortable benches. There were colonnades resembling those in the Palais Royal, the most extensive market for sexual pleasure that existed in France before the Revolution. The tombstones of the cemetery could be used as private letter-boxes. Beneath them reposed the remains of Athenians who had fallen in battle. But the surfaces, recording the feats of dead warriors, remained available for combats with weapons of a different kind. The *hetairai* were in the habit of inscribing upon the stones, with eyebrow-pencil, the names of men to whom they were ready to listen, while the citizen would write the name of the *hetaira* who attracted him.

The sex market

The working day of the *hetaira* accordingly began with the despatch of a slave girl to the 'post office' in the Ceramicus. The messenger would not have to be literate. It would be enough if she could recognize the marks forming the name of her mistress. If she did, the *hetaira* herself would go to read the inscription. It would usually be of a flattering character and quite frequently included a definite offer in hard cash. If she had no prior engagement, approved of the applicant and found the sum mentioned adequate, she would take a stroll in the evening to the tombstone on which her name had been written and arrangements could then be made for an encounter on more intimate terms. If she were too busy to accept the offer or refused it for other reasons, the consequences might be rather vexing for the applicant. Hundreds of people had read his offer and hundreds had seen him rebuffed. All the same, that happened to everyone sooner or later. We think of Athens as constituting a whole world. But it appears from the gossip of the comic dramatists to have been actually a microcosm where scarcely anyone could hope to keep his private activities a secret.

This state of affairs, however, implied that all the *hetairai* were well known, since any mention of their names immediately evoked a clear notion of their personalities. Little of what they did, accordingly, could escape public attention. Dufour stated that in the golden age of Athenian civilization 'no other woman, so to speak, existed. For the virgins and matrons remained obscure in their special accommodation, while the *hetairai* dominated the theatres and market-places. Most of them were of middle-class origin but had come down in the world, while retaining traits of beauty and cosmopolitan mentality . . . It was especially in the time of Pericles and influenced by his example that the Athenians adored these sirens and enchantresses, who did so much mischief to Greek morals and so much good to literature and art.'

25

Aspasia

The 'example of Pericles' was provided by Aspasia. The daughter of a certain Axiochus, she came from the Greek city of Miletus in Asia Minor to Athens. She is repeatedly cited by later defenders of the *hetairai* as a class, yet she was the most dangerous of all. For while her less educated and intelligent colleagues merely took money from their lovers, Aspasia cherished political ambitions. She schemed, prepared wars, and after the death of Pericles turned her next lover also into a 'tribune of the people'. She surrounded herself with a group of younger women who obeyed her orders and learnt so much from her that their very names were uttered with awe by the citizens. This exalted circle can hardly be regarded as a school for harlots, such as was maintained by Nikareta (see p. 15), but rather as a training college for *hetairai*.

Aristophanes blames Aspasai for starting the wars against Sparta and Samos. He declares that the second of these campaigns had begun because two of Aspasia's pupils had been abducted before obtaining their leaving certificates. Pericles had been granted a divorce for Aspasias' sake. He was obliged to fight hard, again and again, to hold his position, for she represented his exposed flank. Many attempts were made to attack him through her. He had to employ every resource of his masterly persuasive eloquence to save both her and himself from being condemned when a sensational suit was brought against her on political grounds.

Nevertheless, the personality and activities of Aspasia cannot be ignored in considering the Athens of Pericles. Socrates cultivated her society. Plato wrote favourably of her. No such evidence can be offered on behalf of any other member of her trade. The testimony is enough to ensure Aspasia her unique situation at the summit of the pyramid.

Thais

But she was by no means the only one of her kind to hold what may be called a 'court' or 'salon' and to exercise political and economic influence with a view to guiding the destinies of a city or a country. Thais, too, contributed to the history of civilization. She was a beautiful young Athenian who accompanied the victorious campaign of Alexander the Great through Persia.

Plutarch wrote:

At this time Alexander was again contemplating a further extension of the war against Darius. He and his friends arranged to indulge in yet another feast on a great scale. Prostitutes and their companions also came to take part in the carousal. The most famous of them was Thais, who later became the mistress of King Ptolemy. She flattered Alexander in judiciously chosen terms and jested with him. At last wine gave her the courage to make a suggestion thoroughly characteristic of her native city but over-bold for such a creature to utter. She exclaimed that all the hardships which she had been compelled to endure in her wanderings through Asia in the train of Alexander had been most richly recompensed by the present occasion, which enabled her to express her scorn for the proud capital of the kingdom of Persia. But it would give her even greater satisfaction, she added, if in a triumphant and riotous progress through the streets she could with her own hand, in the presence of Alexander himself, set fire to the palace of Xerxes, who had once laid Athens in ashes. Then, she concluded, the news would run through all the world that a weak woman in Alexander's retinue had taken sterner vengeance upon Persia for the invasion of Greece than ever the Greek generals and admirals of that time had been able to inflict.

A palace in flames

The proposal was greeted with exultation and applause. The guests crowded round Alexander and exhorted him to authorize the plan. At last he gave in to them and sprang to his feet. Garland on head and torch in hand, he led the revellers to the palace, which they surrounded. Other Macedonians, hearing what was afoot, ran, full of joyful excitement and carrying torches, to join them.

Such women demanded wars and palaces. They had the heads of executed prisoners handed to them on silver platters. Yet at all times the most bitterly reviled were those who merely asked for money. Such requests were regarded as the basest possible. The supposedly high-minded Thais, who avenged her native land more effectively than the Greek commanders-in-chief, married Alexander's general, Ptolemy, after the former's death, and so founded the Lagid dynasty. (See p. 21.) Another Greek *hetaira* bore a son who became King of Cyprus. The mother of Philetairus, King of Pergamum, was yet another. Themistocles, who is reported to have harnessed four *hetairai* to his chariot, which he then drove through the Ceramicus park, was not the son of a *hetaira*, though he is often said to have been. His mother was a *deikterias*, who charged only a few drachmae for her favours.

27

Luckily those *hetairai* whose superior intelligence and education attracted poets, thinkers and artists were more numerous and less troublesome than those who were taken up by statesmen. The rise of the former, non-political women to wealth was not so rapid, for even in classical Athens artists enjoyed no special material advantage in society. But their feminine companions acquired a less equivocal reputation than that of the richer minority of *hetairai*.

Such fame in its highest form was bestowed on the mistresses of sculptors and painters. The Greek artist could draw on a permanent supply of models from the ranks of the *hetairai* and *auletrides*, who were especially useful to their employers on account of the attention such women had always given to the cult of beauty in general and their own personal charms in particular. Many Greek statues seem eternally young, classical and ageless in the type of beauty they represent. One reason may well be that the models who posed were not just ordinary good-looking girls paid by the hour for undressing, but queens of the realm of love who unveiled for the express purpose of enchanting the spectator and were well aware of the effect produced by every line of their figures. Their friendship with an arist did not mean that they were either subordinate to or dependent upon him. In antiquity such relations carried no trace of the glumness so often evident at later times in Montmartre or Montparnasse. On the contrary, it is clear that many originals of the marble statues still extant were worshipped like goddesses.

Phryne of Thespiae

The most famous of the women thus adored was nicknamed, with a freakish humour due perhaps to a superstitious fear of excessive beauty, 'The Toad', for the Greek word *phrune* has no other meaning.* She transformed this appellation into one of honour and from all the accounts of her which survive her intelligence gave her every right to do so.

Like Aspasia, Phryne was not an Athenian by birth. She came from the small town of Thespiae, the ruins of which can still be seen near Erimokastro in Boeotia. Although the god Eros had always been preferred in Thespiae to all others, the most famous woman ever born there lived for a considerable time in poverty. The beauti-

---

* It was also applied to other *hetairai* in Athens. [J.C.]

ful Phryne had to earn her living as a girl by gathering capers. The back-breaking labour of plucking these buds from their tangled, thorny and low-growing bushes was at that time relegated to the poorest of the poor. Phryne's intense social ambition must have begun during those harsh years.

Her subsequent career proves that she had unusual self-control for a girl of her class and also a strength of character which, unless tradition has grossly idealized her, suggests that she, not Aspasia, should be regarded as the most resolute, independent and effective of all *hetairai*.

She never tried, like so many of her colleagues, to gain a reputation for intelligence or quick wits. She knew that nature had endowed her with a figure of rare perfection and realized from the start that it represented capital which she could invest to the greatest profit. In a country where nudity was not daily on view but where it was nevertheless not yet subject to Christian taboos, she avoided every occasion on which she would have been obliged, by local custom, to strip. She never visited the public baths, where it was hardly possible to exclude spectators from the corridors. Even her lovers were only permitted to embrace her in the dark. But whenever she was not acting simply as a *hetaira* but representing, as the most beautiful woman in Athens, the earthly incarnation of love, she had no hesitation in revealing every part of her person.

Phryne at Eleusis

Incontrovertible testimony exists that she appeared in the gateway of the temple, at the solemn climax of the Eleusinian Mysteries, as if she were a goddess, and laid aside her garments one by one in the presence of the assembled multitude. As soon as she assumed, after this ritual, the veil of purple, the ceremonies ended. During the festivals in honour of Poseidon and Aphrodite it was again Phryne who stripped on the temple steps and then walked naked, clad only in her black hair, through the crowds down to the seashore, where she dived into the water and re-emerged as Aphrodite. Those who had once seen her brushing the drops of moisture from her body on the beach and wringing out her wet hair never forgot the spectacle. It inspired painter after painter, from Apelles to Botticelli, and it was with Phryne's behaviour in this scene that the series began.

The proceedings at the sensational lawsuit against her can only be understood by realizing that all Athenians were familiar with the rites just described. Like all much envied persons Phryne was exposed to the machinations of blackmailers, then called sycophants. A man named Euthias acted, it seems, in this affair under the pressure of certain married women who were much disturbed by the Phryne cult, though Euthias may have been a rejected suitor, for Phryne was most fastidious and could not be persuaded, at any price, to receive those whom she disliked.

Euthias charged her with 'godlessness', one of those elastic legal terms the interpretation of which depends entirely on the atmosphere in court. Pericles, for instance, had been obliged to resort to the methods of an undisguised demagogue in order to clear Aspasia from the same accusation. Euthias maintained that Phryne's conduct during the Eleusinian Mysteries insulted divinity. But above all, he declared, she injured the State of Athens by her inroads on the wealth of its foremost citizens and her diversion of their attention from state business.

It appears incomprehensible today that Phryne should have been arraigned instead of the citizens who neglected public affairs. But to the ancient Greek mind it seemed quite natural for exceptional beauty in a woman to be irresistible and for those so spellbound to be acquitted of guilt. The whole decision then depended upon whether the indisputable beauty of Phryne could be regarded as exercising witchcraft or divine inspiration. Proof of the latter was scarcely to be obtained by mere rhetoric. But Hypereides, a former lover of Phryne, happened just then to be on intimate terms with two other famous *hetairai*, Bacchis and Myrrhina. Phryne asked her colleagues, with whom she was friendly, to intercede on her behalf. They recognized the danger which would ensue for all *hetairai* if Phryne were convicted and persuaded Hypereides to undertake the defence.

A sensational trial

The *Heliaia* ('Supreme Court') at Athens bore no resemblance to a modern tribunal. It comprised hundreds of members, who sat in unrestricted publicity. This enormous jury consisted of men who had to be over thirty but were not required to provide evidence of any special training. Nothing that Hypereides could allege against the prosecutor Euthias and in defence of Phryne had any effect on the cautious reserve of the assembly. His statement that Phryne had participated with all due piety, almost as a priestess, in the Mysteries, was received without enthusiasm. He had no choice but to try to recreate there and then, in open court, the solemn mood in which the ceremony in question was enacted. Accordingly, he walked suddenly up to Phryne, tore the veil and tunic from her body and showed her to the jurymen in the same state as that in which she had been revealed at the Mysteries.

It is possible that Hypereides actually took this step on the spur of the moment. But Phryne probably expected it, for the letters of Bacchis and Myrrhina show that his own speech had already been rehearsed, before the trial, in the form in which it was later published.

The scene in court, and Hypereides himself, acquired much celebrity. The *hetairai* had gained an important success by their concerted defence. Their solidarity is proved by the scorn which Myrrhina's action aroused when she accepted, probably through jealousy of Phryne, none other than Euthias, the prosecutor, as a lover.

May our lady Aphrodite see to it [Bacchis wrote to her], that you never find a lover with better taste than that Euthias whom you so revere, but go on living with him to your life's end. Silly woman! You are ruining yourself by such stupidity. However could you have brought yourself to pick on such an oaf? ... It looks as though you're deliberately trying to antagonize Hypereides, for I notice that he's not paying much attention to you these days. Well, he has a mistress worthy of him and you also have the kind of lover good enough for you. Just you ask him for something he doesn't want to give you and you'll soon find that you've been setting the docks on fire or undermining the security of the State. Mark my words. We all of us, we who serve the benevolent goddess Aphrodite, hate you like poison!

The model of Praxiteles

Phryne did not need the trial to make her famous. If she had not been famous already it would hardly have taken place. But it seems that thereafter she concentrated still more exclusively on the society of the great contemporary artists, where she was largely exempt from such plots as had brought her before the Supreme

31

Court. She revealed to the sculptors and painters what she withheld from her other lovers, for the artists gave her more than money. They gratified her ardent desire to shed the squalor of her humble origin and the mud which stuck so persistently to members of her trade. She admits this secret and yet unmistakable aspiration in a most admirable letter to the sculptor Praciteles.

Don't worry! You have created a work unlike any that has yet proceeded from human hands. You have set up the statue of your mistress in the temple grove. There I stand, between your Aphrodite and your Eros. Do not grudge me this honour. For all who see me there praise Praxiteles and on account of the skill with which you have created my likeness the Thespians now consider me worthy to stand among gods. Only one thing is lacking to render your gift to me complete. Come to me and let us go and lie together in the grove. We shall commit no sacrilege, by so doing, against the gods whom we ourselves have created.

She was not blaspheming but merely expressing a religious feeling different from our own, at a period when people still believed in meetings with gods and goddesses on hillsides and at the springs of rivers, when demigods were believed to inhabit the earth and the thrones of divinities might be found at a central point in any country. No priest could grant Phryne the increased respect she longed for. But Praxiteles, the carver of gods, could give it her.

She had nevertheless once deceived him for the sake of that grove in her native town of Thespiae, if we are to believe the story reported by both Pausanias and Athenaeus. Praxiteles had promised her one of his works, according to this anecdote, and she demanded the one which he himself considered his finest. But he prudently declined to answer. Accordingly she arranged that one day while she was with Praxiteles at his house one of her slaves should rush in with a cry of 'Fire! The studio's burning!' The sculptor turned pale. 'If my Eros and my Satyr have been destroyed,' he exclaimed, 'I shan't want to live any longer!' Phryne soon reassured him. But afterwards she told him that she wanted his Eros.

The nude Aphrodites
As the town of Thespiae was devoted to the cult of Eros and Phryne soon afterwards presented her birthplace with a splendid statue of the god, wrought of Pentelic marble, there is no need to suppose

that her choice of this work had been determined in so dramatic a fashion. It would have been quite natural for her to have decided on an Eros. Owing to the exceptionally high fees which Praxiteles commanded in his own lifetime the gift was of the highest possible value. The price paid for a statue by Polycleitus was a hundred talents. The cost of the Eros of Praxiteles at the time of its production may therefore be estimated as at least some £40,000. So great a sum can no longer be regarded as a payment to the artist but rather as a gift to the woman most intimately associated with the production of such works. Others presented by her were figures of herself. In addition to the portrait-bust she mentions in her letter there was a statue in pure gold dedicated to her in the holy city of Delphi. Whether she also served as the model for the well-known statue of the Cnidian Aphrodite, a Roman copy of which is preserved in the Vatican, remains a matter of dispute. Athenaeus declares that this work, with which representations of Aphrodite in the nude began, combined physical features derived from a number of different *hetairai* whom Praxiteles had assembled in his garden.

The scene was illuminated by the melancholy light of the moon. The group of girls suggested a gathering of nymphs. One lay carelessly on her back. Another was dancing, the night wind lifting the jealous folds of her tunic. A third, quite naked, glittered like a goddess, dazzlingly white against the shadowy background. Of a fourth, fully clothed, nothing could be seen but alabaster-like arms and shoulders. The bosom of a fifth was covered, but the most stimulating contours could be glimpsed through the openings in her robe.

The walls of Thebes

Phryne, fastidious as she was, remained nevertheless in such great demand that she grew very rich. But she used even her wealth to promote her ambition. Accordingly, just as Thais had taken vengeance on the Persians for the invasion of Greece by hurling a blazing torch into the palace at Persepolis, so Phryne, as a provincial patriot, meant to put to shame, through her ample funds the city of Thebes, more renowned than Thespiae and its long-standing antagonist. In the year 335 BC the Thebans had revolted against the young Alexander, who had then only recently come to power. Within twelve days the Macedonian king, not yet called the Great, had reached the city, stormed it and destroyed its fortifications. Six thousand of the citizens are said to have fallen, thirty thousand to have been sold into slavery. This punitive act caused Phryne to offer to restore the walls of Thebes at her own expense, provided that the city fathers would pledge themselves to have a slab affixed to the rebuilt fortifications inscribed with the legend: DESTROYED BY ALEXANDER AND RECONSTRUCTED BY PHRYNE THE HETAIRA. But the Thebans would not permit the *hetaira* from Thespiae to enjoy such a triumph. They preferred to wait twenty years, until in 315 Cassander, the new King of Macedonia, built new walls with Athenian help.

Phryne's good sense and self-control enabled her, in her declining years, to avoid the poverty and humiliation experienced by so many other once famous *hetairai*. She appears, moreover, to have remained beautiful, a matter which perhaps meant more to her than any amount of money, until the end. Her figure did not degenerate. Her complexion stayed fresh. Her favours never ceased to be coveted.

The city with love for sale

The only careers comparable with that of Phryne for prosperity were those of three *hetairai* called Lais, the last of whom had been lucky enough, while still a child, to attract the attention of the painter Apelles about 320 BC. The artist is said to have first noticed the girl while she was fetching water. The extraordinary grace of her movements as she came down the street with the pitcher on her head could not escape his professionally expert eye. That same evening he introduced the adolescent girl to the circle of his boon companions. When they demanded, with some annoyance, why he had brought a virgin to join their revels instead of a *hetaira*, he answered: 'Patience! In three years she'll be one!'

He seems never to have lost sight of her after that and to have supervised her education to the level required by any peasant girl for success in the exacting trade he had mentioned. She would perhaps have remained a slave all her life if Apelles had not bought her freedom. It is to his credit that he did not pay the ransom in order to possess her himself but set her at complete liberty.

Another Lais had been born in the seaport of Hyccara (now Carini) in northern Sicily and carried off to Greece in 414 or 413 BC during the disastrous Sicilian expedition undertaken by Athens.

The eldest of all was born in Corinth, where girls were trained in the temples for the service of Aphrodite and the citizens were used to immigrants, for the native women alone had long since been found insufficiently numerous to meet the needs of the seamen who transported their merchandise across the isthmus at this point. Corinth was not in general so important a city as Athens, but it was a regular metropolis for prostitution. Lais of Hyccara was accordingly soon provided with renowned lovers. One of her patrons, Aristippus of Cyrene, who later became a most celebrated philosopher, met her while he was still quite young and had to engaged in bitter polemics with the philosopher Diogenes for her sake. The latter sage, a member of the Cynic School, conformed with the precepts of its doctrine in being as unkempt and poverty-stricken as Aristippus was well-groomed, sophisticated and rich. Athens soon began to hear of the disputes of these two learned men about Lais the *hetaira*.

A failure by Demosthenes

The reputation of a subsequent Lais induced the great Athenian orator and statesman Demosthenes (d. 322) to visit her in Corinth. But instead of the thousand drachmae he had expected she demanded ten thousand for a single night (about £800). Demosthenes is said to have replied with dignity: 'I am not prepared to pay so high a price for the shame of having to regret an action.' Lais allegedly retorted: 'And I am not prepared to sell myself to you more cheaply, for then the regret would be mine.'

The story does not explain why she treated Demosthenes, of all people, so harshly. The stammer which had impeded his rise to political eminence in his youth had probably been cured and the questionable sources of his income would certainly have been a matter of indifference to Lais. Perhaps she disliked his politics.

Myron as father and son

It must have been the original fifth century Lais of Corinth whom the elderly sculptor Myron persuaded to pose. But her beauty when unveiled deprived the great man, who had produced mainly bronzes of athletes and splendidly modelled animals, of his common sense. He offered her everthing he possessed if she would surrender her person to him. But the capricious *hetaira* declined to grant him this favour, probably because by then he must have been quite old.

Next day he strutted into her presence reeking of scent, with his hair dyed, and repeated his offer. But she only laughed. 'My dear fellow,' she told him, 'it was only yesterday that I rejected your father. To accept his son today would be hardly decent.'

She was usually bad-tempered with old men, however famous they might be. The poet Euripides, for example, had referred unfavourably to *hetairai* in one of his plays. Lais resolved to avenge her colleagues by ensnaring him. But when they met he only growled at her. 'Get out of my way, you vile creature!' She answered him with one of his own lines. 'Vile actions are only committed by those who know them to be vile.'

These three Laises provided gossip, legend and the poets with nearly as many themes as did the renowned Phryne. Consequently, sayings and proceedings may have been attributed to one which should really have been ascribed to another or even to a differently named *hetaira*.*

Murder in a temple

One of the *hetairai* called Lais, at any rate, came to a terrible end. So many details of the event have been handed down that it cannot be regarded as pure fiction. According to Plutarch, Pausanias and other sources, this Lais fell in love with a Thessalian, left Corinth for his sake and lived with him as his wife. Either her beauty or the discovery that she had other lovers turned respectable women against her. She was induced by false information to visit the temple of Aphrodite and there murdered with a footstool.

The poets and philosophers were so enraged by the perpetration of this 'lynching' that they report with satisfaction that a deadly epidemic thereupon infested all Thessaly and only ceased its ravages when the desecrated temple of the goddess of love was purified by propitiatory rites.

The tomb of this Lais on the bank of the Peneius (now Salamvrias), the biggest river in Thessaly, has disappeared. But its epitaph

---

* The confusion may be to some extent elucidated if it is recalled that Myron, Euripides and the first Lais of Corinth all flourished within the fifth century B C, while Aristippus (d. 356), Lais of Hyccara (born about 421) and Diogenes (d. 323) spent most of their adult lives in the fourth century. Demosthenes (c. 384–322) was a later character of the same century and Apelles his younger contemporary. [J.C.]

is stated to have read as follows: 'Invincible Hellas, land of so many heroes, was enslaved by the beauty of Lais, born of the god of love, bred in the school of Corinth, laid to rest in the soil of Thessaly.' The Meteora group of monasteries, an abode of piety, peace and seclusion from the world, overlooks the valley of the Peneius and the unknown spot where the bones of the far-famed *hetaira* lie buried. Her life shows even more clearly than Phryne's how very ready the male, if not the female, inhabitants of ancient Greece were to forgive a truly beautiful woman.

In comparison with Aspasia and Thais, Phryne and Lais, the rest, however famous they may once have been, remain vague figures. They include Gnathanium, many of whose delightfully witty sayings are recorded; Glycera and Pythionice, who between them squandered the greatest fortune known to the antique world, that of Harpalus, Alexander's receiver-general, who escaped to Athens with plunder from the expedition to Persia; and the good-natured Bacchis, who gave a necklace of hers to a certain youth whose mistress had probably only asked for it to annoy her. Far more written information survives about these *hetairai* than about any respectable women. Statues and temples, tombs that cost eighty talents (over £30,000), as well as palaces and theatres, were erected in their honour. One inspired Praxiteles, another Apelles and a third Myron. Socrates and Euripides conversed with them. The dramatist Menander was kept by Glycera. The philosopher Aristippus would wait patiently at Lais's door if she happened to be engaged at the time and pretend that the delay did not worry him. 'I'm prepared to pay a lot for the happiness of possessing her, but I don't require others to be deprived of her for that reason,' he said.

The age of the hetairai

Those were centuries in which Greece flourished as it never did again. The nectar then harvested was quaffed by a few hundred beautiful women. No wonder they despised the men who made life so easy for them and who laid at their feet all the prizes they had collected for themselves or for the glory of their city and their country. A Phryne or a Lais could accordingly enjoy the sensations of a despot and a foretaste of divinity. During this era of incessant warfare and merciless exploitation of slavery very few women exceeded the degree of emancipation achieved by the *hetairai*.

Many women who became truly free, such as the oriental autocrat Semiramis or the poetess Sappho who ruled an island, had been *hetairai*. Others, like Cleopatra, were descended from *hetairai* and openly admitted the fact. In a society so frankly devoted to exaltation of the male, to the masculine physique and masculine virtues, the *hetairai* could freely celebrate their lesbian revels with girl flute-players. Mania, of whose sayings a whole volume was composed, could coolly tell a couple of mutually jealous athletes: 'I slept with you, Leontius, at the same time as I did with Antenor, for I was determined to find out once for all what two winners at the Olympian Games could do with me in a single night.'

Rome, the City of the she-wolf

'In general most people do wrong whenever they
have the opportunity.' – ARISTOTLE

The rivalry of the ancient civilizations of Greece and Rome extended to their darker aspects, their night-life, so to speak. A
modern mind can scarcely credit the naïvety with which Rome for
a thousand years embraced the myth of its foundation, in which an
itincrant prostitute, such as were already known in Greece as 'she-
wolves', played a special part under the name of *Lupa*.

The secret of the she-wolf

According to the annalist Valerius Antias:

Rhea Silvia, the violated Vestal Virgin, gave birth to twins and named
Mars as their father. She either believed this to be the case or considered
that association with a god would be less dishonourable to her than that
with a man. Yet neither gods nor men saved her from the cruelty of the
king. He had her seized and fettered and her children thrown into the
river. But by divine intervention the Tiber had already overflowed its
banks and formed extensive swamps. The river-bed itself remained
almost inaccessible. When the royal attendants arrived, they considered
the stagnant, shallow water deep enough to drown the new-born twins
and dropped them in the nearest pool. The site is that where the 'ruminal'*
fig-tree now stands – [i.e. at the western angle of the Palatine hill, where
the Lupercalia festival was held].

The place was at that time uninhabited wasteland. After the flood had
ebbed and the previously floating basket containing the two exposed
children came to rest on dry land, the boys' crying, according to the well-
known story, attracted a she-wolf which had come down from the neighbouring hills to drink. The animal suckled the infants with such tender
attention that the shepherd in charge of the royal flocks is said to have
noticed her licking them. His name, it is added, was Faustulus.

* The adjective *ruminalis* is derived, like the modern English 'ruminant', from the old
Latin noun *rumis*, found only in inscriptions and philological works and meaning a teat.
The fig-tree was called *ruminalis* because under it a she-wolf was supposed to have
suckled Rhea Silvia's children. [J.C.]

He took the children to his hut to be brought up by his wife Larentia. Some say that she was called Lupa by the shepherds because she had many lovers. Now, a further meaning of *Lupa* is 'she-wolf'. Such is the origin of the legend and the miracle it relates . . .

If the annalist is right, the legend would not be the only one that began with a play upon words. But he goes so far as to affirm that Larentia gradually acquired, through the profits of her trade, the very hills upon which Rome still stands. She is alleged to have presented this property, which she had no means of exploiting, to her two foster-children. They may accordingly be said to have founded Rome on Lupa's savings, derived from the proceeds of the first Roman *lupanar* ('brothel'), an establishment older, therefore, than the city itself.

Etruscan brothels

It was not unusual at that period for prostitutes to exercise their vocation in rural surroundings. In the land of the Etruscans, which was the first the Romans had to obtain by conquest, brothels were only permitted outside the city walls, a stipulation which is stated to have been imposed in order to prevent young men from visiting such establishments too often. In these circumstances it was natural enough for the women in question to be closely associated with the local shepherds and no doubt in some cases to live with them.

Foundlings may well have often fallen into the hands of such *lupae*, many of whom might have looked after them with characteristic good humour and generosity. At any rate this hypothesis is a good deal more likely than the story that Romulus and Remus were really brought up by a wolf. The latter belief only became current when, as time went on, it began to be thought shameful that a great and indeed imperial city should have arisen from the activities of a *lupa* and a *lupanar*. It was then that the double meaning of *lupa* would be recalled with relief and the dissolute female of the legend transmuted back into the prowling, predatory animal to which she owed her nickname. Thus the honour of a city destined to be called the 'Eternal' or the 'Holy' in later times would be restored for some thousands of years.

Ancient Roman fertility rites

Yet the true character of Lupa and her abode survived in a sphere from which it is hard to eradicate truths recognized in very ancient times. The cult of the spot at which the children were supposed to have been found developed into the festival known as the Lupercalia, all the recorded details of which have an unmistakably sexual character. At certain times the formal assembly of priests and congregation degenerated into an undisguised orgy. The *Luperci*, clad only in loincloths, would then beat all the women they encountered with leathern straps. The victims of this chastisement pressed forward delightedly to receive it, believing that the strokes would render them fertile and their offspring be favoured by the gods.

Even prominent Romans did not disdain on occasion to act as fertility priests. The strikingly handsome Antony, idolized by a proportion of Roman citizens, is related by Plutarch to have wielded the leathern scourge at the Lupercalia.

This festival and everything that could be connected with it were studied with enthusiasm for decades by historians of religion and philologists, for the ceremonies seemed to reveal the very soil upon which Roman institutions arose. It was argued, for instance, that the shepherd Faustulus, who appears in the legend of the foundation of the city, should be identified with Faunus, and his loose-living consort, the prowling Acca Larentia of the many love-affairs, with Flora, goddess of the fields. Consequently Faunus and Flora could be regarded as an innocent couple dwelling upon the Seven Hills and acquiring immortal glory by founding Rome as a result of their rescue of the twins exposed to death by drowning.

Hercules and the prostitute Larentia

A special feature of the Flora-Lupa-Larentia case, proving that she was at any rate a devotee of Venus, a goddess hitherto unknown on the banks of the Tiber, appears from an interesting legend linking Ancus, the fourth king of Rome, with none other than Hercules. It was alleged that the latter, already represented by tradition as having wandered all over the Mediterranean region, arrived in due course at the court of King Ancus, was by him challenged to a game of dice and won it, the prize being the fair Larentia, the most beautiful prostitute in the city. Hercules, by way of reward for the pleasure she had afforded him, prophesied to her that the first man

41

she happened to meet that morning would bring her luck. This turned out to be one Tarutius, a wealthy man, whom she subsequently married, eventually inheriting his estate, a vast fortune which she proceeded to pass on to the Roman people.

The fact that prostitutes figure so often in these early traditions is remarkable in view of the exceptionally high reputation for moral purity generally attributed to the Romans at this stage in their history and also because the town itself had not yet become the metropolis of later times but might be better described at this date as a wide community of farmsteads, small independent units often at odds with one another but nevertheless preserving their rustic character as persistently as the later Romans did.

The apparent contradiction may be explained by reflecting that the mere existence of prostitutes in a city does not by any means prove it to be a Sodom. It is not prostitutes, however numerous, who dictate the ethical character of a society, but the behaviour of the rest of the population. This point is convincingly exemplified in Roman history. Prostitutes were allotted a special position under Roman law. They were subject to a quantity of special regulations which for the most part have remained valid, in various forms, up to the present day. On the other hand the ordinary female citizen of Rome, the so-called 'decent woman', was exposed to several pernicious influences which led to a general decline of morals over the centuries.

Frivolous circus girls

Under the Roman Republic, long before the example of the imperial households affected the ethical standards of other families so disastrously, prostitution could only be observed in public on special occasions. As a rule it operated in considerable secrecy. During the Lupercalia and still more at the Floralia festivals the unwritten laws against indecency were broken in brief outbursts of violence, but never abolished for that reason. An incident at the Floralia affords very clear proof of this attitude. The temple of Flora stood near the Circus Maximus and it had become customary for an exuberant crowd of prostitutes from the temple to invade the Circus and continue their riotous merrymaking there in full view of the public. On festive occasions, therefore, they did not, like the Greek *hetairai*, confine their celebrations to their own colleagues, but deliberately provided a spectacle which the Romans, who had long been fond of theatrical performances, good-humouredly applauded. But the public were deprived of their enjoyment on one such occasion during the Floralia. For Cato, the Censor, was present in the Circus and when the prostitutes burst in they did not dare to begin their usual erotic dancing and other antics. Instead, an awkward silence prevailed. Thereupon the Censor resignedly lifted his arm, covering his eyes with the sleeve of his toga, and left the Circus. It is most improbable that after this episode the festive atmosphere which it had overshadowed returned to the gaiety characteristic of former years.

Censorship of morals at Rome

Moral censorship began at Rome during the fifth century B C, in other words at the very time when at Athens, in the golden age, social relations with the *hetairai* were in full swing and the most eminent men in the city, its leading statesmen, thinkers and artists, unblushingly cultivated the company of these female devotees of love. Any Athenian would have thought contemporary Rome a rustic and backward community, especially as the Romans themselves obviously considered it most important to remain so. Their censors were not actually so much concerned with instances of open incontinence, as Cato's behaviour shows. In such cases they merely veiled their faces. It was the general level of conduct that they chiefly investigated. According to Schmähling:

> The superintendence of morals by the Censors affected every Roman citizen without exception and indicates in the clearest possible fashion the unlimited claims made by the State upon the individual and the indissoluble links that bound him to it. In principle his private life was regarded as an affair which did not concern him alone but was deliberately made subordinate to State control.

Little as this view may appeal to modern opinions of the proper functions of government it proved highly effective under the Roman Republic. The fact that Roman history records a practically unbroken rise to power over a period of five hundred years is primarily due to the device of imposing a positive regulation of morals. The censors wasted no time in prosecuting a war, which they could see from the start must be unprofitable, against the

43

practice of selling sexual favours. On the contrary, they concentrated upon the respectable section of the population. In conformity with the ideas of honourable life which had been current among their rural ancestors, they recognized marriage as the natural foundation for the existence of a community and inflicted penalties upon bachelors as soon as they had reached a certain age. On the conclusion of wars they brought vigorous pressure to bear on widows to remarry, while drastically obstructing the careers, whether political or otherwise professional, of unmarried men, who had always provided the main source of moral infection. Just as in modern democracies leading statesmen must be able to prove that they are happily married and a thrice divorced man, even if he were the political genius of the century, would never be able to gain the support of an electorate, so also in Rome, in the year 184 B C, a senator named Manilius was expelled from the senate simply because he had been seen to kiss his wife in front of their daughter.

Those who may suppose that Manilius was thereby setting a touching example of matrimonial affection which could only exercise an edifying influence upon other minds, particularly youthful ones, mistake the nature of the basis of ancient Roman morality. Though not precisely Spartan, it was consciously directed to military ends and whatever increased the power of the State as a whole was automatically recognized as virtuous activity. No attitude could have been less concerned with women or even with respect for them. One of the most famous of all the Censors, Quintus Metellus Macedonicus, openly proclaimed:

Citizens! If we were able to live without wives everyone would no doubt evade the burdens of marriage. But since Nature has ordained that we can neither live in perfect peace and comfort when we have wives nor go on living, in any circumstances, without them, probably the best thing we can do is to pay more attention to the continued welfare of the State than to the material delights of this world.

Marriage as a nuisance

He might just as well have exclaimed: Sacrifice yourself for the State and marry! It is intelligible enough that the Roman bachelors only obeyed such instructions with reluctance. Masculine unanimity in this respect, however, which the Censor himself admits, is rather surprising. He does not commend matrimony as a condition worth striving for, but as a necessary evil. The number of male residents in Rome – females, apparently, were disregarded – is alleged not only to have not risen over the thirty years between 164 and 136 BC but actually to have decreased by twenty thousand. The private fortunes of widows were accumulating, so that they could afford to dispense with male guidance and grew more and more self-supporting. But the real reason for the Censor's advice does not appear in the brief fragments of his speech which have been preserved. The true occasion of it was the rapid spread of pederasty under the Republic.

Underclothing was abominated as enervating. Extravagant dishes at table elicited curses and comparisons with the good old days of pap and broth and manly virtues, which in their turn were contrasted with the mentality of contemptible females who thought of nothing but luxury goods. Yet at the very same time boys began to be praised at the expense of girls and the import of young male slaves to serve their masters' lusts grew to alarming proportions. The State intervened by recording the value of any slave of an age rendering him liable to such treatment as ten times his purchase price in the list of his master's possessions. This remarkable expedient could be applied because the slave himself was a mere chattel and a master could treat such property as he pleased without incurring any legal penalty. All that happened in consequence of the measure was that it became quite expensive to keep a male prostitute.

Adultery heavily punished

The contrast of light and shade becomes even more striking when the dreadful sentences passed on wives found guilty of adultery are considered. A husband's lapse in this connection would be a stain upon his honour or an impediment to his success in life. In certain circumstances it might prove economically disastrous for him. But a woman who committed adultery, unless she belonged to one of the leading families of the community, was given over to ill-treatment by the dregs of the population. Her husband does not seem to have been in a position, at any rate if she had been caught in the act, to save her from being carried off by a jeering mob to be outraged in one of the small goal-houses on the outskirts of the city. Numbered dice decided the order of admission of her assailants.

Those awaiting their turn crowded to stare through the barred windows. If the victim survived until the evening, she had as a rule no choice but to go into exile. Many adulteresses are also assumed to have turned to prostitution after such shocking experiences. The origin of this punishment is to be found in the oldest sources of Roman law and it continued to be inflicted on adulterous wives as late as the fifth century A D. 'Lynch-law' therefore lasted for a thousand years in a civilization which has contributed more than any other to the establishment of protective legislation in society.

Feminine vengeance

Women developed their own methods of revenge. They used their immemorial weapons to defend themselves in a republic exclusively controlled by men. Within the space of only a few years three eminent male citizens, the Consul Calpurnius Piso, Claudius Asellus and L. Postumius Albinus, were poisoned by their wives. If husbands concentrated upon boys or public women for their sexual pleasures, the wives, whose behaviour outside the home was considerably restricted and closely watched, turned to their domestic staff. At the Circus men and women sat together. The cruel and voluptuous spectacles to be witnessed there provided a high degree of excitement. Prostitutes waited outside the arena for the men, so as to take advantage of so favourable an opportunity. Women, on the other hand, had to arrange their liaisons within the building. Ovid has described, with many details taken from actual life, what then occurred. Comedy, farce and mime were sometimes even more stimulating sexually than fiercer scenes.

> When the tender Bathyllus leaps as he dances the Leda,
> Tuccia can't hold in her bosom and Apula moans
> as if in the arms of her man, consumed with passion, and
> even the rustic Thymele long gazes and learns—

The athletic gladiators, however dubious their antecedents, made just as much impression as the elegant dancers and actors. Fashionable Roman ladies eloped with prisoners of war, slaves and criminals after the show at the Circus. No sea was then too wide for them to cross, no mountain range too high.

> When a husband pleads, it's hard to go boarding a vessel,
> for then it's so smelly, her head goes round and around.

46

But if with a lover she flees, her stomach's in perfect order.
One spits at the thought of her husband, another sits down with the
    seamen
or romps all over the deck and plays with the heaviest ropes.

Broken homes

The evidence of Tacitus, Cassius Dio, Martial and other Roman writers could be cited in support of these verses by Juvenal. Such testimony as a whole depicts a society under the later Republic and the emperors which contrasts notably with that of Athens. Sympathy may indeed be felt for the Greek matron who had to sit at home without taking any part in public life, while helplessly watching her husband chasing *hetairai* or *deikteriades*. Yet the domestic sphere as managed by Penelope and her successors retained a certain amount of point and remained relatively free from disagreeable features. In Rome on the other hand a similar lack of respect for women, their deprivation of rights and in fact complete subordination to the head of the family, led to a ruinous degree of liberty. The tyranny of the censors was exercised only over men. Women had no need of it since they were subject to domestic jurisdiction. But it was actually women who brought about the relaxation of the strict rules which the censors had tried to impose and maintain. Sumptuary laws could not restrain luxury if women were perpetually demanding new dress materials, cosmetics, ointments and perfumes. It was of little use to recall the ancient Roman virtues when their very foundation, that of the contented and happy family, no longer existed except in the censors' lists and the home was being practically crushed out of existence among favourite slave-girls and boys, complacent litter-bearers and provokingly handsome actors.

Juvenal on Messalina

Dost thou rage at middle-class crime and the sins of an Eppa?
Turn to the rivals of gods and hear how Claudius suffered!
So soon as his consort saw him sleep she lightly remembered
in the self-same hour the harlot's mat and the emperor's couch
with nocturnal hood abandoned and a single serving-maid.
O most illustrious of strumpets, dark-haired but golden-wigged,
off to the steamy-curtained brothel's chamber long reserved,
imperial gold at bosom but all else naked flesh for sale!

47

There, Britannicus noble, the womb is shown that once bore thee.
Smiling she welcomes her clients and claims the chinking coinage . . .
When at length the keeper dismissed his girls, ah, how sorrowful
she then departed, yet still whenever she could as the last,
closing the door behind her, still all agog with her lusts
on homeward way, for the men had wearied but never appeased them.
Hideous she looked, with filthy visage all smeared with the lamp-soot,
bearing the sultry stench of the brothel to the emperor's bed.

The Empress Messalina, to whom Juvenal refers in this famous
passage of his Sixth Satire, would today be called a nymphomaniac.
Her behaviour is accordingly less significant than the fact that it
was even possible. That so direct an association between gutter and
court existed and was evidently maintained for so long and that
Roman society as a whole had so close a connection with prostitution is most remarkable.

Money-grubbers of the Tiber

The approach to this situation had been paved with victories. The
Republic had been growing progressively stronger and wealthier.
The spoils of war, gold and merchandise streamed into the capital
from the provinces. Anyone who managed to acquire a fortune
could think of no better place to squander it than the Eternal City,
for which so many had longed during their service in the East or in
Spain.

It's money-grubbing [wrote Petronius in his *Satyricon*], that has been
responsible for this mode of life. In the old days, when simple virtue was
still respected, the liberal arts flourished and men vied with one another
most zealously to discover anything that might be of use to future ages.
Democritus, for instance, extracted the juice of every plant and spent his
life in experiments designed to determine the specific properties of stones
and shrubs. Eudoxus grew old on the summits of the highest mountains
in order to investigate the motions of stars and the firmament . . . Lysip-
pus starved to death while preoccupied with the modelling of a single
statue and Myron, who almost gave souls to his bronzes of persons and
animals, left not a single farthing to his heirs. We, on the other hand, are
utterly given over to wine-bibbing and servitude to harlots and can no
longer even appreciate the works of art made in the past . . . so it's no
wonder painting has gone into a decline, seeing that a gold nugget seems
finer now to everyone on earth or in heaven than anything that such
funny old Greeks as Apelles and Phidias ever created.

Hetairai *as models*

The sense of a decadent age has rarely been more uncompromisingly conveyed than by Petronius Arbiter in his sometimes disconcertingly frank novel of manners. He had himself served as proconsul in Bithynia and knew the fashionable society of Rome at first hand. Almost everything there came from abroad, money from the provinces, luxury from the East and culture from the Greeks. The very courtesans assumed Greek names, even if they actually came from some little country town near Rome. They called themselves Glycera, Chloe or Citheris, like their models in the Athens of Pericles or Alcibiades. They were no less greedy than a Lais or a Phryne, but they never showed the least disposition towards higher things. They gave no sign of any independent outlook, discretion or even an occasional interest in more elevated subjects than their trade. On the contrary, they remained entirely subordinate to its dreary mechanical operation, which drove them into the hands of the highest bidder and so down to the level of common prostitutes.

There may be some injustice in this view. For Roman literature has not preserved any such affectionate studies wholly devoted to *hetairai* as have made some of those who dwelt in Athens, Corinth or Alexandria so vividly familiar to posterity. Perhaps Roman courtesans have all been regarded as much alike because no Roman Alciphron ever collected their letters, and their behaviour can only be judged from the recorded evidence of a few perpetually disgruntled lovers. But on the whole the decadence of fashionable civilization seems also to have permeated the sphere of the higher-ranking prostitutes – those of lower rank could not have fallen lower – in other words all the courtesans who were unquestionably in a position, owing to their exceptional material prosperity, to have salvaged some traces of intellectual interests and cultural ambition. It would not have been the first nor was it to be the last time that such an opportunity presented itself to the *demi-monde*.

Propertius and Cynthia

Although there were no such great sculptors and painters in Rome as had endowed the Greek *hetairai* with much of their immortality, the art of poetry flourished during the last century of the Republic and the first of the Empire. Very few poets of distinction disdained to frequent fashionable circles in the capital, at least from time to time. But they came only as guests, to enjoy the lavish hospitality of the rich. They themselves could offer the courtesans nothing but posthumous fame, the mention of a Lesbia, Cynthia or Delia in their verses, though they all wished they could do more.

> Cynthia, can that which all say of you really be true?
> Everyone seems to be sure that yours is a life of shame.
> Have I deserved this of you? O faithless one, you shall rue it
> and I shall be borne elsewhere on some fortunate wind
> there of your fickle company to court some other
> ardently longing for glory in poetry's praises,
> one who will never so vex me with cruel, injurious words,
> but will tear your good name to pieces. Then too late your tears!

It is to be feared that these threats by Propertius did not alarm his Cynthia unduly. She certainly seems to have been one of the best educated of her colleagues. Her father, Hostilius, was a professional historian and had sent her to a good school. Yet this same Hostilia, under the name of Cynthia, preferred a career under the protection of an official who had made a fortune in Illyria. Whenever the latter happened to be in Rome a mere poet like Propertius was simply not admitted to her apartments. Young, gifted and successful, he raged at her in letters and poems, cursing her in the most exquisite phrases. But his love, so far from raising Cynthia to his own level, brings him down to that of her protector.

Plunder from Illyria

So now he's back again, is he, that praetor of yours, Hostilia, your spoils from Illyria? Couldn't he have gone and broken his neck in those Acroceraunian Mountains? [Albania is meant.] Ah, if he had, what wouldn't I have sacrificed to Neptune? Now I suppose you'll be revelling day and night, as usual, without me. Well, at any rate you'd better be reasonable enough not to lose a moment in reaping the harvest he offers you and skin the fool as he deserves. And as soon as he's got through all his money and hasn't a bean left, tell him he'd better set sail for another Illyria.

The passage already sounds like something by Villon. But Propertius was more deeply involved and the mistress who ruled his short life was not simply a woman of the world but a practising courtesan who betrayed him, not with a single rival, but with so many that not even Thais of Corinth, he exclaims in ludicrous despair, could have had such a swarm of admirers crowding other door as his Cynthia.

Inhibitions of the beautiful Cynthia

Cynthia's intellectual training had left her with a strange inhibition, though it may well have been, as in the case of Phryne, shrewdly calculated on professional grounds. She would never strip entirely naked, but covered herself at times when no patrician dame would dream of doing so. She did not even listen to the entreaties of Propertius when, intoxicated with her beauty, he pleaded with her in deathless verse, citing the examples of every goddess and demi-goddess he could think of, to render his coy mistress obedient to his wishes. On the other hand he had no cause for complaint in the dark. 'Do you consider,' he once asked a friend, 'that it is beauty alone which kindles the most ardent passion?' But he himself answered the question without waiting for the other's reply. 'Ah, how much more she gives me than that, till I almost die of it! She glows with fervour in desire, her skills are many and delightful, how eminently she participates in those pleasures which it would be indiscreet to mention.'

Cynthia-Hostilia's pride was her undoing. For not all the admirers whom she rejected put up with her scorn or merely retaliated with rude letters or poetic laments like her faithful Propertius. At some time or other she must have offended a certain powerful personage who saw no reason why he should swallow her insults. The man in question can hardly have been the somewhat commonplace praetor from Illyria, who had known her too long and too well to quarrel with her. A much more likely figure would be one of the freedmen then so influential at court, people who would never forgive an impudent courtesan for hinting that she knew where they came from.

Nomas the female poisoner

A certain whore, by this time so old that she could only pick up clients for a few pence in the most murky alleys, and was obliged therefore to undertake all sorts of shady work to get enough to eat, wormed her way into Cynthia's confidence by talking of former times and gave the unfortunate girl a dose of poison. All Rome knew that the poisoner's name was Nomas and anyone could see how well she had been paid for the murder. For the ancient harlot, free from all interference, thenceforth paraded in silks and jewellery, as though she had been suddenly restored to her earlier prosperity by a new lease of youth. As for the beautiful Cynthia, she was hastily buried beside the little river Anio, on the way to Tivoli.

Propertius was absent from Rome at this period, perhaps luckily for himself, since the prostitutes who ventured to take flowers to Cynthia's grave were brutally beaten and subjected to all kinds of persecution. Such is probably the reason why Propertius never mentions the name of the aged Nomas's paymaster, though the poet records that he was tormented by nightmares in which Cynthia appeared to him and demanded that he should avenge her murder. He lived before the period of the despotic emperors, when the mere hint of imperial displeasure would be enough to drive such a man as Petronius to suicide. But Propertius knew Rome. He was well aware that a man who had enjoyed the intimate favours of a famous courtesan in the capital continued to live there at his peril.

Who was Lesbia?

An atmosphere of peril and secrecy also envelopes the name of Catullus's mistress, the young woman whom he calls Lesbia in his poems. But she is generally believed to have been no other than the beautéous Clodia, sister of the unscrupulous Publius Clodius Pulcher. As a patrician whose mode of life had earned her the reputation of a prostitute she was known as the *Quadrantaria*, since anyone could buy her favours, it was said, for the insignificant coin representing the quarter of an *as* (less than a halfpenny).

This rumour was of course an exaggeration. But no less a personage than Cicero had publicly denounced her numerous love-affairs and all Rome, consequently, considered itself entitled to use her nickname. Catullus himself, however, was not disturbed by it.

> Never shall any woman e'er boast of so ardent a passion
> as that which burns me for thee, my Lesbia, adored one.
> Never was love returned with a loyalty deeper than mine,
> Lesbia, when love for love I rendered thee back again.

Every lover believes his own love to be uniquely passionate. But undoubtedly Clodia, who was some ten years older than Catullus, could be proud of having inspired the greatest lyric poet of Rome with dozens of glorious poems, which might never have been written but for her. It is equally certain that he would have been less stimulated in these compositions if the course of his love had always run smooth, instead of undergoing such shocking changes of temperature as were imposed upon Lesbia's young adorer by that experienced woman of the world.

Catullus came from Verona. But he was by no means the sort of innocent provincial who so often migrated to Rome. He belonged to a cultivated and wealthy family. His father occupied a high post in Cisalpine Gaul and maintained friendly relations with Julius Caesar. Catullus was twenty-two when he first came to Rome in 62 BC, though he pretended to be slightly older. His affair with Clodia began in the same year and at once plunged him into the very centre of the eddying vortex of political and social intrigue. In fact, he arrived just in time for one of the worst scandals in the whole history of the Republic.

Clodius at Caesar's house

Plutarch described it as follows:

Clodius was a man of aristocratic birth, still young in years but of an audacious, haughty and presumptuous character. He fell in love with Pompeia, Caesar's wife, and entered his house by stealth, disguised as a female cithara player. For the women there were celebrating at the time the secret rites of the festival of the Bona Dea, from which males were excluded and in fact no man was present. Clodius hoped, since he was still a beardless youth, to be able to mingle unnoticed with Pompeia's attendants until he could reach her . . .

His plan miscarried. For actually he was already thirty and in spite of the closest possible shave looked thoroughly masculine and in particular continued to speak like a man. Unfamiliar with the extensive premises, he lost his way and when a female attendant asked him his name made the mistake of evading the question. The woman, on hearing his voice, screamed to warn her companions, who had thought they were unobserved and were absorbed in the performance of the private ceremonies required for the service of the 'good goddess', the Bona Dea.

Indulgent as the Romans were in general to youthful follies, they were extremely sensitive to interference with their ancient religious observances. The Bona Dea was one of the local divinities piously worshipped in Rome for centuries and the maintenance of her cult was regarded as more important than that of many of the Greek or oriental sects which had been introduced into the city. The invasion of her Mysteries, the spying upon women engaged upon such intimate matters in the house of a distinguished family, and the fact that the intruder's object was the seduction of another man's wife, were regarded as misdemeanours so serious that Cicero, so far from attempting to protect his friend Clodius from their consequences, censured him in open court.

The great orator, at about the same time, ceased to woo the fair Clodia. Thenceforth, accordingly, open war raged between Clodius, his circle and especially his sister on the one side and Cicero on the other. As the latter's outstanding eloquence did not spare his opponents, all Rome soon knew all about the conduct of Clodia and her brother.

Lesbia mourned by Catullus

Adroit bribery and intimidation enabled Clodius to secure his acquittal. But it came out at the trial that he had committed incest with his youngest sister and also in all probability with his sisters Tertia and Clodia. As for the latter, so many stories now became current about her that Catullus in his perplexity could only shield his eyes from contemplation of his adored one.

> My Lesbia, Caelius, ay, she, Lesbia,
> the sole love of Catullus, loved yet more
> than even his very self and all his dearest friends,
> lurks in the public squares and narrow lanes
> to trap the glorious progeny of guiltless Remus.

The still self-consciously glorious progeny of the city's founder were the citizens of Rome. If the beautiful, rich and even, through her family connections, powerful Clodia had really come to make no distinction between them, her propensities can only be explained as pathologically excessive, as was later the case with Messalina and other ladies of the imperial households. Yet it may well be that Catullus did not mean his verses to be taken literally. After all Caelius, who had now succeeded him in Lesbia's favour, knew the truth as well as he did. Perhaps the squares and lanes referred to were only metaphors he resorted to in his distress, for the circumstances in which Clodia prostituted herself were of no consequence. In any case her proverbial immorality could no longer be doubted. It was only her beauty that remained as brilliant as ever, in spite of her utter degradation. The more she was seen in the company of other courtesans, since, patrician though she was, she could no longer keep them at a distance now that she herself had been contaminated, the more evidently her beauty exceeded theirs. It seems that Catullus had been present in some such scene of rivalry in the theatre and had passed round a rapidly scribbled poem in defence of the Lesbia he still admired, a kind of lover's broadsheet, such as has seldom been recorded.

> Many think Quintia's a beauty and myself I'd never deny
> she's handsome and tall and quite slim. I grant you
> those separate items, but 'beauty' I'd cut from the list, for
> grace has she none and her shape's too commanding to charm us.
> But Lesbia's a beauty all right, free from all blemish or fault,
> she's robbed all the rest of their points, stands alone in her glory.

Portrait of Clodia

Beautiful and depraved, suspected of murdering her husband and doubtless guilty of many other crimes, such as slander, conspiracy to defraud and incest, Clodia, for all her recklessness, showed plenty of sagacity when it came to the choice of a husband or a steady lover. She indulged in innumerable casual love-affairs because her temperament demanded variety. But her longer-lasting associates were such men as Metellus Celer, who had distinguished himself in the suppression of Catiline's rebellion, had been Governor of Cisalpine Gaul and even became Consul in 60 BC. Marcus Caelius Rufus, the successor of Catullus in Clodia's favour, was also a most eminent personality. Some of his letters, which have been preserved, prove him to have possessed political abilities of a high order. But during the merciless struggle for power in Rome between the two giants, Caesar and Pompey, his luck deserted him. In the course of an attempt, with only a few adherents, to get the upper hand in Italy himself, he fell into the hands of his adversaries and was beheaded at Thurii in the year 48. Caesar's dramatic end followed four years later.

Catullus did not live to hear of this event, though he did not die at thirty, as was for long assumed, but at nearly forty. His life had been dominated by Clodia-Lesbia ever since he had taken wing as a fledgeling, from his native province to settle in the great foreign metropolis. He made several attempts to free himself from her toils. But they all failed, from his flight back to Verona to his various fleeting associations with courtesans who never succeeded in casting so permanent a spell upon him as did Clodia. Not even the Greek Ipsithilla, reckoned an expert in love, could hold him, though for a while he fell completely under her influence. Another of these young women caused the sensitive poet the most acute distress by declining to receive him in a brothel which she had entered, though she admitted everyone else who applied for her favours.

Poets under the yoke

The pictures of Catullus helpless with longing outside the brothel and of Propertius at the door of a mistress revelling within at the side of a rich lover illustrate the treatment which poets had to endure at the hands of Roman courtesans. Not even the sharp-tongued Tibullus proved any exception. In fact he suffered twice as much. For while Catullus might well console himself with the un-heard of erotic delights experienced in the company of a beautiful Greek girl and also had enough stamina to appreciate all the novelties to which she introduced him, the frail Tibullus had already so exhausted his energies at an early age that he frankly confesses he found himself quite impotent in a woman's company. Yet he returned to the charge again and again instead of seeking consolation in verse-making. Such was his personal tragedy. But it was also that of his era. A young poet living at the centre of the fashionable world, with no friends elsewhere, could hardly hold aloof from its diversions. He preferred to put up with the abuse of his Delia's greedy exploiter, actually her husband, and the jeers, ultimately, of Delia herself.

Petronius and his Satyricon

Albius Tibullus resembles the person described by Petronius in one of the most delightful and historically valuable scenes of his *Satyricon,* as a lover who took the most desperate measures to overcome his impotence by magical means but nevertheless failed to do so and was treated accordingly.

The old woman took a twist of threads of different colours out of her dress and tied it round my neck. Then she mixed some dust with spittle, put it on her middle finger and made a mark on my forehead despite my protests.

Then, after uttering a spell in verse, she bade me spit three times and throw pebbles, three times, into my bosom. She next pronounced a second spell in verse over the pebbles and wrapped them in a purple cloth. After this she laid hands on my sexual organs to test the response. They acted faster than she could speak and a powerful movement started in the old girl's grasp. She jumped for joy, exclaiming: 'Hey, Chrysis, darling, just look what pleasure I can give other people!'

The old woman then handed me over to Chrysis, who was beside herself with delight at the restoration of her mistress's lost jewel. She hastily led me to the most charming apartment in all the world, where everything that nature produces to gladden the eyes of men lay before me . . Extended with the nape of her neck, white as marble, against a golden cushion, my mistress fanned her placid countenance with a spray of flowering myrtle. As she gazed upon me she blushed a little, probably remembering how I had vexed her the day before. After sending everyone else out of the room she asked me to come and sit by her. Then she placed the spray of myrtle across my eyes and, as if a wall had sprung up between us, grew bolder. 'Well, paralytic,' she enquired. 'Have you come to see me all of a piece today?' 'Try me!' quoth I. Thereupon I flung myself without restraint into her arms and enjoyed kisses which did not have to be extracted by spells in verse.

I was drawn to the act of love by the sheer beauty of her body. A rain of kisses resounded as our lips met. Our clasped hands discovered every kind of sexual pleasure. In a close physical embrace even our souls were made one . . .

The mistress of the house, stung by my open taunts, at last broke into a vengeful fury, summoning her chamber footmen and ordered me to be hoisted for flogging. Not content with subjecting me to this terrible insult, she bade all her spinning-maids and the most abject of her female domestic staff to come and spit on me.

An incompetent sorceress

In the end the impotent lover, the incompetent sorceress and the weeping Chrysis herself were all ejected from the premises. The superb description of this scene also leaves us in no doubt that the

Roman courtesans made no secret of their trade, so much so that their entire households would share in their joys and sorrows. Since no one was ashamed even of male prostitutes, there could be no reason why a good-looking woman should only receive her lovers in secrecy.

Many widows determined to have a private life of their own registered as prostitutes, not in order to practise the trade, but merely to ensure that the men who came to see them were not charged with pursuing a respectable woman. For so long as a man kept away from virgins and matrons of good repute he ran no risk of scandal. Ovid would never have been banished to the shores of the Black Sea if he had limited himself to courtesans. But his attentions to only one girl who led a sheltered life, though she was, to be sure, the grand-daughter of an emperor, caused his downfall. His famous poem, *The Art of Love*, rendered it certain, moreover, that the emperor would never forgive him.

Ovid

The blow struck him at the height of his career, when his *The Art of Love* had just rendered him, in the eyes of all Rome, the leading expert in sexual questions and the acknowledged head of the group of erotic lyrists. He had not only been the friend of Tibullus, who had died early, but was also popular with other poets. The experiences he relates and the secrets he reveals, whether of a delicate or gross character, in his *Ars Amatoria*, could only have been derived from frequenting the society of courtesans. It is therefore greatly to be regretted that he only names one of them, who has achieved immortality as Corinna. That may or may not have been her real name. Only he himself could say and it must be remembered that Ovid destroyed a certain number of his manuscripts. It is also possible that he intended the name Corinna to stand, in his verses, not for a real person but for the general idea of a courtesan. No actual woman who played a part in his life need have been named Corinna, though no doubt he had relations with very many in addition to his three legitimate wives.

In his poetry, at any rate, Corinna's circumstances are typical. She has a husband who also acts as her *souteneur* and is therefore regarded by the poet as his natural enemy. For although Ovid belonged to a prosperous family, having been born into the class of knights, he always remained short of money. Corinna also disposed of the services of one of these ancient procuresses who have scarcely ever been so ingeniously reviled as by Propertius, Ovid and Martial. That poets of all people should have been jealous of the courtesans who obviously led this kind of life is a constant surprise to the modern reader. They never seem to have realized, so far as we can tell, the senselessness of such feelings in this connection. Their jealousy is repeatedly in evidence, casting them into the lowest depths of despair, so that, however elegantly their verses express it, one can only feel amusement that such a sentiment could arise in the circumstances given. It is not tragic, for instance, but absurd, if the lover of an extremely busy courtesan declines to bestow on her any more intimate caresses than a kiss, on the ground that any further attentions would only increase his jealousy. It is much more intelligible when the poet, kept waiting by his Corinna, as so often before, for an unconscionable time, is attracted, in his boredom, by one of her attendants. A Greek girl named Cypassis had the good fortune to please Ovid on such an occasion, so that for a few weeks he didn't care whether Corinna remained satisfied with a mere kiss or not. It was probably Cypassis of whom he was thinking when he wrote in Book III of his *The Art of Love*:

The maid deputises

> She, I may tell you, who sets in good order your bed
> and your chamber has often been there alone with me.
> So take care the girls at your service are not over-pretty.
> She's more than once taken her mistress's place with me.

Ovid was already familiar with Rome and a man of the world when the imperial edict banished him. He had studied in Athens and travelled in Sicily and Asia Minor. He was sixty-five when he undertook the long journey to Tomi, one of the most distant outposts of the empire. It stood on the Danube estuary and he was obliged there to consort with semi-savages, Geti and Sarmatians, and suffer in winter from its icy winds. He tried to keep in touch, by correspondence, with friends of happier days. In petition after petition he begged for recall or at any rate transfer to some other place of exile. On the other hand he himself records that the inhabitants of

Tomi treated him with such consideration that it might have been his birthplace.

Last Act in Tomi

It is unlikely that the brilliant courtesans of the metropolis took any interest in Ovid's last productions, the *Tristia* and the *Epistulae ex Ponto*, so often expressive of his longing for life in Rome and the people he had left behind there. Corinna's rivals had once done their very utmost to be praised as eloquently as herself by the famous poet and she had once been delighted at being pointed out as the muse of the great Ovid. For her sake he had strenuously opposed Augustus's decrees against immorality. He had contested, on behalf of the fashionable society of Rome, the reforms and revivals of old customs advocated by an emperor who was far from restricting his personal self-indulgence. But no sooner had the citizens, after a brief stage of alarm, started sinning again, than they forgot the scapegoat sent into the wilderness. Ovid himself, however, does not seem to have forgotten Corinna. He continued to lament her downfall. Her decline had started while he was still in Rome and no doubt he heard of her further deterioration from correspondents. He had spent enough nights on Corinna's doorstep to know where her career must end. He had long recognized her lack of consideration for others, the indifference with which she ignored his fervent prayers and turned to more fortunate lovers, the reckless ostentation with which she paraded the most daring fashions at the theatre and the complacence with which she received intruders at the Circus. Her behaviour had deeply wounded him. Since all Rome gossiped about his association with her, he pleaded: 'I have no right to ask you to live chastely and cultivate modesty, but I do beg you to conceal the cruel truth from my own knowledge. The lowest common prostitute has shame enough to do in private what you expose to the eyes of all the world.'

Corinna falls on evil days

After Ovid had been banished to Tomi, the brilliant Corinna had been obliged to take up work as a barmaid. She lived on the sailors coming up the Tiber to the city. Neither her own avarice nor any single one of her circle, from *souteneur* to eunuch, saved her from this fate, for Ovid, so far as all the evidence about both of them

60

shows, had been the only man with whom she had formed any kind of truly affectionate relationship. If this were in fact the case, Augustus's sentence of exile had brought about a third sacrifice. Ovid died at Tomi; the emperor's granddaughter Julia died after twenty years on the island of Tremesus, to which he had banished her; while Corinna, reduced to destitution, could not even summon up enough energy to manufacture love-potions or sell beauty preparations, expedients resorted to by many others of her trade who in their prime had been able to live on its practice alone.

Martial the avenger

Almost exactly a hundred years after the death of Catullus a poet was born who took vengeance on the courtesans of Rome for their treatment of his colleagues. He was Marcus Valerius Martialis, the greatest epigrammatist of all time, a master of the brief, stinging comment in verse. He was born about AD 40 in the Roman garrison town of Bilbilis, near the modern Calatayud on the River Jalon in Aragon, leaving Spain for Rome when he was about twenty. Little was heard of him in the metropolis for a considerable time. He lived in needy circumstances on the proceeds of versified flatteries composed for several clearly not over-generous citizens. It was not until the year 80 that he acquired some small reputation and at last found himself in a position, after purchasing a modest property at Nomentum, to the north-east of Rome, to escape the direst poverty.

So long as he remained poor he seems to have exercised a certain amount of restraint and refrained from indulging in the excesses of the early imperial period. But as he grew older he began to develop a taste for the delights available to dissipated Romans, even if they had only a few coppers to spare, and made up for his previous austerity. He continued, however, to regard himself as a respectable person, proclaiming in one of his epigrams that *Lasciva est nobis pagina, vita proba est*, 'my writings may be obscene, but my life is decent'. Nevertheless, according to the evidence of his own poems, Martial must have had a good deal to do with courtesans, with brothels and their inmates and above all with the world of male prostitutes. These experiences do not exclude the probability that he was quite sincere in claiming to be an honourable citizen. For he had never murdered or informed against anyone. He neither kept a brothel nor lived on the earnings of a mistress. He had plenty of friends and yet little money. So his morals were higher than those of very many of his contemporaries who tried on a small scale and in their private misdeeds to rival the conduct of the emperors.

Basis for a catalogue of hetairai

In the hands of so relentless a satirist his exceptional knowledge of affairs and personalities might be very dangerous. Martial knew all the female devotees of Venus, whatever their status. He knew not only their names and where they came from but also their individual traits of character, admirable or otherwise, what they liked and what they might be disliked for. His epigrams as a whole would furnish sufficient material for one of those catalogues of *hetairai* rumoured to have existed in every century and yet surviving in so few examples. He may even himself, since he was always in need of money, have compiled some such *guide galant* for fellow provincials who had come to Rome in search of enjoyment.

No doubt he was able to preserve the aloof and cool attitude of a mere onlooker for the reason that at heart he preferred boys to women. He certainly paid the latter visits and frequented their society. For two or three of them he even seems to have felt a certain affection. But in general it was not courtesans he favoured but good-looking boys. One of his most biting epigrams is addressed to a man who ignored such lads and concentrated on being supported by elderly women.

On this view his sarcastic contempt for the entire class of *hetairai*, common prostitutes and their hangers-on would be a perfectly genuine sentiment, though it may not have arisen on moral grounds as in the case, for instance, of Cato the Censor, nor even out of respect for male virtues and the male principle, as in the case of many republican critics concerned with morality, but simply as a consequence of his personal predilections. Martial's refined cruelty in the depiction of Roman prostitution at all its levels springs from a hatred rooted in sexual feeling. The blind rage of his hostility to women is all the more remarkable in one who was no true homosexual in the pathological sense, but merely bisexual, as were indeed most of his contemporaries in the upper classes of society.

His well-aimed shafts of wit and above all his brutal frankness made his scandalously satirical verses famous almost as soon as his first books of epigrams were published. The first eleven books came out in quick succession after the year 86, when he was approaching the age of fifty. Some were furnished with prefaces. From others he compiled a relatively mild anthology for the emperor Nerva. But as a rule the material was new and the publisher could hardly keep pace with the demand for it. How many women and of course men too must have seen themselves pitilessly reflected in the following passage, which at the same time obliterates their own view of themselves!

> The smell of Thais, worse than bad,
> exceeds that of a dyer's pail that's had
> long use, or rutting he'goat, rotten fish
> piled higher up on quays than we could wish,
> a lion's jaw well gorged, a carrion dog
> or foetus perished, in the womb a clog.
> When naked in the bath the wench,
> to counteract this plaguy stench
> will use a skin-refreshing lotion
> and plaster over it with urgent motion
> a three or four-fold layer of thick paint
> hoping to banish thus our noses' taint.
> But the result of all, I must say, is
> That Thais still stinks of – well, of Thais.

This abusive ditty, which all Rome was soon repeating as if it were a street-corner ballad, Thais had brought upon herself simply because she had dismissed Martial with the taunt that he was too old for her. She must have bitterly repented that she ever said such a thing. A certain Celia, who had pretended to be a Greek because Greek *hetairai*, like Greek actors, commanded high prices, did not fare much better. She had gone so far as to refuse admittance to any Roman and had to undergo the humiliation of being asked by Martial what sort of an opinion she could have of the people she dealt with if she thought they could believe a lie so transparent as to be obvious whenever she tried to utter a single sentence in Greek.

Like many men attracted by their own sex Martial was repelled by
women unless they were still in their first youth. He repeatedly
reproached them, in particular, with their offensive importunity, in
such contrast with the shy, demure bearing of male prostitutes, who
allured him for that very reason. He censured his mistress Lesbia
– who had nothing but her name in common with the woman beloved by Catullus – for being more shameless, though she was a
renowned courtesan, than the cheap whores who frequented
cemeteries in order to receive their lovers in the dark. One of
Lesbia's characteristics was never to draw the curtain when a man
was with her and she enjoyed most of all being surprised by some
unsuspecting visitor while she was already entertaining another
lover. Owing to this habit, as recorded by Martial, social historians
have added the name of Lesbia to the rather short list of women
noted for sexual exhibitionism.

Every refusal that Martial met with elicited an abusive poem
from him. When Saufeia declines to go bathing with him the reason
can only be, says he, that there are features of her figure, usually
veiled, which she does not dare to exhibit. If Marulla rejects him,
it's simply because he's not rich enough for her. If Chione does not
respond to his ardour when they are together, he takes care that all
Rome shall be assured that he is not the guilty party.

> You ask me whether Phlogis or Chione
> gives the best value for love's hard-earned money
> I answer that Chione has the looks,
> Phlogis the charm. Grey-bearded spooks
> she'll turn to boys again and Priam's old
> ashes could fan to glowing heat, however cold.
> She's got that something which in girls no man
> could ever strive against in counterplan.
> But fair Chione in your arms is dumb,
> feels nothing and remains quite numb.
> With absent gaze she scrutinizes space
> as if she had a marble statue's face.
> O gracious gods, pray grant me this my plea
> if for us mortals such a boon may be.
> Either lend beauty charm or be so kind
> as to add beauty to the charm we find.

Martial's dislike of old age caused him to conceive a furious hatred of courtesans who used the money they had made in their prime to cultivate the society of young people. He himself seems to have received offers of this kind in his youth, which he had no doubt sometimes accepted when hard up. The disgust he felt on these occasions, both with the woman concerned and with himself, found expression in a number of particularly rancorous epigrams. In a few of these there are unmistakable traces of his vexation at being himself regarded by the women in question as too old. He tells a certain Chloe, who was spending her fortune on an ancient Roman species of 'gigolo', that her 'Lupercus' will one of these days take the last shift off her back. The name Martial maliciously gives him was not his own, but that applied generically to any of the naked priests officiating at the Lupercalia, whose whips were supposed to render fertile any of the women they struck.

The poet's tendency to lash out with vituperation in all directions is less intelligible than the antipathy he shows, in common with Propertius, Tibullus and Catullus, to elderly procuresses. It would not be altogether easy to decide which of these writers has depicted the type – by no means confined to ancient Rome – in the most striking terms.

> And so she's off to hell at last. that she-beast,
> high on the scale of Nestor's years and only
> three months the Sibyl's junior. Think of it!
> That glib, loose tongue lies now for ever silent!
> So wise a hag we shall not see in future,
> so expert in the pairing of the love-lorn.
> Lie light upon her, earth! I mean by that phrase
> the soil should strew her grave with such sparse cover
> that the dogs won't have so hard a time of it
> when they come scrabbling for her bones, their supper!

These verses, a neat combination of hatred and 'black' comedy, might have been jotted down in the Subura (a quarter of Rome where provisions were sold and many prostitutes lived) or even possibly scribbled on the wall in a brothel. But both their energy and their discretion are most remarkable. Martial repeatedly succeeded in detaching himself from the quagmire which he not only describes but inhabited for three and a half decades. When he at last gave up the struggle and in his seventies realized that a poet's weapons were doomed to defeat, he sought peace and security, at the side of a wife, in his native Spain.

He longs for Rome

It was there, in the hill country south of the Ebro, in the depths of a province still only slowly undergoing Roman influence, that he composed the twelfth and last book of his Epigrams. They were inspired partly by his longing for Rome and partly by his recognition that so gifted a poet as himself might have been able to derive more from life than a mere distillation of its dregs. His thoughts turned, perhaps with envy, but in any case with melancholy, to the great lyrists of love in former days, who were moved by the *hetairai* of their period to indite the glorious songs that bestowed as lustrous an immortality on the girls they praised as on the poets themselves.

> If thou would'st have my line to wheel
> and soar on a mighty wing
> and live for ever in youthful zeal,
> then give me a love to sing!
>
> The rake Propertius found his Muse
> in Cynthia's beauty bright.
> Fair Nemesis planned no other ruse
> to bring Tibullus to light.
>
> 'Twas Lycoris who woke the first
> Gallus to genial life.
> Catullus by a Lesbia nursed
> dreamed of their amorous strife.
>
> Trust me, I'd gain a Vergil's crown
> for the skill of my verse, if led
> some Corinna like his to own
> or Alexis to my bed.

A significant summing up

This lament may not have been intended very seriously by Martial, but it provides a significant summary of his views. For all the female names he cites are those of *hetairai*. Not one of them is that of a girl or woman who could have been anything but the mistress of her

66

poet. The most powerful poetic talents in Rome were inspired by such easy conquests for two centuries, comprising the entire extent of the golden age of Latin verse. Yet so far as we can judge Clodia-Lesbia was the only one of such women who could lay claim to comparable intellectual status. Many Athenian *hetairai* developed a considerable degree of intelligence, wit and artistic sensitivity, which delighted their male admirers. But the fashionable Roman courtesans seem to have been more like moons, drawing their brilliance from the men of genius with whom they associated. Poets, however, have always been glad enough to bask in the delusions of such reflected glory.

The biographers of these writers occasionally deplore the prevalence of homosexuality, regret the exhaustion of Tibullus in precocious dissipation or ascribe the early deaths of certain poets of the epoch to reckless debauchery. But it is generally believed today that it was not so much the leading spirits of intellectual society in Rome who were particularly dissolute. The whole imperial period, on this view, clearly shows a breakdown of inhibitions in every direction. Prostitution proper almost disappears in the intoxicating fog induced by sexual obsession. The trade being a permanent institution which had been practised ever since the foundation of the city, even specifically social histories of life under the emperors omit the customary touching anecdotes of mercenary love. For no one could be expected to take much interest in any particular courtesan when an actual empress was in the habit of occupying a harlot's pallet, when a brothel was set up in the imperial palace itself and an emperor disguised himself as a eunuch in order to serve liquor in the cubicles of a whorehouse.

Connoisseurs at court

Messalina, Caligula and Commodus were not of course obliged, any more than other empresses or emperors, to go in search of direct contact with public prostitutes. It would have been possible for such despotic rulers to find at home in the palace, with less risk and more comfort, what they were looking for in such places. Commodus in fact had a private harem of three hundred women and three hundred boys. The atmosphere that attracted Messalina to the Subura and caused Caligula to establish a gambling-hell, complete with cubicles for fornication, in the imperial palace, was the odour of corruption, filth and squalor, quite possibly also the typically Roman brothel-stench, which is alleged to have been impervious to even the strongest perfumes of Arabia once it had settled firmly in the hair and skin. But neither Nero nor Otho nor Galba nor any other emperor or empress ever became truly addicted to this sort of thing, however often the avaricious Messalina might accept payment from deck-hands and gladiators. Nor would an imperial client ever have been satisfied with what the ordinary Roman prostitute could offer – so much less than the stimulation required by the excessively exigent temperaments of such libertines as Tiberius, Nero or Heliogabalus.

Prostitution at its height

While, therefore, the Roman upper classes and in particular the imperial court indulged in more and more new refinements of eroticism and thus provided the social historians with their most sensational stories, ordinary prostitution continued to exist on many levels and in many forms, though on the whole without undergoing much modification. In the course of centuries the ramifications and range of the market had reached a perfection of development only comparable with that of Alexandria at the same time or that of Georgian London later on. It would certainly be possible to compile an exhaustive doctoral thesis on the single subject of the various kinds of prostitute and their often highly expressive designations.

The vast numbers of girls and women who adopted the trade can be deduced from the strict code of morals drawn up by the Emperor Augustus, which clearly distinguishes between women who could be legally frequented and all the rest. The criminal law of the Republic had made no special provision for the punishment of the violation of female chastity, action in such cases being in general left to the sphere of domestic jurisdiction. But after the passing of the marriage laws formulated by Augustus offences of this kind were made the subject of criminal proceedings – that is to say, they were prosecuted by the State. Mommsen observed that this innovation was one of the most fundamental and lasting in human history. It applied to every free woman of good repute as well as to the man concerned. Freedwomen could be prosecuted under the new law in the same way as the free born. But a special regulation dealt with female slaves. Anyone associating with a female slave who did not belong to him could be charged with wilful damage to the property of another citizen. The law made no distinction between persons thus charged. A woman of good repute could even be proceeded against if she had encouraged one of her slaves to make love to her.

Exceptions to the chastity laws

These measures did not apply to certain definite, relatively restricted groups of women and girls, including harlots regularly engaged in their trade. But if such women retired, married and then began to associate with one of their former clients, the crime of unchastity was held to have been committed. As Roman law afterwards became a model for all civilized countries, this limitation of a whore's ill-fame to the period of her professional activity acquired special importance. In later times, for instance, it allowed veteran prostitutes to enter a nunnery or become respectable citizens. Another class exempt from prosecution under the chastity laws of Augustus was that of the female brothel-keepers. The landladies of inns and their female employees, since these establishments almost always functioned clandestinely as brothels, could also claim immunity, as could, surprisingly enough in modern eyes, any actress or female dancer or female musician.

If a woman wore the dress of a prostitute, dyed her hair blonde and behaved in public like a genuine street-walker, the man she thus deceived incurred no penalty. But she herself was arrested unless she registered as a prostitute. The consequence was that hundreds, perhaps thousands, of the names appearing in that long list belonged to women who did not actually practise the trade. Their object in reporting that they were whores was simply to evade interference and punishment for associating with men.

Ingenious subdivisions

Genuine prostitutes, however, continued to exist in such large numbers that they were obliged to organize themselves into separate groups in order to earn any sort of a living. Dozens of them have been distinguished by classical scholars who took more interest in the philological aspect of their task than in its subject. Their ingeniously contrived designations are admirable examples of the flexibility of the Latin tongue but unfortunately serve no practical purpose, since it is impossible to explain them to schoolboys.

Apart from the 'freelance' operators, for instance those gay ladies who often pretended to be Greeks and the ancient Roman equivalent of the 'good time girl', the most important of the true professionals were the *meretrices*. They lived like respectable women for most of the day, until the time came for the afternoon meal (*merenda*), from which they derived their name.* As in Paris at a later period, so also in ancient Rome the question 'What does one do at five o'clock?' only too often led to a discreditable adventure. The *meretrix* left her quarters at about five and repaired to a brothel, like an employee going on night shift. She paid her taxes regularly, never made a fuss and always did her very best not to come into conflict with the police. Her most dangerous rivals were the *famosae*, the 'notorious ones', women of good family who pretended to be prostitutes in order to amuse themselves in a brothel or earn pin-money. Many had begun by using such an establishment as a house of assignation in which to meet a particular lover and ended by indulging in a promiscuity which they often found themselves unable to give up.

The much envied delicatae

A class still more hated than that of the amateurs who took the bread out of the mouths of the undisguised professionals was that of harlots so young and pretty that they could afford to aim at the fattest purses. The dainty aspect and fastidious natures of these girls caused them to be known as *delicatae*. Men who wished to obtain their favours were not expected to haggle over the price. It often proved cheaper, in the end, to marry them. Even one of the emperors, Vespasian, sank to the level of this expedient. Flavia Domitilla had been a freedwoman and the mistress of a knight when she first smiled upon him, prior to his accession. She bore him three children, of whom Titus and Domitian were subsequently made emperors, though their mother had been a *delicata*.

* The future participle passive *merenda* (from *mereo*, 'I deserve' and therefore meaning 'that which will be deserved') was the name given to an afternoon meal taken between four and five o'clock in ancient Rome. *Meretrix*, also from *mereo*, meant literally 'she who deserves', i.e. earns a cash reward for services rendered. This name does not therefore refer primarily to the alleged habit of the *meretrix* in starting operations at the hour of *merenda*. [J.C.]

The *Dorides* (plural of *Doris*, a common feminine name in Greek) must have been as young and beautiful as the *delicatae*. It was the habit of the former to take a pride in practising their trade in the nude, as though they were really nymphs. To the wrath of many straitlaced Romans they used to exhibit themselves on their doorsteps in this state, that of goddesses who needed no clothing in the balmy atmosphere of Mount Olympus.

Another speciality at Rome was that of the *alicariae* (mill-girls) who not only ground the corn for the bread to be offered on the altars of Venus and Priapus but also sold it and remained at the disposal of the purchaser, in their own persons, for so long as he wished. These women may be regarded as the last survivors of temple prostitutes. For the loaves they sold were actually symbolic of the two divinities mentioned, so closely concerned with sexual enjoyment. The girls who supplied these grotesquely formed, saltless and unleavened wares had found it perfectly natural for centuries to accompany their presentation with the offer of their own bodies.

Eros among the tombs

The *bustuariae* considered themselves servants of the gods of the dead. For these women followed their calling in the great Roman cemeteries, either lying in graves which had not yet been filled in or else simply on the grass, with only a few tombstones to shelter them from view. The gravediggers and cemetery gardeners must have been their usual clients. It is difficult to imagine that many Romans were attracted by the strange conjunction of death and erotic proceedings in these places.

The mystery of the popular term *putae* for prostitutes has still not been fully elucidated. All that is certain is some connection or other with the Latin word *puteus*, meaning a well or tank, coupled with a passage in Plautus where that eminent reporter on the society of his day rattles off in jest a number of pet names for a harlot, the last of which is 'love-tank'.* French and some other modern Romance languages have borrowed and brought into general use the word *puta* from among the many which the ancient Romans employed to designate prostitutes.

* It seems probable that this expression carried a burlesque suggestion of the vagina. [J.C.]

The torrent of Latin technical terms employed in antiquity becomes overwhelming when those relating to whores are augmented by synonyms for their masculine or semi-masculine competitors. There were homosexuals of every age and variety of colouring, at least three kinds of eunuchs, depending on the method of castration adopted and its outcome, together with other weird specimens of this dismal form of life. Sometimes brothels could actually be found in which trained dogs, apes, donkeys and birds were put at the disposal of sodomites. Two lines by Juvenal suggest that the rabid salacity of the donkey in particular had a certain importance during the celebration of the Bona Dea Mysteries. In the archaic period a Roman adulteress was punished by being forced to submit to assault by this animal, which added the belabouring of its hoofs to the painful nature of her experience. This tradition may account for the special attention paid to the donkey in Rome over a prolonged period.

Slavery and castration

There were times at which the numbers of boys in Roman brothels exceeded the quantities of women and girls, at any rate until the Emperor Domitian forbade this variety of prostitution and prohibited the castration of children and slaves. The severity of the penalties for emasculation proves the depth of degradation to which society as a whole had fallen at this date. A slave who was castrated at once obtained his freedom and half his master's fortune was confiscated. Those who undertook the operation, not only slaves and persons of humble rank, but also doctors, were sentenced to death, as were also those who voluntarily submitted to the process. Castration of a foreign slave could not be regarded as damage to property, since the man's value would be increased by treating him in this way. Accordingly, the act fell into the category of *iniuria* (offence against the person). The Christian emperors at last succeeded, though only by slow degrees, in clearing the streets, at any rate, of male prostitutes. Within doors they lasted just about as long as slavery itself.

The army of male and female prostitutes was naturally reinforced at all times by an immense troop of 'camp-followers', hangers-on who comprised not only such whores as were no longer young and appetizing enough to fight in the front lines, but also panders and ponces, brothel-keepers and other shady opportunists.

Fate of the aged harlot

Whores grew old younger, if such a paradoxical phrase can be allowed, in Rome than in Athens or Corinth. For the Athenian custom of curtained windows and darkened rooms, current at any rate in the Piraeus and at Corinth, with its mass production of prostitutes, enabled many a veteran she-warrior to eke out a meagre existence as a *didrachma* (twopenny trollop). But in Rome the supply of women was more copious and varied, as well as being continuously strengthened by youthful contingents from the provinces. These girls took the fullest advantage of their superior physical attractions, without a thought for the future, so that by the time a Roman prostitute reached the age of thirty or at most forty she had to look round for some other way of earning a living. She was compelled to do so on account of the clothing she wore. For as soon as the new recruits began to prosper they went in for the Syrian or Babylonian garments which the Greeks had first made fashionable. These extremely thin silks, woven on the islands of Amorgos and Cos, elicited contradictory opinions from men of talent. Horace praised them. 'In Coan raiment they appear as if unclothed. With eye alone canst thou assess the harmony of line in leg and foot.' Seneca on the contrary storms. 'A multitude of wretched female slaves laboriously toil to enable that company of voluptuaries to reveal nudity under transparent veils of gauze, so that any stranger can be as familiar with their secret charms as a husband with his wife's.'

Such materials were of course expensive and at the same time much too flimsy to stand up to the hard wear to which they were exposed in the brothels. They were accordingly assumed only out of doors or at banquets, in order to allure clients. At the bawdy-houses and especially in the warm inner courts and under the colonnades whores were in the habit of promenading naked until they met an Adam to join their representation of Eve. Their older colleagues could not compete in such displays and therefore preferred to turn to auxiliary trades, of which there were plenty.

Love-potions and poisons

The most popular and no doubt most profitable of these alternative occupations, which accordingly came to be practised almost as soon as prostitution itself, was the preparation of various kinds of beverages, from entirely ineffective love-potions to more or less powerful aphrodisiacs and from remedies for diseases of the genitals* to deadly poison. The magician specializing in the sexual field, as described by Petronius, was an especial favourite. Persons who did not feel up to the mark erotically consulted some old woman who had the reputation of an expert and a similar authority was called in to apply a troublesome sexual weakness, by magical means, to a successful rival. Since these veterans in the mercenary service of Venus did not hesitate to silence a witness who might prove a nuisance or to cause some recalcitrant lady to experience disturbing dreams in bed, clients were probably never in very short supply and the most celebrated of the consultant sorceresses, if they had powerful protectors, might become very wealthy.

For some considerable time the preparation of poisons and the dispensing of philtres only incurred penalties under Roman law if they resulted in bodily harm or death. At this period, accordingly, the witches who concocted such brews had already begun to work on the development of the slow poisons which afterwards acquired such notoriety. It was difficult to discover by what means they had been administered and the delay allowed the poisoner enough time to make herself scarce.

But many of the methods used were quite harmless, though as a rule disagreeable to the subject. For example, a paste compounded from the soil on which a bull had urinated would be applied to the loins of a man suffering from impotence. Such were the principles upon which the stimulants of those days were manufactured. Anything which had a shape resembling even in the remotest degree a phallus was held to be useful in counteracting sexual deficiency, a shortcoming often really only due to anxiety or lack of confidence. The symbols thus employed included the dried and pounded skins of certain lizards, the trunks of elephants and of course the testicles of such animals as the wolf or the hedgehog. The women who prescribed remedies of this kind were mostly experienced

* It is not yet at all clear that diseases today recognized as 'venereal' were prevalent in antiquity. [J.C.]

enough. But not one of them had any scientific training. They can hardly be blamed for what they advised, especially as the contemporary doctors still advocated the most peculiar assortment of ingredients. Serenus Sammonicus and even Xenocrates of Aphrodisias were fond of prescribing dung, both human and animal, while Galen himself recommended the external application of that of goats to relieve tumours of the neck – though not in the case of city-dwellers; only of patients from the country.

For every wizard a thousand witches

Since anyone was permitted to practise medicine in ancient Rome there was no way in which the abuses perpetrated by female quacks could be controlled. They employed both true poisons and traditional domestic remedies, exploiting both contemporary superstitions and especially the difficulty of tracing the cause of any particular death or illness back to the potion they had prepared. Michelet's statement that for every wizard there must always be a thousand witches no doubt also accurately describes the Roman situation. No other occupation would be open to the experienced old women who knew their former trade only too well.

Those who did not understand how to brew potions undertook the more primitive and sinister operations of abortion and infanticide. Among thirty-five thousand registered prostitutes a great many unwanted children must have come into existence. Many a charming *delicata*, finding her career impeded by the swelling of a pregnancy, must have summoned one of the *sagae*, from whose designation Dufour may be right in deriving *sage-femme*, the French word for a midwife. If any such unnmarried mother still retained some natural feeling, she would venture upon the somewhat tricky expedient of exposing the infant in one of the traditional areas set apart for this purpose, for by so doing she could count on the possibility of the baby being noticed and rescued from its fate.

All these practices, the preparation of poisons and potions, spell-casting and infanticide, combined to give the world of the prostitute the character of a criminal society ready to carry out any assignment, however illegal or shocking. Its members would commit murder and arrange or at least promise to arrange any operation which a doctor would refuse to perform. Many investigators

75

of the frequency of mania in the imperial families relate this disorder to the absurd stimulants to which the exhausted voluptuaries in question resorted. Apart from sheer lunacy, serious diseases often resulted from the potions they drank and the ointments they applied to their bodies and were transmitted to their children.

Superstition and human sacrifice

The worst feature of these superstitious proceedings was without doubt the considerable number of innocent persons who were sacrificed in the course of such experiments. An adult might, after all, voluntarily and in full consciousness of the risk he was taking, expose his person to the dubious arts of a female poisoner or street-corner apothecary. But a foundling or the child of a slave could not defend itself against the fancy of a sick mind that a certain malady could only be cured by the blood or liver of a young, still vigorous human being. It would be unreasonable to exaggerate the total number of those who fell victims, in the course of centuries, to such dangerous and expensive operations. But thousands of children may well have succumbed to medical superstition alone between the time when secret remedies from the ancient East were in vogue and that of the infanticides perpetrated at the court of Louis XIV.

In comparison with the monsters who were capable of any atrocity for pay, whether or not they believed that their operations would effect cures, the panders for the most part appear relatively harmless in modern eyes, for their disgusting trade was strictly supervised. The aediles had of course other matters to attend to in their municipal duties, besides the control of prostitution. But modern practice in this connection seems to have been current even in ancient Rome. Prostitutes appear to have been regarded there as a necessary evil which it was impossible to prohibit. But for that very reason it was considered essential, so far as can be gathered, to restrain the activities of panders.

Brothel keepers at Rome

The obscure quarters of narrow lanes surrounding the Circus, and the Esquiline Hill and constituting the Subura resounded with the lamentations of procurers and brothel-keepers. They complained of the low fees earned by whores, the high costs of fitting out a brothel, though the cubicles rarely contained more than a big wooden bed and a shabby blanket, and the scanty consumption of refreshments by clients, etc.

But on the whole it was not adverse commercial conditions that worried the brothel-keepers. They had other troubles, one of which was diseases affecting the sexual organs (see note on p. 62). Such maladies had reached Rome from the Near East about the middle of the second century BC. After conquering the Levant the Roman armies had marched far into Persia, accompanied, like all victorious troops, by girls and boys who formed part of the spoils of war, many of these young people having been already infected. Hardly any great city of the antique world could match Rome in the variety of nationalities represented by the inhabitants and in addition the rabble of its native population, living in the most unhealthy circumstances, could be numbered by the hundred thousand. Consequently the metropolis became a centre of contagion unequalled in all Europe. Medical science was not yet equipped to deal with epidemics of such magnitude and such repeatedly novel symptoms. Women in particular, it appears, succumbed more often than men to these diseases, or if they recovered had a worse convalescence. Some reputable scholars are of opinion, therefore, that the popularity throughout the ancient world of pederasty and brothels for male prostitutes is to be ascribed to fear of infection by women. If such institutions barred all females, it might be supposed that one could take one's pleasure there without danger.

Registration by the aediles

Should any brothel-keeper be lucky enough to have only healthy inmates in his charge, there was always the possibility that some newcomer from the country might not have duly complied with the registration laws and would consequently be fined by the aedile. It usually fell to the lot of the pander to settle the penniless girl's debt, with the result that even at later periods many of the inmates of brothels were never able to clear themselves of obligations incurred at their first arrival in the establishment. The register of prostitutes is stated by a particularly industrious investigator to have also fixed the price which any harlot was entitled to demand for her services, a figure which would certainly require a more than ordinary degree of connoisseurship on the part of the aedile to assess.

At any rate disputes over fees were usually determined by reference to the register and the aedile concerned.

The main areas for prostitution

One consequence of this strict regulation was the prohibition of 'homeless or roving' prostitution. It lurked in so many and various byways in Rome that the aediles were particularly concerned to keep such women off the main streets at any rate. Their efforts, like all supervisory measures of the kind, were partially successful. The easier it proved to sweep the humbler practitioners into dark corners, the more conspicuous and impudent the smarter courtesans became. They had themselves carried through the streets wherever they pleased, borne in litters with the curtains drawn back to reveal the occupants reclining in hip-length cloaks of gleaming blue silk. Meanwhile their male competitors trotted about, uttering seductive murmurs, so that even a blind man would know the kind of pseudo-masculine fellow-citizens with whom he was rubbing shoulders. By day such scenes took place in the Via Sacra, while in the evenings they were transferred, just as in modern times, to the Appian Way, which led out into the Campagna and provided plenty of shadowy spots favourable to dalliance among its bushes, tombs and sepulchral monuments.

Streets and roads

These streets were regarded as pleasure-grounds by the Romans, so it was impracticable to clear them of courtesans, easy as it was to recognize such women from the brilliant blue colour of their garments. Nor could the boy stroller be eliminated, with his toga gathered about him in much the same way as a woman's robes. Panders, too, were almost ubiquitous, for every water-carrier practised this trade as a sideline and any innkeeper, barber or seller of perfumes could be consulted in the same connection.

In the shops of the dealers in scent and the hairdressers both male and female employees performed any service a client might require of them. The atmosphere of intimacy which still prevails in establishments for manicure, chiropody, hair-stripping and other aids to physical well-being or personal attractions favoured familiarities. At Massilia, for example (the later Marseilles), both boy and girl slaves were trained at special schools for this employment.

While it was only with difficulty that the urban streets were kept respectable, the country roads presented no such problem to prostitutes. There at last they found regions, the main arteries of communication across the Roman Empire, where no one even attempted to interfere with them. They and their followers could operate quite freely there. Such roads, though not paved as they were in the city, remained, so to speak, as visible branches of it, connecting the whole vast domain under Roman rule, all its numerous and mutually diverse provinces, with the metropolis. The highways were used by military officers and soldiers, by civil officials, by couriers and merchants. These travellers were therefore typical representatives of the imperial power as a whole and generally based on the capital. But there were also humbler citizens who lived on the road and made a living out of it, wandering interminably from one part of the empire to another and timidly making way for any vehicle or litter demanding precedence.

Horace on the move

The journey from Rome to Naples took four days if one was in a hurry and travelled light. But as a rule wayfarers were on the road for weeks or even months, during which they were supplied by the local traders with everything they could possibly want, including sexual gratification. Horace's account of his journey from Rome to Bari, which took thirteen days, has survived. He went by the Appian Way, one of the most famous lines of communication in the antique world. He complains, like many other disgruntled travellers, of the smoke-filled, filthy and bug-ridden inns, packed with all sorts of riff-raff, run by surly landlords and infested by complacent females. These domestics, called *copae*, were on hand in enormous numbers at Rome, where their favours could be bought for a glass of wine. But in the lonely country inns, to Horace's wrath, they put on such airs that sometimes they kept a customer waiting indefinitely. But as a general rule, at any rate along the country roads, there was so little difference between a tavern and a brothel that the landlords of such places were regarded as following a dishonourable profession and at a later period, after laws had been passed for the protection of slaves, the informal hiring of girls at inns was forbidden.

A comprehensive view of all the alternative accommodation

available for the oldest of trades renders it perfectly intelligible that though there were only forty-six officially recognized brothels in Rome under the empire there were more than thirty-five thousand harlots. The brothel in the restricted sense of the term had in fact a great deal of competition to meet. However much the few genuine bawdy-houses might extend the services they offered and assume such pompous appellations as *Libidinum Consistorium* ('Sexual Pleasures United'), thus alleging that they catered satisfactorily for all tastes, the fact was that vice had by this time become rampant in every quarter of Rome. It is of course not true that life under the empire could be described as constituting a single huge orgy, as asserted with pious horror by Schlichtegroll and other respectable middle-class nineteenth-century authors. In a metropolis so eminent in so many directions as Rome there must always have existed a majority of hard-working people, an efficient bureaucracy and an uncontaminated nucleus of ordinary citizens. Nor was it the male or female prostitutes of Rome who destroyed the power of the city in the fifth century. Many immoral emperors, moreover, were nevertheless strong and prudent rulers.

Ineradicable abuses

Yet it remained a characteristic feature of the metropolis that its swarms of whores and panders, of *souteneurs*, quack doctors and brothel-keepers, could not be eradicated and expelled from the venerable buildings to which they clung. They could always find some refuge from which it proved impossible to extract them.

The trouble had started with the most ancient cults maintained in the city, celebrations in honour of local divinities, harvest festivals and the primitive, orgiastic fertility rites in which the masses of the people openly indulged. These riotous proceedings became intensified when the wild debaucheries of oriental religious mysticism were imported by legionaries and traders returning from abroad. A measure of official toleration appeared in the spectacles of military triumphal processions, when all Rome could contemplate beautiful Syrian women, negresses and females of other equally seductive races from Egypt and elsewhere, who were afterwards sold to the brothels. Nor could the evil be extirpated by the reforming emperors, since they themselves were by no means patterns of virtue. Neither Augustus nor Domitian applied their legislation to their own personal behaviour.

Christianity itself, for a long period, could do little to improve the situation. For nothing must have seemed stranger to the antique world than the association of religion with chastity. Temples and priests had been responsible for the first organized prostitution. It appeared perfectly natural to any ancient Roman that sexual pleasures should be offered him, at a price, in the shadow of the Temple of Venus. Even citizens who had throughout their lives carefully distinguished good and evil would have considered it senseless to refrain from sexual intercourse on any grounds except perhaps those of ill-health.

The notorious lure of great cities

The plundering of Rome by nomadic armies and later by pirates from North Africa broke more deeply the continuity of the gay life of the city's underworld than the influence of its first Popes, who introduced few changes into the habits of ordinary people, or that of the Christian emperors, who had more important matters to attend to than keeping the Subura or the Via Sacra clear of prostitutes. Consequently the conviction became stronger in Rome than elsewhere that no large city, least of all a metropolis, can ever dispense with 'the oldest profession'. It might even be held that this trade had contributed in a not altogether negligible degree to the notorious fascination of the great cities of antiquity, where each house, not excluding 'disorderly' ones, could be regarded as deserving a social history of its own.

BOOK II

FORBIDDEN FRUIT

*

The wandering scholars and the townsfolk

'All the faults of humanity are more pardonable than the means employed to conceal them.' – LA ROCHEFOUCAULD

The word inscribed on the banner of Christianity, the new religion of the Mediterranean world, was 'Chastity''. This idea was not derived so much from the Old Testament, where the Jewish kings, with their concubines, feminine bed-warmers and other oriental specialities do not seem to have been much more morally austere than their heathen neighbours, as from the pagan sensualists of the ancient Roman Empire, against whom Christianity had declared war. The chastity ordained by the early Christian Church was proclaimed in the manner of an election slogan, on the tactically sound premiss that in this sphere the strongest arguments could be deployed and the clearest demarcation lines drawn.

The vessel of sin

The principle in question actually at first caused most bewilderment among its own adherents, for no one knew or could know to what extent chastity should be practised. Ascetics being liable to draw exaggerated conclusions, some people considered that a refusal to indulge in sensual pleasures necessarily implied a general condemnation of women. St Clement declared that the only object in marriage was procreation. But the prospective parents, he added, 'must always remember that they are in God's presence and should pay due respect, by guarding against all unchastity, to the bodies with which HE has provided them'. Origen, one of the early fathers of the Church, was a particularly zealous champion of sexual restraint. He eventually took the view that in the Beyond at any rate one ought to be safe from contamination by such vessels of sin as women obviously were. This attitude led straight to the belief that women could not have immortal souls or any hope of eternal bliss, a doctrine which was one of the reasons why the teaching of Origen was pronounced heretical three hundred years later.

But the assertions of the 'man of steel', as Origen was called, decisively influenced the adoption of celibacy by the higher dignitaries of the Christian Church. 'It was resolved, in general . . . to command all clerics included in the ministry to refrain from intercourse with their wives and the procreation of children and that those who disobey this order be excluded from holding clerical office.' (Canon xxiii of the Synod of Elvira.) Some far-sighted princes of the Church notified their opposition to this decree. Synesius of Cyrene, for instance, boldly confessed about 410, on his proposed appointment to a bishopric, that he had a wife.

God and the Law and the sacred person of Theophilus, Archbishop of Alexandria, have given me a wife. I declare and testify to all men that I utterly refuse to separate from her. Nor shall I have to do with her only in secret, like an adulterer. Piety forbids the one and the Law the other. Furthermore, I both wish and pray that I may be granted very many and admirable children.

Resistance to asceticism

Other objections were based upon the certainly natural enough question how such restraint, demanded of a husband in relation to his wife, could be enforced. For while he had his ministry, his faith and his aim in life to consider, she was merely a woman and could not fully exercise even that narrow vocation unless she became a mother and lived a normal married life with the husband of her choice. Bishop Paphnutius frankly stated that 'not everyone would be able to practise abstinence . . . the chastity of all wives of (clerics) could probably not be maintained in these circumstances'.

We know today how this thousand-year-old dispute over the possibility of sexual abstinence in the clergy was eventually settled. Celibacy was the answer. Marriage being forbidden to priests, there need not, at least, be any mock marriages, legions of dissatisfied wives of priests and priestly cuckolds. The renunciation in principle of any dealings with women, expressed by so many documents of the early Christian era, remained, however, an intractable position. The Christian view of women continued and still continues to be the most ticklish feature of the new morality and involved Christian communities in the most desperate straits, for instance that arising from the delusions of belief in magic.

The courtesan discovers her soul

The good-time girls and obliging ladies had no suspicion, apparently, that they were about to fall victims to new and terrible forms of proscription. For they turned to the new faith more readily than their habitual patrons. Male representatives of the smart set in Rome resisted for a considerable time the temptations of leading a life of humility and chastity. But the courtesans not only of Rome but of the whole empire discovered that they had souls. They were delighted to find that, contrary to all expectation, there was still something left in the world that had not been soiled. They retrieved their humanity at last.

The legends of the saints supply so many examples of this kind of self-communing and revulsion of feeling among prostitutes of all people that there can be no doubt of the peculiar attraction of Christianity for this section of the population, which had been downtrodden for centuries. Despite all the eulogies of them in Greek and Latin verse, despite all the immortality they had acquired in stone and their innocent appearance in paintings, it was only now, perhaps, ever since such venal women had existed, that they became conscious of the iniquity of their lives and simultaneously realized that when they surrendered their bodies they did not at the same time give up the essential and most precious possession of any human being.

It is hard to imagine any type of person or professional group more susceptible than prostitutes of every kind to the sense of liberation and exaltation which may be conveyed by the idea of an earthly envelope inhabited by an immortal soul. For the very reason that many harlots felt themselves sinking deeper and deeper into the mire of their trade and saw no chance of finding any way out of it, they eagerly grasped at the opportunity offered them by a new road to salvation and changed their mode of life. In the absence of hope no one would do such a thing. For a life already lost cannot be transformed. The Christian *hetairai* fortified by the new faith provided it with a series of martyrs and saints as indomitably courageous in their altered careers as they had been of necessity utterly submissive in those they had abandoned.

If a new religion were to be founded today its advocates and preachers would probably refrain from visiting quarters mainly occupied by prostitutes. But in the ancient world the *hetairai* were simply too conspicuous to be ignored. It also came natural to the missionaries to aim at making converts in the citadels of vice, which they felt to be at the same time the citadels of paganism. For the conflict between Christian and heathen had long been raging most furiously in the field where chastity faced its opposite. There were of course other spheres of contention, the world of the slaves, that of the temples and that of the Circus with its baiting of wild beasts and its combats of gladiators. But the special power of attraction exercised by sexual activities had very soon caused both antagonists to realize that a decision gained in this direction would have the widest repercussions. Whenever, therefore, the Christians triumphed by converting a courtesan, the pagan Romans took their revenge, not by simply executing the convert forthwith, but by first marching her through the streets of their cities naked and next planting her among the inmates of a brothel.

A wealth of legends

So many stories of this kind have survived from the early Christian centuries that it may fairly be assumed that the narrators took a secret, unacknowledged pleasure in describing the incidents in question. The monkish scribes led such uneventful lives that they can hardly be blamed for turning with special zeal to themes of a licentious character, provided the adventures had an edifying conclusion. For example, our excellent fellow-countrywoman Hrotswitha of Gandersheim,* for all her pious fervour, gives a distinctly exuberant colouring to her pictures of pagan depravity when she narrates the life of Mary of Egypt, rescued from prostitution to become a recluse.

Mary began as a harlot in Alexandria, a city which had something of the reputation in the ancient Mediterranean world of Marseilles today. For seventeen years, like thousands of other

* A tenth-century German nun. [J.C.]

girls, she led a wretched existence of subservience to sailors from Spain or Gaul, Italy or Syria. Then she saw the light and abandoned the wickedly gay city. Some conversation or experience, some meeting with one of the Christian preachers then so assiduously diligent in North Africa, was probably the cause of her decision. She took herself off to a wilderness, though not to one of the low-lying deserts immediately to the south of Alexandria, but to Palestine. There she encountered, to the east of the river Jordan, the future Pope Zosimus. Only scanty traces of the beauty of the former courtesan remained. Years of life in the wilderness had destroyed her clothing. The unprotected flesh had withered in the sun. The skin was deeply tanned, the hair whitened and unkempt. She told Zosimus that she had desired to make a pilgrimage and after reaching Jerusalem had decided not to return to Alexandria, where every dwelling had witnessed her shame.

The patron saint of repentant prostitutes

The festival of Mary of Egypt is celebrated on 2 April. She is said to have died in 422, after forty-seven years as a hermit in the wilderness. She is represented by painters as sunburnt and naked, sometimes as a negress, holding the three loaves with which she set out for the desert. Yet strangely enough neither she nor the New Testament penitent, called alternatively Mary of Magdala or Mary Magdalene, became the patron saint of repentant prostitutes. This function was allotted to a certain holy woman from Syracuse, who does not seem to have been a prostitute at all. Her name was Lucia and she is related to have so provoked her betrothed, a Roman living in Syracuse, by her chastity, that he denounced her as a Christian. In the age of Diocletian this charge meant almost certain death. Lucia accordingly, after being tortured in various ways, was finally executed on 13 December 304 by a sword-thrust in the throat. The legend proves that chastity alone, at that time, was enough to reveal a woman as a Christian. Chastity and Christianity were as closely associated as unchastity and belief in the ancient gods.

Condemnation to compulsory prostitution

In the same year in which Lucia suffered, the sisters Irene, Agape and Chionia were martyred at Salonica as a result of their chastity, while in Egypt the Prefect Hierocles treated Christian women with such severity that he regularly sentenced them to compulsory prostitution. The most remarkable and embittered struggle between paganism and Christianity, the pleasures of the flesh and their renunciation, took place in the brothels of the empire under Diocletian. Prostitutes who had seen the light of the new spirit fled from the establishments in which they had hitherto lived. A courtesan who had taken the famous name of Thais betook herself to a walled-up cell in a monastery, where one of the monks, called Paphnutius, made her repeat a single short prayer for three years on end. Pelagia, an actress, consulted a hermit, who showed her the way to salvation. The prostitute Theodote was compelled by the Roman authorities to continue her trade in spite of her conversion to Christianity. Afra, one of the camp-followers of the Roman forces at Lechfeld near Augsburg in southern Germany, on refusing to admit any more clients, was carried off by the enraged troops to an island in the river Lech and burnt alive. Her bones are preserved at the church of St Ulrich in Augsburg under the altar called by her name.

The gaps which the new religion of chastity had opened in the ranks of the devotees of Venus were only partially closed. Although the majority of the Christian women denounced were sentenced to the brothels, at any rate at certain periods, the trade of the *meretrices*, which had been so flourishing under the first emperors, came gradually to an end. It was not much good, for instance, sending seven Christian virgins at once to a brothel at Ancyra. No one could be found to patronize them, for they were all between seventy and eighty years old. In other cases the superstitious Romans, Greeks, Syrians and Egyptians were repelled by manifestations of the faith of the converts. The basilica of St Agnes in the Via Nomentana at Rome commemorates a virgin of that name. The Prefect Sempronius ordered her clothing to be torn from her body. But it was immediately covered by a miraculous growth of her hair and so became invisible to the onlookers. When she was taken to a brothel no one except the Prefect's son dared to approach her. But when he did so he is alleged to have been struck down by a thunderbolt.

Propaganda for the new faith

The questions whether all these legends are true or not and to what
extent the names of the persons involved and the events described
have been confused are not very important. What is important is
that they were common gossip. For in a world in which very few
people could read and neither newspapers nor any other modern
methods of influencing the masses existed it was only such stories,
legends, rumours and traditions which eventually, in the course
of decades and centuries, consolidated the new, specifically
Christian, attitude to life. They did more than merely introduce
the populations of the empire to Christian doctrine. For in that
case Christianity would have remained only one of the many
religions which had come to be associated with faith in the gods of
ancient Rome. It was the psychological bases of that faith which
the tales of the Christian martyrs undermined. The casual pagan
outlook passed away, as defeats on the frontiers multiplied, imperial power declined and the loss of valuable provinces brought
economic disaster. The decision whether or not to cultivate
chastity depends in the last resort upon what principles of conduct
are considered essential. In former times the Romans had gone so
far, in their dread of diseases affecting the sexual organs, as to
prefer boys to the Asiatic women provided by the brothels. Now,
when they felt obliged to believe in the existence of the soul, they
began to be anxious about their spiritual welfare.

Continued existence of the brothel

Nevertheless, to suppose that the houses of prostitution thereupon
closed their doors and that the inmates packed up and travelled
back to the homes they had left for the great vicious cities of Rome,
Corinth and Alexandria, would be to underestimate the primitive
strength of survival latent in their ancient trade. The establishments remained open and a new thrill, that of the consciousness of
sin, was added to the carnal encounter with the girls on sale. What
had previously been regarded as entertainment, hygienic necessity
and a pleasant change became an excitingly wild and 'wicked' spice
of life in the growing tedium of the dawn of the Middle Ages.
Christianity had intended to destroy carnal pleasure. But only
delight in it had been found vulnerable and laid low.

Such psychological changes were hardly more important than

those brought about by Christianity in the social structure of Europe during the early medieval period. These were not so evident in the Mediterranean world, where the ancient cities still remained in being, as in the north of the continent, where the heathen Teutonic and Slavonic tribes, after conversion to Christianity, ceased their migrations, founded cities and for the first time grew familiar with the higher standards of civilization which had long prevailed among Greeks, Romans, Egyptians, Syrians and other peoples.

Small and impecunious as these first settlements in the north were, they attracted astonishingly large numbers of citizens. The towns did not offer much in the way of freedom. But there was more of it to be found there than in the country, where every labourer was subject to some lord or other. In urban groups on the other hand, a certain amount of provision for those without property gradually came to be customary. At Rome persons without possessions had got used to living on the bounty of the State and its free distributions of corn. In France and the Netherlands, in Germany and England, these members of the population were also homeless. If they left the service of their lord they could only find security in the territory of another. Municipal authorities for long refused to admit serfs to their communities. The serfs accordingly roamed the roads and crowded daily through the gates of the towns, where they begged at the church doors and however they got on were repeatedly expelled. In times of distress a thousand or more would invade a single town, often constituting more than a tenth of the population according to the statistics compiled at this period.

Wandering scholars and beggars

This roving population, of both sexes and various age-groups, supplied medieval settlements with venal girls and women. At many places they were only permitted to ply their trade in darkness and had to carry small lanterns. At Nuremberg they could operate, officially, during the first two hours after sunset in summer and during the first three in winter. But on the whole improvised measures of control were the rule everywhere, owing to the enormous numbers of migrants who filled the streets. Compassion led to their being given food and humanity forbade their slaughter. They followed goods to the markets, pilgrims to the south and the armies into conquered enemy territory.

In France, by the year 806, warnings to beware of these bands were already being issued. Within a few centuries of the downfall of the Roman Empire the Christian doctrine of poverty and the examples of pilgrimage and mendicant friars had combined with ecclesiastical charity and the provision of victuals for the poor to create one of the most typical phenomena of the European Middle Ages in this nation of beggars, which became a nursery of rogues, a crucible of races and a seething multitude of vagabonds, among whom wandering scholars, Jews and gipsies were conspicuous and therefore repeatedly mentioned in surviving records. The no less numerous girls and women formed a dumb and submissive train of camp-followers.

No organized prostitution

Organized prostitution had not yet begun at this period. The institution was so unfamiliar to the Teutonic peoples that they only very gradually adopted it. But as at all times and places there were panders among them who exploited girls. In this case it was mainly the horse-dealers who arranged the sale of young women. A few of the fair-haired type were even exported to the East, though in view of contemporary traffic conditions the obstacles to this trade must have proved considerably more troublesome than nowadays.

In the year 973 the Spanish Jew Ibrahim ibn Jaqub, who had been converted to Mohammedanism, travelled through Bohemia, Central Germany and the Baltic lands, then still inhabited by Slavs. He does not expressly admit, in the surviving fragments of his report at any rate, that one of his objects was to purchase blonde prisoners of war captured by Baltic tribes in battles with the Teutons. But this conclusion may be drawn from certain indications in his text. If he were in fact so engaged he could not have been alone in his enterprise. The Rani of the island of Rügen, the Pomeranians and the Liutici waged almost continuous war against the Danes and the Swedes, carrying off very many of them after a victorious conflict. But even in times of peace such girls, in particular, as had been involved in some scandal, were regularly sold to Arab merchants by the Teutons of northern Europe.

The still heathen Vikings and the Arabs who did business with them combined to solve, to their mutual profit, the problem of what to do with dissolute women. But within the empire, where the protection of the Church extended to both the just and the unjust, traders in this connection had to be more discreet. For centuries the authorities preferred to put up with the nuisance of strolling females rather than provide whores with a fixed abode where they could settle down. In Italy itself, however, the Church had long since come to terms with prostitution. Even the Papal Treasury enjoyed a revenue from premises which it had leased to brothel-keepers – such an income amounting in good years, when many pilgrims visited Rome, to as much as 20,000 ducats. Meanwhile, in central Europe the wanderers had it all their own way, under no obligation to anyone and paying no taxes, but constituting a menace to security and morality alike. Whenever such a band of rovers sat down to feast on the common stock it had acquired, the strolling harlots took advantage of the opportunity.

Ballad of the beggarwomen

> The beggarwomen come to call,
> tough and upstanding one and all.
> The leather bottle passes round
> till every pocket's empty found.
> And drunk we get I'll warrant ye
> with miracles for all to see.
> For the blind will watch and the dumb will shout
> and the lame and halt are straightened out.
> Then fast and furious we prance
> as up we rise for the beggars' dance.

The scene is one which we have all witnessed, even if only on the stage in *The Threepenny Opera*. It presents the most colourful picture of the life of the masses in medieval times and the most forceful poetic minds have always been attracted by it. In France François Villon, himself a member of such circles, lived in brothels and was at least once nearly hanged. In England Marlowe, the son of a shoemaker, is alleged to have been stabbed in a brawl over some woman.* In Germany behaviour of this kind was dealt with by Sebastian Brant, author of *The Ship of Fools*, and the incisively

---

* It was definitely established some years ago that the quarrel arose over the payment of a bill at a Deptford inn. [J.C.]

eloquent preacher Johann Geiler of Kaisersberg.

In the writings of Villon, Brant and Geiler, together with those of Pamphilius Gengenbach and some other authors whose names are unknown to us, the horde of vagabonds they described begins to assume a certain significance in the history of ideas and civilization. The wanderers came under close investigation. Their talk was listened to and it is probable that a few of the better educated were induced to impart instruction in thieves' and beggars' slang. Some of the strange forms taken by prostitution among beggars and vagrants generally are recorded by Brant and in still more precise terms by the anonymous *Liber Vagatorum*. The ordinary process of simple prostitution for cash went on inconspicuously among the rest, being mainly documented by the use of a considerable number of old words for features of the trade. The bawdy-house was indicated by several such coarse expressions, its female keeper and her charges by others. But as competition was severe and prostitution has always provided a free field for every kind of perversity, the most inventive of the roving harlots figured out their own specialities, some of which are illustrated by the *Liber Vagatorum*.

Tricks of the strolling trade

Some of the girls were known as 'sin-scourers', being 'whores who roamed the countryside announcing that although they had taken to a dissolute life they wished to mend their ways and begged to be given alms for the sake of Mary Magdalene'.

The 'bedsters' also appealed to the sympathy with self-sacrifice and the piety of the Middle Ages by spreading a blanket, if possible near a church, but always in some crowded square, and throwing themselves into fake convulsions, as if they were in agony. One of these women thought of an interesting variant of such a display, after she had collected a group of respectable, kind-hearted females around her. She declared that she had recently given birth to a toad and presented her miraculous offspring to the monastery at Einsiedeln, a place of pilgrimage. She now needed a pound of meat every day to feed it. It turned out, however, that the meat-swallowing monster was nothing more nor less than a *souteneur*, who was awaiting in an adjacent inn the result of his supporter's fairy-tale.

The 'crazies' and 'strippers' relied on the love of staring that characterized the inhabitants of small towns, who were offered very little distraction by the ecclesiastical and municipal authorities. The 'crazy' behaved as if she were a lunatic and accordingly adopted indecent attitudes and exposed parts of her person, giving the onlookers to understand that such pledges could be redeemed at nightfall for due payment. The 'stripper' went in for less strenuous methods by simply exhibiting herself got up as a shabby waif, practically nude, on the steps of a church until someone, posing as overcome by charitable feelings, signed to her to follow him.

As no legalized prostitution existed, while there was a great demand on the part of ordinary citizens, young artisans and even priests for dealings with women unprotected by law, makeshift solutions of the problem were devised. They were planned, with the ingenuity of persons who had nothing else to do but think, to suit local customs. The peculiarities of the inhabitants of a region, their local traditions, were exploited, as in the case of Einsiedeln, with unerring precision. The beggars, harlots and wandering scholars made use of everything they came across on their roads from town to town, for by this time they knew such localities far better than any of the people they met there.

Roving multitudes

No one knows how many there may have been of them. At certain places they were counted by panic-stricken officials, but as a rule only their vast numbers were deplored. They crammed the highways with primitive tumult and the unrest of the rootless. Jews and gipsies contributed oriental subtlety. Persons displaced by the endless wars of the Middle Ages and deserters from feudal duties added to the common stock of resources the tricks and subterfuges learned by the cunning of peasants during centuries of servitude. Everyone had his own speciality and the women and girls, in addition, had their own persons, which they used as trump cards when high stakes were in prospect.

Those 'tough and upstanding beggarwomen' of whom Nicodemus Frischlin sang, must have occupied the serious attention of several German city councils at various times between the eleventh and thirteenth centuries. The glittering and clinking coins that poured into the laps of the strolling charmers must also have added up to a considerably larger sum than that gained by the sturdy ruffians who begged on the church steps, alleging as an excuse that they had once been hangmen. The male beggars could be got rid of. No one wanted them. But why should the hard-earned money of the citizens be thrown away year after year, even month after month, on strolling harlots, when it would be so easy to plant a few of them, under municipal protection, in a single building and share in their earnings?

These typically middle-class arguments, with their spice of prurience, were found convincing. They were based on the consideration that whores, after all, were necessary and could easily be replaced – from abroad, naturally – as soon as they grew stale. For there could be no question of training local girls for such a trade. It was in this way, in the shadows of the walls of small towns, cosily enough, that the traffic started which today causes headlines when practised under the neon-lighting of St Paul's.*

Origin of the bawdy-house

The individual encounters which occurred in these buildings, at that time known as 'women's quarters', could not have been unprecedented in German life, otherwise there would have been no such places available. The existent accommodation itself was however an innovation, though it was adopted so long after the Roman brothel had become general that it can scarcely be regarded as having been imported from the south. Medieval Germany was intensively and consciously self-centred. An international outlook was not yet feasible, for even other nations were still in the process of formation and consolidation. Nor did Germans yet think along metropolitan lines, for they had no big cities. No particular horizon attracted them, education being still at the stage of imparting only the most elementary information. All the conditions were therefore favourable for the creation of national, unalterably German brothel. It became so German, in fact, that at first the name, a word of French derivation* did not apply to it at all.

In the age of Charlemagne the 'women's quarters' meant simply a building or room, situated on the lord's estate or in the village,

---

* i.e. San Paolo fuori le mura, the oldest church in Rome. [J.C.]

* Fr. *bordel*, Ger. *bordell*. It may be observed, however, that the English equivalent, 'brothel', is of Anglo-Saxon derivation. It meant in Old English a 'wretch'; this noun having been formed from the past participle *brothen*, of the verb *bréothon*, to destroy. [J.C.]

where women and girls of the serf class gathered to work under supervision. Their spinning, weaving, flax-dressing, pounding, cutting out of garments, needlework and other activities were undertaken in common because a serf's accommodation would only exceptionally provide space and light enough for such occupations and also because in any case simple-minded employees of this kind needed guidance by a manageress.

So conspicuous a collection of the female subordinates of a lord must have proved a temptation both to him and his guests, even if they happened to be in other respects good-natured and law-abiding. The incitement to sin would be much more powerful in the case of petty landowners brutalized in the numerous wars and plundering expeditions of the period. After an all-night banquet, when they had drunk deep, there would be no point in riding off at once in broad daylight to attack the nearest town. They would be much more likely to remember some maidservant in the women's quarters. They might even leave after their first carouse to inspect the female serfs occupying the building and apply such pressure as might be necessary to their feeble resistance.

From the estate to the town

The women's quarters on an estate developed accordingly into something like a pool of girls, on the lines of an oriental harem. Any man who heard the expression 'women's quarters' soon began to connect it with the diversions which might be obtained there, provided by its spinning and weaving maidservants. Consequently, when the municipalities began, during the central and late Middle Ages, to erect pleasure resorts for soldiers, travellers and probably also for the more prosperous class of citizens, no more suitable name than 'women's quarters' could be found for the establishments in question.

As they could not be set up without the aid or consent of the town council, the keeper of such a place invariably depended on that body, often as its tenant, but always anxiously concerned with the payment of his taxes, since his licence could be withdrawn at any moment by the council. The urban 'women's quarters' also afforded protection, quite essential in that rude age, to the virtue of the virtuously inclined. Respectable housewives and their daughters ceased to be molested, since a few steps would take any

95

importunate fellow to a building where for a trifling sum he could satisfy his lusts with impunity.

But even the strolling charmers, once they had agreed to lodge at the bawdy-house, were protected by the council. No one was permitted to do them any injury or defraud them of their earnings. Moritz Bermann actually reported in his *Old and New Vienna, The Story of the Imperial City and its Environs* that the girls concerned, 'in consideration of their sacrifice for the common good', were accorded civic rights.

Many such harlots might have regretted their free and easy life on the highways. Yet the advantages just mentioned were not to be despised. Security was important in those days and the prospect of a warm room after years of roving was undoubtedly attractive. The councillors also kept competition at a distance from their chosen contingent. Unauthorized 'women's quarters' were closed and amateurs caught at the trade were escorted to the town gates, where they were birched and formally exiled.

Jews excluded

Apart from married men, who in most towns were not allowed to visit brothels, and priests who did not dare to do so in the smaller settlements, everyone was satisfied with the situation. It should also be recorded that in certain towns Jews also were forbidden to enter the 'women's quarters' and risked their lives if they ignored this prohibition. For it must have been issued not only on religious but also on racial grounds.

The extremely ancient trade of harlotry seems, in view of all these considerations, to have been organized in the towns of medieval Europe almost on the lines of a guild, being similarly taxed and protected against unauthorized practitioners. Although the 'libidinous women', who were certainly less libidinous in their behaviour than their male clients, wore distinguishing badges on shoulder or arm and were occasionally provided with short cloaks, red caps or veils to show their difference from respectable women, yet no less a personage than the great organizer of the German State, Rudolf of Habsburg, forbade in 1276 any 'offence' against a whore. Now that someone had at last taken their part they were no longer outlaws. The closed community of the medieval town would never permit the demoralization of anyone who had once belonged to it. Difficult as it may have been to escape from such a backwater, one would have to be extraordinarily unlucky to be utterly ruined there.

The Church's excellent digestion

These municipal and imperial regulations have to be borne in mind when it is realized that even towns under ecclesiastical control could not ignore the need for 'women's quarters' and that consequently it was to the bishops themselves that the keepers of such establishments paid rent. The Archbishop of Mainz pocketed revenue from this source until 1457. In that year however a new occupant of that delightful see on the Rhine felt the arrangement to be incompatible with his dignity and passed on his rights in this connection to the Prince-Counts of Hennegau. At Frankfurt the Leonhard monastery owned a brothel adjacent to the Mainz Gate and administered by the municipal authorities, who were accordingly obliged until 1561 to pay a proportion of their profits of management to the monks. In 1309 Bishop Johann of Strassburg actually built one of these places at his own expense, thus becoming not only the lessor but also the founder of the establishment.

In Tiefer Graben, Vienna

Bigger cities needed several 'women's quarters'. In Vienna until well into the sixteenth century there were three. Two stood close to the so-called Wieden Gate, in the modern Naschmarkt. The third was situated, quite contrary to the usual practice, in the centre of the town. It is now Number Twenty-three in the Tiefer Graben. Each of these houses had a manageress in addition to the male keeper and was governed by a strict set of rules. Among those persons already mentioned who were not allowed to enter such places the Viennese regulations included bakers, perhaps for reasons of public health.

The establishments in Vienna were owned by the Dukes of Austria and held on feudal tenure from them by the Pauperger family, which also enjoyed a substantial income from the property. A proportion of the profits was of course returned to the whores themselves or at any rate to the penitent among them. In 1384 a committee of 'pious and wealthy citizens belonging to important Viennese families' determined to render palatable to the girl inmates of the brothels a return to the troublesome responsibilities of an honest life by erecting a home for those who repented of their sins. It was built at the end of the Singer Strasse, near the present day Seilerstätte, and a certain Frau Klara Pauperger, belonging to the lessee's family, added a chapel. The latter was used chiefly for celebrations of the weddings of women formerly members of the local brothels. Any man who rescued a girl in this way was highly esteemed, with pious logic, by the citizens of the Middle Ages. No loss of social respect would be incurred by such a step. But if his wife ever returned to her former habits she would risk being drowned in the 'Blue Danube'. Many only too merry wives of Vienna probably started the last of all their trips to Budapest in circumstances of this kind.

Tolerance also accompanied strict regulation on the banks of the Spree in Berlin, where the brothels stood in a row in the narrow Spree Street leading to the Virgins' Bridge. Wilhelm Ostwald believed this last name to have been an invention of the satirically-minded citizens of Berlin. 'The Virgins' Bridge,' he wrote, 'was certainly so called from the character of those who dwelt near it, just as Rose Street in Berlin was called after the women who lived in it.'

As soon as it became generally known that now at last there were places where one could go and sin and at the same time make a profit for the State, markedly stern measures were taken against those who ventured to behave immodestly anywhere else. A monk from Magdeburg on holiday in Berlin invited a girl to accompany him to the public baths. Although this offence against female decency had only been verbal, it cost the monk his life. The man, whose name was Konrad Schütze, occupied the post of scribe to Theodor, Archbishop of Magdeburg. But that made no difference at all. He was 'seized by the constables, who were accompanied by a great multitude of the citizens and, forthwith removed to the market-place, where he was beheaded'.

The Berliners of those days do not seem from this report to have been particularly friendly to the Church. They even appear to have been prepared to pay for what amounted to little less than their lynching of the monk. For the archbishop naturally demanded financial compensation from the city. On the other hand a Berlin woman, after pacing up and down in front of the Greyfriars Monastery, shouting in the voice of a town-crier: 'Girls for the priests!' was merely driven away with a few strokes of the birch, despite the indignation she had aroused among the monks.

Versatility of the fair and frail

The municipal authorities soon realized that brothels were a good investment. The establishments proved so popular that legal disputes about the distribution of their profits broke out between ecclesiastical and secular dignitaries. There were festal occasions, too, on which the fair and frail sisterhood was employed in many more capacities than could ever be required of modern airline or dance-hall hostesses. When the famous Wend family of the Quitzows from Priegnitz once more repulsed the Pomeranians, the grateful citizens of Berlin offered the victors a triumphal reception. The supply of food and drink presented no problem. But that of billeting, even in those days, proved serious, however generously lodgings were made available by the local population. Accordingly Dietrich von Quitzow and his men were escorted by the 'daughters of the city' to the latter's quarters, and the municipality paid. In Vienna, too, similar ladies had to prepare their premises for important visitors. It is nowhere recorded that such accommodation had to be evacuated. The city fathers footed the bill for housing and entertainment, a tradition still in force at the period of the Congress.

Professional prostitutes were also employed by the towns to embellish processions and festivities of all descriptions. Newcomers were always glad to see pretty girls. There was no point in exposing the daughters of councillors and guildmasters to the public view since everyone knew them and always would know them. Consequently, the 'daughters of the city' had to be put on show. For those young women obviously did not mind exhibiting themselves and in fact approached the emperor himself with astonishing self-assurance.

Some experiences of great men

On one such occasion a couple of them seized the Emperor Frederick III in a Nuremberg street, tied him up and facetiously demanded ransom. They addressed him in words which sound almost like those of a corporation. 'Your Grace must submit to being bound.' The monarch replied courteously: 'We dislike being bound and wish to ransom ourselves.' This answer guaranteed the two impudent harlots a generous reward. The Emperor Frederick Barbarossa was received in the tiltyard of the palace at Vienna, even before the guests of honour could greet him, by a band of lightly-clad charmers carrying bouquets. In this case the girls had no great distance to cover, for their headquarters in the Tiefer Graben stood close by.

An especially brilliant spectacle was organized for the entry of the Emperor Charles V into Antwerp. The population of the city amounted at that time to about a hundred thousand. Four thousand five hundred ships and an annual revenue of 130 million florins rendered it the richest community in Europe. The display presented to the emperor was talked of for centuries. The procession which met him outside the city gates was led, not as one might expect by the notables of the town, but by hundreds of prostitutes. They were clothed, according to contemporary reports, partly in scanty garments and partly in nothing at all. But they were all crowned with garlands of flowers, which they threw at the emperor and his escort. The city of Paris proved equally inventive in 1431, when the ten year old King Henry VI of England was unexpectedly confronted at the St Denis Gate by a fountain in which three nude girls swam round a centrepiece representing a fleur-de-lis.

Countless other local variants of such celebrations, with more or less decently arrayed harlots participating to a greater or less extent, imply that something more than mere frivolity and diversion was involved in these displays. When the legendary Greek hero Bellerophon crossed the plain of Xante in order to assault the royal castle, 'the Xantian women lifted their garments above their hips and ran to meet him in this attitude, offering him their persons if he would only allow his wrath to be appeased. Bellerophon was so abashed by this behaviour that he turned back and rushed away.' (Ranke-Graves.) Again, when the Irish hero Cuchullin, returning from his victorious expedition, rode up to Conchobar's castle in a glow of mettlesome excitement, the wise king said:

'Here comes Cuchullin. He has dipped his hands in blood. So he is full of the rage of battle and if we cannot quench his fury all our young men will fall by his hand.' It was therefore resolved in great haste to send Cuchullin thrice fifty stark naked women, led by the lady Scandlach, in order that the sight of their nakedness might assuage the warrior's ferocity . . . Then Cuchullin turned his face away from the naked women, gazed down upon his chariot and drove on past them . . .' [Löpelmann.]

Public functions

The city fathers of Viterbo, who had to think out new diversions every year, and those of Verona, who organized annual races, always on the same lines, between nude prostitutes, knew nothing of Bellerophon or Cuchullin. But they knew that a furious bull in the arena could be tamed by the presence of cows. It was not simply females, but accessible females, who caused this tranquillizing effect. Lords and heroes alike experienced it, much to the gratification of castles and towns. But in a rigidly ordered class structure like that of medieval Europe only prostitutes were available for tasks of this sort. It was at a later period that Caterina de' Medici for the first time dared to form a 'flying column' of young noble-women.

But apart from all such, so to speak, representative functions performed by whores, they embellished the lives of two large classes in particular, those of priests and of soldiers.

Transitional difficulties

Compliance with the demand for a celibate priesthood had for long been sluggish. But after the Second Lateran Council of 1139 more and more clergy began to separate from their wives and consequently, if the flesh proved weak, to resort to concubinage or the services of whores. As a rule monks also could only rely on the 'women's quarters', though in certain regions the nuns lived such a gay life that the local prostitutes felt justified in complaining of competition. The Chronicle of the Lords of Zimmern records a highly entertaining story. After the convent of Our Blessed Lady at Strasbourg had been struck by lightning, this exceptional occurrence revealed 'a person of the male sex and moreover of tender age naked in bed with a nun, each of the couple having been suffocated by the fumes arising from the thunderstorm'. The investigation which followed disclosed that the nuns were in the habit of training the male foundlings introduced into the convent (through the humane device of the revolving box) to become assiduous bed-companions. The same chronicle is responsible for an account, now famous, of a certain 'evening dance' held in a darkened hall at the convent. While the local lords were enjoying themselves, in these circumstances, with the nuns, one of the former, probably fearing that someone might show a light, suddenly called out: 'Not so fast, boys! Let's have another change of partners! I've got hold of my sister!'

Fathers in disguise

This affair cannot have been altogether unusual, for reports of similar proceedings have come down to us from Hans von Schweinichen, Rosenplüt and others. The monks were not so lucky. They could not admit partners, but had to leave the monastery in search of them, so that they were certain to be noticed in the streets. It is known from a decree of the Zürich Council issued in 1433 that the holy men liked to disguise themselves on such occasions. This practice might prevent their being recognized. But it could not prevent certain other consequences, such as the vast numbers of children they begot after being forbidden to marry. This result presented both Church and State with a particularly intractable problem. If the males so procreated wished to become priests they had to obtain papal dispensation. Pope Clement VI distributed 484 such documents in the year 1342 alone, a record which suggests at least a slight idea of clerical life at that time. For not all the children of priests were male. Nor did all the male children wish to become priests. It is likely that they would more often choose occupations for which they did not require dispensation.

The above figure has been quoted in support, certainly not of any particular theory, but of a most important fact of social and moral history. A large group of men, undoubtedly the best educated of their day, had been forced by the rule of celibacy into an exceptional situation. During the transitional phase they experienced considerable difficulties for centuries. Many rural communities which had no brothel demanded with rustic common sense, and quite logically, that their priest should take a woman to live with him. They did not care whether he would be allowed to marry her or not. All they wanted was to avoid the sort of trouble in their small parish which was likely to be caused by the presence of a bachelor by compulsion, especially seeing that the authority he wielded and his superior mental training guaranteed him a privileged position.

102

Concubinage prohibited

On the other hand the Church again felt obliged to intervene. For example, at the Provincial Synod of Trier in 1423 Archbishop Otto von Ziegenhain announced:

Although many new and old laws have been passed against duly ordained clerks who notoriously keep concubines or other women of questionable character in their houses and several have been punished for so doing, yet many clerks today pay no heed to such penalties but on the contrary continue to dishonour themselves by commission of the said heinous sin. Much indignation has been caused by such conduct and will almost certainly increase if no preventive measures are taken.

At the same Synod a period of twelve days was set for the clergy to get rid of their concubines, though these women, as the bishop himself proclaimed in so many words, constituted the least of the evils to be dealt with. In Paris, if a whore accosted a monk or priest and he did not immediately join her, he had to endure a flood of abuse as a sodomite. Again, the penal code of the German Order of Marienburg reveals the knightly members of this military corporation in as dubious a light as the priests. Satiated with their 'women's quarters', they felt no shame, on occasion, in approaching honest housewives and virgins with libidinous intent or even in seducing children.

Seven thousand whores in Rome

It may have been such considerations that caused Pope Sixtus IV to cancel an order issued by his vicar forbidding concubinage. For Sixtus, the son of a seaman of Albisola near Savona, though no pattern of moral austerity, had one of the acutest brains that ever ruled from a papal throne. During his pontificate, when his nephew Pietro Riario, in particular, lived in great splendour, an official census of Roman prostitutes was taken. Some seven thousand mercenary females were counted among a total population estimated at seventy thousand. This ratio is about ten times that prevalent in most modern capitals. Consequently, a city where almost everyone was connected in one way or another with the Church kept more prostitutes busy than any other, the reason being that a high proportion of the male inhabitants were deprived of the natural satisfactions of marriage and its restraining influence on licentiousness.

The position indicated by these figures was common knowledge at the height of the Middle Ages. No one made any secret of the matter, from Pietro Riario, who had gilded chamber-pots placed under his mistresses' beds and died of his debaucheries at the age of twenty-eight, to the obscure priest of Altenrüthen in Westphalia who was stated at his trial in 1458 to have made improper advances to four housewives and five spinsters.

Craftsmen's fun in the churches

The masses treated these failings with indulgence, sometimes even with amusement, for it was not the common people who had issued the orders resulting in such disorder. An anonymous mason working on the magnificent cathedral at Strasbourg carved the figure of a reclining monk on the pulpit stairs. But this image was represented as making very free indeed with a nun, also of stone, reclining beside him. He was able to carry on like this for another three hundred years, since it was not until the middle of the eighteenth century that the two shocking figures were removed. A similar stone couple in a dark corner of the cathedral at Erfurt, probably from the hand of another facetious craftsman, escaped ecclesiastical censure for an even longer period. Images of this and related types may still or could once be found in churches at Wetzlar, Nördlingen, Worms, Bremen, Magdeburg, Doberan, Zerbst, Basle and elsewhere. Such productions were of course more than a mere jest. Quite deliberate, they are not illustrations of rumour but attempts to give secular expression to the profound discord of which the Christianized peoples of Europe were conscious. Their religion had excommunicated the lusts of the flesh. But not even the anointed servants of the Lord could ever really conquer them.

Soldiers

If any social class could be said to be practically unconscious of the conflict in question, it was that of the fighting troops. In that age of mercenary armies warfare was not a special state of affairs but a constant preoccupation. Nor was there any lack of opportunity, throughout the medieval period, to practise the military profession.

Anyone who decided to do so led a practically pagan life under the protection of a great masculine corporation dedicated to providing for his needs. The attentions paid to his welfare, both digestive and genital, were applied on principles tested over centuries, if not millennia, and whenever any particularly pious commander tried to enforce a different scheme, at any rate for crusaders, he was simply ridiculed – as was, for instance, St Louis of France.

Medieval armies needed even more women than gatherings of the clergy. The greatest of the latter in the Middle Ages, that at the Council of Constance, numbered fifty thousand participants, who had to be satisfied with a mere fifteen hundred whores in all. But Charles the Bold of France, when besieging the stubborn town of Neuss, had one prostitute in his camp for every four of his soldiers. Consequently, the receipts of the ladies who had chosen to serve the Church were considerably the higher.

Whether the high density of harlots in Charles's camp accounts for the fact that he could not storm Neuss even after a siege of eleven months remains a matter of dispute. It is certain however that the number of these non-combatants was regarded as relatively large, with the result that they were set hard to work digging trenches, to which labour they were marched off behind drummers and flags. Even the Duke of Alva did not disdain to enrol whores in his Most Christian fighting forces. All he did was to organize them into companies for supervisory purposes. Four hundred on horseback and eight hundred on foot are said to have accompanied the invasion of Brabant. But even so, as the behaviour of the imperial troops showed, their camp-followers were not enough to prevent the brutal outraging by the soldiery of the Dutch women and girls.

Prostitutes in camp and their sergeant-major

But the camp-girls were almost always placed under the strict discipline of one man, the so-called 'whores' sergeant' who may therefore be regarded as the direct precursor of the modern warrant officer or quartermaster in charge of supplies. The duties of the whores' sergeant, more politely called in French *roi des ribauds* and in contemporary chronicles actually *rex ribaldorum*, were every bit as multifarious as those of his modern successor. The medieval officer thus designated had usually grown grey on active service and added the habit of command to his experience and practical knowledge. A young subaltern officer was generally appointed to assist him. He himself drew a captain's pay, but also enjoyed certain not inconsiderable casual earnings. He had to keep the swarms of dissolute women, who were of course not easy to control, hard at work 'cooking, sweeping, washing clothes, in particular tending the sick and lending a hand smartly at tent-pitching, fetching fodder and solid and liquid rations and whatever else may be necessary ... as well as cleaning out latrines and other quarters which may require it'. They also had the task, not always without danger, of filling in holes or pools which might impede the advance of troops to an assault. At other times they helped with the transport of artillery.

It is clear that they were not superfluous. In fact their availability was the answer to a whole series of problems which constantly arise in modern warfare.

The camp-followers were the colleagues, still at a loose end, of the other sisterhood, those who had decided to stay put in one spot, the brothel. On special occasions, however, both travelling and sedentary sections acted together, as when, for instance, at a Diet of the Holy Roman Empire, the martial lords brought their camp-followers with them out of sheer habit, while the scribes and minor officials preferred to patronize the local brothels. This was the case at Regensburg in 1471, where fifteen hundred camp-followers proved hardly enough for the assembled nobility of the empire to vent their lusts upon, and again in 1298 at Strasbourg, whither King Albrecht took some eight hundred whores, to ensure that there should be nothing to complain of.

Grimmelshausen's Courasche

The feelings of these women, who led a masculine life and had been obliged to give up all thought of any household, home or country of their own, are expressed by Grimmelshausen's Courasche, who so longed for marriage. 'A young fellow came to see me, whom I thought quite attractive, strong-minded and not at all short of cash. I set up all my nets to entrap him, using every hunter's trick I knew, till I had fairly noosed him and made him so mad about me that he'd have eaten salad out of my hand without feeling sick. Well, that chap swore that the devil might have him if he didn't marry me.'

The verdict of history which many a camp-follower would probably have been unable to express is given with amazing insight by Bertholt Brecht, when he makes his own 'Mother Courage' say:

Perhaps things will actually turn out all right in the end. We're caught, but only like a bug in a rug. The ups and downs of the big boys up aloft and the others down below don't all happen at the same time, far from it. There are even cases in which, when the underdogs are beaten, it's actually a victory for them. Honour is lost, but nothing else . . . On the whole you can say that victories and defeats both cost us common people dear. It's best for us when politics doesn't make much progress.

Resignation is already apparent in this wish. But in the Middle Ages it actually came to fulfilment, for the troops just as for the camp-followers.

For France the Middle Ages were the Teutonic phase of its history and many French historians accordingly deal very harshly with this stage in the development of their nation. East of the Rhine the tendency is to ascribe positive influences and effects to the influx of Frankish and Norman blood into Gaul. But scholars in France censure the unconstrained habits of Merovingian society, where the murders of kindred, incest and atrocities of all kinds were everyday occurrences, and they consider the Vikings who settle in Normandy to have been the real originators of the spread of homosexuality in France.

Dubious import from the North

Anyone desirous of standing up for the Merovingians must first refute the chief contemporary witness to their behaviour, the wise and judicious chronicler Gregory of Tours, a feat which would only be possible on points of detail today. The Vikings, who lived on their warships for months in isolation from their women, may have been susceptible, like other seamen, to certain harmless forms of the vice mentioned, which would vanish like the wind at the first sight of a petticoat. It is also more than improbable that the Gauls, during their five hundred years of Roman rule, never once laid eyes on a male prostitute. The frequent wars after that period undoubtedly made further contributions to the brutalization of men, the breakdown of family life and the disturbance of the natural uniformity of small village communities.

But, whatever causes may have been operative. France unquestionably fell, until about the beginning of the eleventh century, into a moral decay that appeared irresistible. Even if a man lived with several concubines at once he felt no need to be ashamed of doing so. *Fornicatio simplex*, normal sexual intercourse, was not only, in those days at least, a perfectly admissible sin, but positively a form of alibi against the suspicion of giving in to worse inclinations.

Paris and its students

In Roman times Paris covered only the Seine islands and the adjacent banks of the river, an area in all of some twenty acres with about two thousand inhabitants. But after the confusion of the Merovingian epoch the city grew fast. Its encircling ring of abbeys was absorbed, together with the extensive mercantile settlement on the right bank of the Seine. Certain famous teachers who came to live on the left bank were responsible for the flow of students to the 'Latin Quarter'. Although the teachers already formed a self-contained body in the twelfth and early thirteenth centuries, there were no actual university buildings in existence at that date but only certain decentralized educational institutions scattered over a wide district occupied by students' lodgings. This part of the town, as well as the Île de la Cité, where the clergy lived, was named by a leading citizen as early as 1270 the local prostitutes' playground. No fewer than twenty of the streets of Paris, then numbering three hundred, were believed to be inhabited by whores and the students were the chief instigators of unrest and insecurity.

This early association between prostitutes and rowdy undergraduates created a characteristic setting for future developments. The Parisian whores and their dwellings differed from the 'women's quarters' of the medieval German city, which had begun as a town substitute for the roving foreign beggarwomen and camp-followers. In Paris the harlots had always frequented a certain environment over which the civic authorities had little control Neither the students nor the clergy were much inclined to tolerate interference by the guardians of law and order. The students even repeatedly launched counter-attacks on the municipal officers. In some years disturbances in the city reached such heights that practically no lectures were given. The unemployed students formed gangs to go foraging for victuals in the countryside. They terrorized the citizens, carried off women whom they then held prisoners, threw down monuments and played all sorts of other tricks. A good proportion of them lived, as was the case in later times also, on the earnings of their sentimental Parisian sweethearts.

The ballads of François Villon

One of the greatest poets that France ever produced, Master François de Montcorbier, known as Villon, described this kind of life in his songs and ballads. He had been involved in a case of murder, sentenced to be hanged, but at the last moment reprieved. He then took leave of Paris in a last ballad and it is not even known for certain whether he survived the ten years of banishment substituted for his execution.

Villon's poems prove that students who had run wild in the city maintained close relations with its criminal underworld. Prostitutes may have acted as the cement of this strange connection. Villon himself belonged to the *Coquillards*, a notorious gang in Paris and its neighbourhood, which perpetrated dozens, if not hundreds, of serious burglaries. Whenever he did not happen to be in prison he could usually be found in one of the brothels of the students' quarter.

> If we have guests I sneak out quick to fetch
> bread, cheese and wine, and if they tip the wretch
> who brings the stuff, 'Why, good,' I say.
> 'Fork out like men and you can come and play
> some other time. Don't worry! If you're itchy, well,
> visit this brothel where we both do dwell.'

Etymology of the word 'brothel'

Villon uses the word *bordeau*, which must therefore have been generally intelligible as early as the mid-fifteenth century, for his language is that of the masses, often positive jargon. It is agreed today that the word is of Teutonic origin (cf. Note on p. 83) though what it represents is not! *Borda* in Old Saxon means little houses, houses near water, arbours and so on. In Old French the word appears in the forms *borde, bordiau, bordelet*, to some extent therefore as a diminutive, proving that the 'little houses' or arbours had a special secondary significance disguised by its slyly affectionate termination and yet unmistakable.

These 'little houses' and their inhabitants became the chief weapon with which the French kings combated homosexuality and the various secret organizations and corporations whose members indulged in aberrations of an often highly inventive character. Only the Templars, whose vast wealth certainly interested King Philip Augustus quite as much as their alleged debaucheries, are at all frequently mentioned in this connection, though they were by no means unique in their reputation. The alternative to the activities of such secret masculine corporations and Lodges was certainly no more gratifying to the authorities. But at any rate its shameless frankness rendered it easier to control.

Philip Augustus felt obliged to surround a large cemetery, much favoured by prostitutes for their diversions, with a high wall, so as to protect the peace of the dead. But he was less successful with what went on in the extensive ruins of the Baths of Julian (now the Boulevard Saint-Michel), about which he could do nothing whatever. Nevertheless, contemporary historians make it quite clear that they preferred the wild young men of Paris to 'that frightful vice, that poison and plague' which Jacques de Vitry for instance (1178–1240) denounced.

The 'roy des ribauds'

The whores and their keepers, conscious of being the lesser of two evils equally hard to eradicate, became organized at an early date, perhaps sooner in Paris than in any other European city, though the oldest corporations of prostitutes are known only through oral traditions, not written down until long afterwards. The *roy des ribauds* acted as their representative at court. But for the rest they enjoyed within their own system of regulations a remarkable measure of freedom, as to which there is a great deal of evidence. Rabelais, for one, declares that the shadow of one student would put several constables to flight, so great was the respect then accorded to academic liberty. The professors may well have lamented that their audience took more interest in Circe than in Cicero. But even they were deeply concerned to preserve the autonomy of the Latin Quarter.

Kissing in church

Even in so gay a city as Paris Bohemia is not always left in peace. Accordingly, in the course of the centuries there were repeated attempts by court or Church to curb, if only slightly, the excesses of the *ribauds*, the bad boys and the loose-living girls. The royal measures were the more dangerous, having originated, it was said, in a slight mishap which befell Margaret of Provence, wife of St Louis. She was annoyed to find that, when the kiss of atonement customary at the end of every Divine Service had to be exchanged, her nearest neighbour, a young woman dressed like a member of the prosperous middle class, turned out afterwards to be a whore known all over the town.

It is not very likely to have really been Queen Margaret who underwent this embarrassment. Many of the circumstances indicate that the victim was a royal princess who lived a few decades previously. It is certain however that the aristocratic lady concerned flew into a violent passion. A twentieth-century priest would probably have been in a position to point out to her that the kiss of atonement actually symbolized the bridging of a gulf between human beings, whereby differences of birth or rank might be abolished. But in the Middle Ages even women were subject to the strict laws of honour on behalf of which blood was regularly shed. The lady's disgust therefore set her cavalier in action.

St Louis and the harlots

The French chroniclers, following the example of their not invariably serious Roman forerunners, tried to score rhetorical points at any price. Consequently, they attributed the start of the drive to expel whores from Paris to the kiss of reconciliation mentioned above. But many considerations suggest that the movement did not get under way so precipitately. Louis IX (1215–70), the first important persecutor of harlots among the French kings, was so pious a monarch as to have no need of any such event as the anecdote records to encourage him. He was so proof against all fleshly temptations that he spent the first few nights of his youthful marriage in the castle chapel instead of in bed. His mother, Blanche of Castile, who was excessively jealous of her daughter-in-law, rejoiced to see him kneeling and praying there.

When he took the field as a crusader, though he could not get rid of the camp-followers altogether, he nevertheless prevented them from coming anywhere near his tent and once faced a knight, as the result of a common occurrence, with the choice between humble apology for his conduct and resignation from the army. The apology would have consisted in being led at a rope's end by the harlot concerned, stripped to his shirt, through the whole camp. The valiant knight refused to expose himself to this humiliation, preferring to quit the king's service.

When Louis, who was canonized after his death, returned to Paris from his first crusade, he was peculiarly horrified by the coolly immoral behaviour of his subjects. Having fought against Antichrist in Syria and Palestine, he determined to do so also on the banks of the Seine and never to tolerate in his native land what he had not been able to deny his soldiers.

This was easier said than done. For in the thirteenth century Paris contained more harlots and loose-living girls than ever before, and a high proportion of its one hundred and fifty thousand inhabitants were connected in one way or another with them and their dependents.

Pensions for penitents

The first measures taken by Louis were entirely conservative, being limited to following the example of the Empress Theodora of Byzantium, though as a matter of fact her educational efforts had not proved very successful. The king set up establishments in Paris and elsewhere in France which provided, for harlots who wished to give up their trade, not only safety from persecution but also maintenance and accommodation. The pensions granted them by Louis are said to have amounted to four hundred gold pieces a year. But this would be a very high figure for those days and is probably an error by the chronicler. On the other hand so few Parisian women obeyed the summons of their king and his bishop that even so generous an award would not have embarrassed his treasury. For only two hundred repentant sinners were counted out of at least twelve thousand whores. These two hundred, moreover, had reached an age at which the royal gold pieces were probably all that ever fell into their laps.

The first Sorbonne

The convent of the Béguines in Paris, also known as the House of the Daughters of God, belonged to the chaplain Robert de Sorbon, who was friendly with Louis IX. It was situated in the rue St Jacques, where François Villon was to grow up two hundred years later. Under St Louis the district was still a quiet one of shabby houses, to which poor students were directed, thus practically ensuring the foundation of the Sorbonne School. It was here too that the repentant prostitutes acquired their first Home. But soon, owing to the proximity of university activities, they were obliged to migrate to another quarter of the town.

As this step had effected so little the king issued in 1254 his famous edict against whores. The regulations promulgated by this document were so unreasonable and impracticable that they clearly show its author to have been incapable of governing and a mere fanatic. The king to whom France owed so much in other ways dedicated his last years to an embittered conflict, maintained by a fixed idea. His failure in the struggle would have been no misfortune for France. But his intense preoccupation with this matter led again and again to critical situations in both foreign and domestic politics.

Louis threatened any prostitute who did not abandon her trade after being once warned to do so with the confiscation of her entire fortune and exile from her parish. Anyone who let a house or other accommodation to a woman of dissolute life was fined a sum equivalent to a year's rent of the premises.

Streets with highly significant names

A hundred years later steps were taken which modern municipalities still believe to be the most effective. Instead of issuing an abrupt prohibition like that of St Louis, which merely resulted in the disappearance underground, so to speak, of the entire class of prostitutes, so that they became uncontrollable, the authorities tried to restrict the trade to certain quarters of the town. (*Ordonnance datée* 18 September 1367.)

Many of the streets named in this Order seem to have been already centres of harlotry, judging from their appellations. They included the rue Trousse-putain ('Lift-the-whore's-skirt'),the rue de la Truanderie ('Strollers' Parade'), the rue du Puits d'Amour

('Love's Well-spring') and so on. A rue du Chapon ('capon') among those reserved for prostitutes proves that the male variety could still be found, in spite of the enormous masses of females available. Other street-names were so excessively outspoken that refined ladies like the exquisite Mary Stuart instantly fainted if they ever lost their way in such places. The city of Paris incidentally, as a form of compensation for the offence committed against the fair and ill-fated queen by their local humorists, afterwards called the street with the unspeakable name after her. Today nothing in the aspect of this short thoroughfare close to the busy markets of the *Halles* suggests that it once competed with the rue Brise-Miche for an unusual title to fame, that of habouring a majority of the whores of Paris.

Special clothing

Almost at the same time as the first closed districts for prostitutes were established the authorities hit upon a much less humane way of making life difficult for women of easy virtue. A clear, unmistakable, outward sign of the trade was required to be worn by those engaged in it. The idea is of very early date, having been mentioned by ancient Greek authors, and cannot therefore be attributed to any particular ruler of the Middle Ages. But it was actually a woman, Giovanna I, Queen of Naples and Countess of Provence, who issued the following decree relating to a brothel she herself had founded at Avignon a year before she sold the city to the popes.

'In the year 1347, on the eighth day of the month of August, our good queen Giovanna consented to the opening of a special House of Sin in our town. At the same time she forbids all women of evil life to practise their trade in the streets and whenever they go abroad they shall wear a red trimming to their dress on the left shoulder.'

Shrewd regulations by Giovanna I

In other respects however the articles of this decree prove that authorities since the days of good Queen Giovanna six hundred years ago have not made any progress worth mentioning. Her *maison de débauche* '(house of carnal dissipation') consisted of a small group of buildings, which accordingly constituted a street of brothels. Access to it could be closed by a gate, which was kept shut on Fridays and certain feast-days. An energetic woman called

114

an abbess supervised all the whores, who were birched at all four corners of the city for the slightest fault. Jews who slipped into the street by stealth incurred the same penalty, which must have been regarded as a very severe measure in Provence, where the Jewish element was extremely prominent in administrative and commercial affairs, including the tariff and financial systems. Once a week every inmate of the brothel was medically examined. If any were found sick, they were taken away for treatment. If a prostitute became pregnant, the 'abbess' was responsible for the child being carried for its full term, born naturally and carefully brought up. The fact that the street led directly to the Augustinian monastery might have been found objectionable by contemporaries. But if anyone did take this view he probably also considered the whole enterprise superfluous. For after all the exiled popes with their clerical staffs had composed the ruling class in the small city of Avignon for decades.

Distinctive signs for prostitutes

Distinguishing marks for whores were changed so often during the following centuries that though contemporaries might have been able to identify them, the historian, looking back, is confronted by a scene of hopeless confusion. At times the harlots were only allowed to dress plainly, at times they could be easily distinguished by their garish ostentation. Sometimes they wore a shoulder-knot, sometimes a garter on the upper arm. Paris being at certain periods less tolerant than the provinces, where France looked big and the king a long way off, the first of the luxury brothels in the west and south acquired a reputation which reached the capital. The Abbaye du Château-vert at Toulouse and the establishments in Montpellier, Angers and Provins were famous on the banks of the Seine. At Strasbourg on the other hand there soon arose so many large and small brothels and so many out of the way holes and corners where vice was rampant that prostitutes were to be found even in the towers of the cathedral, for which reason they were called 'tower martins' and given as distinguishing signs a white veil thrown over a black and white cap.

Francis I and his little friends

It was at this period that the last kings of the *ribauds* were replaced by ladies of adroit intelligence, who took charge of the whores accompanying the court. In the time of King Philip Augustus that monarch had much appreciated his *roi des ribauds* and that officer's staff. The prostitutes and their keepers had repeatedly acted as his bodyguard and won many a battle for him through the daring they had learnt in the underworld and the familiarity with which they handled all kinds of weapons. But circumstances had now changed. The accession of Francis I had brought a gay Lothario to the throne of France who was perpetually surrounded by a bevy of favourites including seductive daughters of the nobility, fair-skinned Norman girls, robust young women from Brabant, insinuating feminine representatives of southern France, with their Moorish blood, and merry baronesses from Charente. The common people of France, who had supposed that they knew something about life and love, gazed open-mouthed upon their king's diversions.

The first courtesans

'That vice has often proved an emancipator of the
mind, is one of the most humiliating, but, at the
same time, one of the most unquestionable facts in
history.' – W. E. H. LECKY

At the beginning of the fifteenth century four memorable years
changed the political and cultural life of Europe. They were the
years 1414 to 1418, during which the Great Council in the lakeside
city of Constance was held. Addicts of arithmetical calculation will
remember that five hundred years later the First World War inau-
gurated a change that was probably still more radical. Yet in spite
of the spectacular burning of heretics that took place in the midst
of the solemnities of the conference, its comprehensive labours
really seem to have brought a new era to birth.

The Great Council

The ostensible reason for the calling of the Council was the schism,
which had now lasted for decades, within the Catholic Church.
One pope sat in Rome, another in Avignon. Attempts to dethrone
both rivals by choosing a third pope had actually led, by 1409, to
the existence of three at once. It was at this juncture that the future
Emperor Sigismund intervened. He induced John xxɪɪɪ, the pope
over whom he had the most influence, to call a council, to be held
on 1 November 1414 beyond the frontiers of Italy, the town chosen
being Constance.

When John xxɪɪɪ arrived in Constance three days before the date
specified it seemed as though the conference would be as great a
failure as any of the previous efforts to put an end to the schism
which had begun in 1378. Only forty-eight cardinals and other prelates had turned up. But before the end of the year the emperor had
arrived with his retinue. In January the Danes and Poles were
followed by the extraordinarily splendid deputation from Mainz,
whence its Elector-Archbishop came with a train of no fewer than
six hundred and thirty persons.

The Council became a focus of argument and the exchange of ideas. Constance, a small town of some ten thousand inhabitants, eventually had to find room for more than twenty thousand foreigners. They ranged from those actually taking part in the discussions, and their followers, to those who hoped to make some profit out of so unique an assembly. Travelling merchants and artisans, and of course prostitutes, fell into this category. They found at Constance all who were and had been throughout medieval times their best customers, viz. priests, soldiers, scholars and dignitaries of all descriptions. Consequently, the traders in question appeared in such large numbers that soon the most fantastic estimates of their multitude became current.

Richental's Chronicle

Ulrich von Richental, a much-travelled, wealthy and astute business man, and a respected citizen of the town of Constance, mentioned in his long account of the Council 'over seven hundred prostitutes in the women's quarters, others who hired premises of their own, and finally those who plied their trade in secret, who were beyond computation'. The same authority added that in the Stadelhof quarter of the town many unfamiliar, i.e. immigrant, innkeepers had been granted permission to establish brothels. But they also settled in other districts, 'wherever, in fact, they managed to find accommodation'.

Everyone knows how people are accustomed to behave at such great gatherings. The exceptional character of the occasion gives rise to a certain amount of gaiety and the distance from home also has a liberating effect. At Constance one's doings were noticed, of course. But after all a state of emergency existed and when one came back home all would be forgotten. The crowds were too lively, their numbers too great, to allow one to stand on one's dignity. The emperor was present with a vast secular retinue, the hostile popes had made their entries. There were twenty-nine cardinals, three hundred bishops and other prelates, hundreds of doctors and other learned men. They had come from all over the world. There were Russians, Greeks, Armenians and even Ethiopians. Eighty-three kings, from Europe, Africa and Asia, had sent embassies. Delegations were present from 472 towns in the empire and from 352 elsewhere.

Poggio the Florentine

The crowds surged through the narrow streets, mingling, making friends, quarrelling and becoming reconciled again. The pikes in this thickly populated pond of carp were the clever young secretaries, whose alert minds were already taking the measure of the new century. Perhaps the most knowledgeable of them was Poggio the Florentine. At the time of his birth in the Florentine castle of Terranuova, Boccaccio and Petrarch had just died. It was under their influence and in their spirit that he studied in Florence, making money there as a tutor. He was soon despatched in the capacity of an apostolic secretary to Rome.

Before he was in a position to marry he had already fathered fourteen children and it is easy to understand that he had no desire to enter the Church, though circumstances imposed that career upon him. Poggio was not the sort of man to miss the Council. But he seems to have had more time to spare than his clerical superiors, for he explored the surroundings of the beautiful lakeside city, with the greatest curiosity and enthusiasm. In the abbeys of Reichenau, Weingarten, St Gall and others he ferreted out copies of manuscripts by antique authors, including six speeches by Cicero, the whole of Quintilian, a book of Lucretius and works by Gellius, Lucius Columella, Eusebius and others. Sometimes he dug the scrolls out of dustbins and lumber-rooms. Sometimes he made copies of those he was not allowed to keep. Sometimes he arranged for the purchase of manuscripts, as he did in the case of comedies by Plautus and works by Pliny unknown in Italy at this period.

All this was matter and stimulus enough for endless, eager speculation all down the long Italian peninsula, and while in Constance Wycliffe was sentenced and Hus and Hieronymus were burnt alive, the flames of the spirit of antiquity illuminated the study-chambers of the humanists.

The two great letters

Evidence of the same spirit is also provided by the two great letters which Poggio wrote to friends from Constance. They soon circulated in many copies and began to have effects comparable with those exercised by the ancient authors themselves. One dealt with the trial and execution of Hieronymus, showing undisguised sympathy with the manly apostate and his courageous death. The other gave an account of the baths at Baden near Zürich, manifesting a delight which seemed positively pagan at the proceedings in the fountains of warm water. The baths appear from Poggio's description to have had the character of a luxurious, crowded and extremely spacious brothel. But what scandalized people in his elegant Latin prose was the unmitigated way in which the writer acknowledged his pleasure in the general enjoyment.

One visits three or four baths every day and spends most of one's time singing, drinking or dancing. Some actually enter the water and play their instruments there. But no spectacle is more charming than when young women just ripe for a husband or already fully mature . . . like goddesses in their shape and bearing, sing to their instruments while in the water. Their light garment is thrown back and floats on the surface, so that one would take any of such girls for a second Venus.

Homeward bound to a new era

The spirit of the new century was not perhaps born in the baths on the Limmat. But the heathen proceedings there, which were attended by thousands of the delegates to the Council, certainly gave rise to the idea that life might be lived on different principles. Many a worried visitor became secretly convinced that he had learnt a good deal about them from this encounter with the outside world. Certain serious matters were taken less seriously on the homeward journey. A few hundred children whose fathers were unknown had been born in Constance and being creations of the Council might be said to have had a unique origin. The city of Rome had been restored to a world which had felt much anxiety over its fate after decades of dethronement by the schism from its ancient power.

Pacified, relieved and yet slightly depressed at the termination of a festival that had lasted four years, the delegates set off homewards They were to see their familiar walls again in the light of the new age that was dawning for mankind.

Rome in the Middle Ages

In no city did that dawn arise so brightly as in Rome nor was any other city more drastically changed by it. Medieval Rome, far less extensive than the antique metropolis, was a mere collection of half decayed palaces, ruins used as dwellings and ramshackle hovels. Internal quarrels had caused every house of any considerable size to be turned into a citadel. The general insecurity obliged pilgrims to visit the holy places outside the city walls only in large numbers under armed guard. Foreigners who came to Rome were regaled with the most incredible and idiotic legends relating to the relics of antiquity and also about the Apostolic Fathers of the Church. The popes occupied a vast building in an extreme state of neglect, at any rate until the pontificate of Martin v, who made a great many improvements both in and around the city during the years 1417–31.

The revival of interest in the ancient world brought a kind of release, like that of awakening from an enchanted sleep, to Rome, where the old Campus Vaccarum had relapsed into its original state of a cattle-range, sheep were kept between the basilica of St Peter and the Castle of San Angelo, and the Seven Hills were climbed by narrow pathways. Political parties had been active in the city. But no strong central authority existed until the papacy, making a rapid recovery after the long schism, acquired a growing secular importance. Members of well-known families were elected popes and cardinals. New dignitaries were created in the persons of the pope's nephews. Moral decline in these circles caused little resentment among the people, for during these decades, for the first time since the age of the emperors, games and pageantry were again organized and the masses participated in the general prosperity.

The Colonna family

Martin v, whose pontificate laid the foundations for the rise of the Colonna family, had already summoned distinguished artists, during the early Renaissance period, to Rome, including Lorenzo Ghiberti, Masaccio, Gentile da Fabriano, Pisanello and others. A new life began for the Eternal City, by this time familiar with the results of an absentee papacy. No pope had lived in Rome for a hundred and twenty-nine years before the advent of Martin v. And even he had needed three years to overcome all kinds of opposition, ranging from the Avignon interest to the emperor's insistence on a papal residence in Germany, before he could set foot again in the degenerate city and enter the gardens of the Vatican, where wolves from the Campagna roamed. The Romans knew all about this situation. Consequently, they showed a rare unanimity in their hopes for a revival. They had seen what their city had come to in the absence of the popes. It had relapsed into a cemetery of memories, a quarry, an area of ruins and a paradise for robbers, as the remains of Babylon had been for millennia.

The Colonna had waited so long for power and had endured so much in the hope of its acquisition that when at last a member of their house acceded to the Holy See they seized the opportunity of enriching themselves with reckless impatience. They remembered how Pope Boniface VIII had razed to the ground their lovely city of Palestrina, with its noble buildings, and ploughed up the site. For five hundred years they had been forced to languish in obscurity. Martin V was personally frugal and honest, but when he died his family had become one of the wealthiest and most powerful between Genoa and Sicily.

The new moral outlook, which could also be described as immoral, had already been evident at the Council of Constance, which came to an end on the election of Martin V. The humanist secretaries who accompanied the princes of the Church had given accurate if also slightly amused accounts of the behaviour in question. After the pope and the cardinals had returned to Italy and the humanists to their stronghold in Florence it became clear that the renovated city of Rome would also be capable of exercising a certain force of attraction. The artists whom Martin needed for the re-erection of a glorious city out of the heaps of rubble were followed by the aesthetes, whom no one had summoned. In the train of the cardinals they found a centre where their sonnets could be appreciated, where libraries were being established, and banquets given at which guests would never be counted.

Courtesans from Constance

A third group consisted of courtesans in pursuit of the revived ecclesiastical splendour. It was a natural step for them to take, since such large numbers of them had prospered in Constance for years. Fees of the magnitude of eight hundred ducats for a single night, which had been paid in Constance to a leading courtesan, could not be expected anywhere but at the residence of the new pope. Just as Poggio and Petrarch had ferreted out the writings of the ancients in monastic libraries and found a Plautus at a convent in the process, so the courtesans too turned to the ancient traditions of their calling, emulated their great Greek and Roman predecessors and set up at the headquarters of the papacy the banner of heathen delight in sensuality.

Their resonant names reveal the places they came from, as with Camilla da Pisa, Beatrice da Ferrara and Allessandra Fiorentina. But they also used family names which, though not always genuine, always sounded well, such as Imperia Cognata, Isabella da Luna or even Tullia d'Aragona, called after the cardinal who had been her father.

A Spanish priest named Deligado wrote a single book, surviving in only one copy. Therein he called the Rome of this period 'Triumph of great lords and paradise of harlots, purgatory of young men and hell of all men, mirage of the poor and den of thieves'. But it was a paradise which was largely the work of the harlots themselves and could not easily be defended. A conclave of cardinals might at any moment degrade them once more to their obscure medieval condition. They might now be living under a sovereign whose wealth could never be exhausted. But he was one who enjoyed secular and ecclesiastical power to a degree attained by no other and to whom his subjects were more helplessly subordinate than they would have been to any king.

The courtesans would perhaps have been less reckless if the stake for which they gambled had been merely their status as whores. For after all they could have lived from that trade elsewhere. But in fact the Renaissance courtesan was simply freeing herself as a woman from slavery to the loom and the stove, stepping from the bower into the full light of the piazza.

A truly emancipated class

It required courage, even impudence, to issue challenges which decent unassuming housewives would never have dared to utter. The courtesans therefore joined the truly emancipated women of the past, like the Greek *hetairai*. They could read and write, compose poetry and sing. They captivated bankers, princes and cardinals. They appeared in the most famous pictures. Even the handsome youth from Urbino, that shy painter of madonnas, Raphael is said to have immortalized the radiantly sensuous beauty of Imperia no less than twice, first in his *Parnassus* and again in his *Transfiguration*, both frescoes decorating the Vatican. As Imperia, in addition, was accorded literary honours in a story by Bandello and at the beginning of the *Contes Drôlatiques*, it can hardly be doubted that she should be awarded the palm and take the lead in the parade of Renaissance courtesans.

Imperia in Balzac

Although Balzac can never have seen Imperia, his presentation of her is to be preferred to Bandello's. An obscure cleric from Touraine strayed accidentally into the antechamber of the famous courtesan.

He stood stock still, like a thief caught by a constable. The lady's shift and hood were off and the maids who were busily stripping their mistress to the skin were peeling off her coverings so dexterously and unhesitatingly that the bold priest could not suppress a tender exclamation at the sight of her naked body . . . the beautiful hair rippled down a back dazzling as polished ivory, exposing amidst its thousands of curls the exquisitely white and gleaming shoulders. She wore a ruby on her snow-white brow. But the jewel sparkled less than her black eyes, still quite moist from her delightful laughter. She kicked her pointed shoe, which glittered with gold like a reliquary, high in the air. It was a voluptuous gesture. And the foot, as it rose, looked smaller than a swan's beak.

The bed on which the beauteous lady then reclined is said to have had a black cover, the better to display the white, gleaming limbs. The invention of this diabolical contrast was credited to Imperia, though others refer to Margaret of Navarre as the originator of the trick. Certainly the sister of Francis I and composer of the *Heptameron* would have been just as likely to think of it as Raphael's model.

The historical Imperia and her bankers

Imperia came from Ferrara and had the luck, soon after her arrival in Rome, to become the mistress of the wealthy banker Angelo del Bufalo. He was succeeded by an even richer lover, the Sienese financier Chigi, who lived in Rome. Bufalo had already set up Imperia in great splendour and furnished an apartment for her the walls of which were curtained in brocade, while the tables were of marble and other items of furniture were inlaid with lapis-lazuli. The ornamentation was in fact carried so far that a Spanish diplomat, feeling the need to expectorate, could find no more suitable target than the face of a manservant. 'Pardon me,' he exclaimed. 'But that was the only ugly thing I could see!'

Imperia cannot have been stupid, for Chigi was most exacting and there were plenty of cheap beauties available in Rome. As was the custom of the day she composed doggerel verses, could play the harp and enjoyed taking lessons from such of her admirers as practised any art, so as to be able to live up to the luxury which had so suddenly been showered upon her.

Her daughter Lucrezia, who later achieved fame by a courageous suicide, had a son named Jacopo Sadoleto, a highly gifted and learned young cleric, afterwards made a cardinal. But Lucrezia had to be legitimized and provided for by the banker Chigi.

Imperia distributed her favours generously. She certainly had not the calculating character attributed to her by subsequent generations on account of her wealth. She had to be rich, because the richest men became her lovers, and she was able to stay rich because she died at thirty-one. There is no more to be said on that subject. It may be true that her splendid house bore a legend requesting every visitor to bring wit and good humour with him and on his departure to leave a gift behind. Imperia was a courtesan and did not wish to be anything else. But she must have been exceptional of her kind, for otherwise all Rome would not so anxiously have read the bulletins which were issued from her death-bed by the most famous physicians of the city and ran like wildfire about the streets. Nor would the pope have sent to any other courtesan his apostolic blessing as she lay dying. It was Pope Julius II who did so, the great patron of Renaissance artists, including Michelangelo.

Death in a storm

The fate of Phryne is recalled when history records that on the death of Imperia the heavens darkened and a frightful thunderstorm broke over Rome. The whole city went into mourning and the poets, who included many of the clergy, did not hesitate to associate the tempest with the death of the great courtesan. By so doing they transferred her, almost as soon as she had ceased to live, to the realm of myth, as had occurred in the case of those Greek *hetairai* to whom temples were dedicated in the belief that they were incarnations of Aphrodite.

Giulia of Ferrara

Though Imperia Cognata may have been the most famous of
Renaissance courtesans, Tullia d'Aragona probably deserved and
still deserves the peculiar reputation of the best-looking blue-
stocking of all time. Her mother before her had been very well
known and much talked of as a courtesan under the name of Giulia
Ferrarese. She once had an altercation on the Strada del Popolo, a
Roman street particularly full of prostitutes, with a gentlewoman,
not of her own kind. Giulia had inadvertently pushed against this
lady, who had thereupon burst into a flood of abuse of a very coarse
nature. The cultured Giulia only smiled politely and as soon as the
other paused for breath remarked in a courteous tone and phrases
entirely free from dialect: 'Excuse me, my dear. I see that you have
really more right to be on this pavement than I.'

Giulia had also taken part in the notorious 'Chestnut Ballet'
staged by Cesare Borgia (not Alexander VI) in his apartments at the
Vatican on 1 November 1501. Fifty of the most beautiful courtesans
had been invited. After they had all eaten and drunk well and
enjoyed themselves the room was darkened. The girls then stripped
and crawled about looking for the chestnuts which Cesare ordered
to be shaken out on the floor from baskets. As soon as they became sufficiently excited by the ardour of the chase to start pushing
one another about and the scuffle was reaching its height, attendants who were in the secret brought in full illuminated candelabra.
His Holiness and Donna Lucrezia watched the scene with mingled
amusement and disgust. *Marrons glacés* are still a Roman speciality.

Such was Giulia Ferrarese. Her daughter Tullia, who was born
in 1505, was fathered by Lodovico d'Aragona, one of the best
known cardinals of his day. He legitimized the baby and authorized
it to bear his name.

Tullia the fair blue-stocking

Tullia d'Aragona represented even more clearly than Imperia the
new type of woman whose ideal was neither the pious matron nor
the mistress of a castle surrounded by knightly suitors. Her mother
had contributed to the sum raised by the prostitutes of Rome for
the laying down of a solid pavement along the Strada del Popolo,
so that they would not have to wade through mud on their daily

beat. Tullia herself had been born in a ramshackle house in the picturesque quarter known as the Campo Marzio di San Trifone. The building belonged to the Augustinians and was occupied from ground floor to attic by prostitutes. But Tullia was lucky in having a father who proved most generous, making it his first care, in that age devoted to education, to ensure that the girl learned to read and write and thereafter to study French and Latin as well as singing, playing the harp and elementary dancing.

Flight of a cardinal

When Tullia was twelve years old, although her mother did not put a stop to her fashionable education, it became difficult to raise the fees for all her teachers, for the Cardinal d'Aragona had been obliged to leave Rome. He was rich and feared the fate for his own person which Cesare Borgia had arranged for the Cardinals Michiel and Orsini to suffer, in order that his father might inherit their wealth.

The best way of protecting oneself against such persecutions was to abandon the field and not even stay long in the places to which one fled. Cardinal Giuliano della Rovere, later the brilliant Pope Julius II, had retreated to the Court of Charles VIII in France. Lodovico d'Aragona went first of all to Germany – probably shortly after the strangling of his relative, Duke Alfonso de' Bisceglia, at Cesare's orders – then to Switzerland, France and the Netherlands.

Giulia Ferrarese still had enough money to last some years. But she preferred to enter upon a sound permanent connection at Siena, where she was not so well known. When Tullia's father died in 1519 her still very beautiful mother had again become a woman of means and could continue in Siena what she had begun in Rome, in other words to allow her daughter the best teachers money could buy. Tullia was this enabled to learn the Sienese dialect, the most elegant in Italy.

For the sake of her beautiful and learned daughter Giulia even ventured to return to Rome, where Tullia was received with open arms. Her welcome was all the more effusive owing to the closer relations which now existed, through the Medici popes, between Rome and Florence. During the most brilliant period of her stay in Rome Tullia's apartments were thronged by all possessed of rank and reputation, not Romans alone but also adherents of the still strong Spanish faction. On one occasion, when she was insulted, a whole set of young nobles, headed by an Orsini, sprang to the defence of her honour.

Soon afterwards Tullia committed the most fatal error of her career. She bestowed her favours on an ugly German because he was very rich and had obviously outbidden all the young Romans of noble birth. The gilded youth of Rome never forgave her for this mistake. She was dropped and went out of fashion. She found herself, overnight, with no one to protect her, for courtesans have never in any country been able to count on the support of the authorities.

Tullia leaves for Adria

This crisis in the life of the young and beautiful woman must have been a serious one, for her reaction to it was somewhat irresolute. She went first to Adria, an insignificant little town after which a whole sea has been called. Her mother was living in retirement there. For a metropolitan courtesan it could only be a refuge dictated by despair. Yet even Tullia's further removal to Ferrara, her mother's birthplace, proves her utter lack of planned purpose. Nevertheless, Ferrara was a capital city. For Tullia it meant a return to the fashionable world. The most famous woman writer in Italy, Vittoria Colonna, lived there. Tullia must have cut an attractive figure and taken care not to offend anyone, for a local diplomat wrote:

A gentlewoman has arrived here whose bearing, character and modesty is so refined and who is so fascinating in her submissiveness that one can't help finding something truly divine about her. She sings all sorts of arias and motets at sight. The charm of her conversation is incomparable. She knows everything and one can discuss any subject with her. No one here comes anywhere near her, not even that most excellent lady, the Marchioness of Pescara.

The marchioness in question was the widowed Vittoria Colonna. Since her husband's death a few months after the bloody battle of Pavia which his brilliant tactics had won, her thought, poetry and practical activities had been very largely concerned with religion. It was also evident that she had no intention of competing in outward brilliance with the experienced courtesan from Rome. For Vittoria had accompanied Occhino, General of the Capucin Order,

128

to Ferrara in order to persuade the duke to found a monastery of that fraternity. Tullia became her rival not only in the poetic field, but also in the favour of the holy man. She was always to be found, dressed in the severe robes of a penitent, among the congregation, whenever Bernardino Occhino delivered one of his famous sermons.

From Ferrara to Venice

It is not yet quite certain why Tullia so suddenly abandoned her salon at Ferrara. She exercised there a dominion over men's minds which would never have been possible in Rome. The aristocrats, prelates and intellectuals who met in her apartments were most gratified to find there an arena for the free play of intelligence so close to that of the intrigues of the little court. A high proportion of her visitors, though not all, were granted her intimacy. The rest at least underwent the spell of so beautiful a woman, who united in her person the brains and charm of a woman of the world with the frivolous refinement of a seasoned courtesan.

She found Venice a disappointment after Ferrara. Although old Bernardo Tasso, father of the poet, immediately fell in love with her, there were well-known courtesans in Venice already who would never have dreamed of giving up their palaces on account of the newcomer. Nor could this commercial republic ever have vied with the cities on the Italian mainland as a centre of culture. Tullia's next stop was at Siena, which she had known in her youth and where she contracted an incomprehensible marriage. Her deplorable husband was not even in a position to protect her against annoyance from the local authorities, who demanded that she should betake herself to the prostitutes' quarter and pin the external badge of their trade to her clothing. The importance of this episode lies in the fact that in spite of princely favour and poetic renown Tullia was still regarded as nothing more than a courtesan by those concerned with her in this aspect, the illiterate subordinate employees of the civic offices.

'Dell'infinità d'amore'

She soon saw that princes could be more easily prevailed on than office hacks and sent a sonnet to the Duke of Tuscany, who thereupon gave her permission to settle in Florence. On her departure from Siena she was already forty, but still beautiful, though poor and disappointed. Yet even so her astonishing vitality remained irrepressible. In Florence she retrieved her old radiance in lively discourse with humanists and poets, acquired the protection of the renowned Benedetto Varchi and helped him to return to the city on the Arno from the country estate to which he had been banished for his involvement in a social scandal. There is a portrait of him by Titian, representing a dark, bearded gentleman, with a book, a high intellectual forehead, a sensual mouth and a shrewd, composed expression full of self-confidence. In this character of an omniscient counsellor and reflective ironist he also appeared in Tullia's most important production, her dialogue entitled *Dell'infinità d'amore*, a discussion of the endlessness of love. It was a discourse that probably ended only with her death.

Death overtook her after the greatest passion of her life, that for a twenty-four-year-old Florentine whom she met in Rome, the scene of her first triumphs. The city was no longer the dangerous Rome of the Borgias, the radiant artistic centre of the Rovere and Medici families, but once more the Holy See of an austere pope, Paul III. He compelled Tullia, the courtesan who had now reached the age of forty-four, to wear the prostitute's veil she had escaped in Florence owing to the energetic protests of highly-placed friends. She also appears in the list of Roman prostitutes issued in 1549. Worse still, for seven years nothing more is recorded of her. Probably she wrote no more poems in the absence of a brilliant circle of acquaintances and no more dialogues for the lack of a partner. Silence closed over Tullia and she herself remained silent until she died, in 1556.

Her will, which she dictated in her cramped quarters, only reveals her former glory in its faultless Latin. The articles with which it was concerned might have been bequeathed by a mere 'candle-girl', the poorest sort of whore. They consisted of outer garments, shifts, sheets and table-linen, all old and worn out, a single carpet and a few sticks of furniture. Eleven volumes of notes and thirty-five books may have represented her most treasured consolation in the last years of her life, when wealth had all been consumed and no friends came to see her any more.

Various conjectures have been made as to why she returned to Rome instead of staying in Florence, where she could probably have lived on without falling into such abject poverty. But it would be intelligible enough if this beautiful and shrewd woman had foreseen her decline and considering it inevitable had crept back like an animal to die where everyone can be most certain of being left alone, a big city.

Veronica Franco

During the sixteenth century it was not Milan and Naples, but Florence and Venice, which rivalled Rome. And in Renaissance Italy courtesans comparable with Tullia and the fair Imperia could most confidently be expected to inhabit Venice, which needed no popes to make it rich and no pilgrims to fill its streets.

Of the Venetian courtesans the only distinguished writer was Veronica Franco. She had enjoyed a good education, first at the hands of her parents and then by a doctor to whom she was married off while still almost a child. He must have been no common practitioner, for when she left him at the age of eighteen she was already a fully equipped courtesan. She immediately began to acquire an exceptional reputation for her skill in the particular operation upon which the whole success of a whore depends.

Though she had nothing more to learn in this field, in the mental sphere she was all the more anxious for improvement. Poets and abbots were therefore her favourite visitors, provided they were not incapable of disbursing the prescribed fees, which were not exactly low. Veronica's name may be assumed to have stood at the top of the long list of Venetian *hetairai* in the sense that the highest of the usual charges made by Venetian harlots were noted as hers.

Henry's unexpected recovery

Veronica wrote in a pleasant style and gained the applause of her contemporaries. Montaigne browsed with amusement in a little book of letters she sent him after his visit, recognizing that she had entertained a distinguished man. In short, she knew what was considered appropriate in the intellectual world, while she also knew more about improprieties than other people. She was no doubt both attractive and expensive and would have deserved an asterisk in the history of morals even if she had not been as successful as she was reported to be in her greatest exploit, that of rousing King

Henry III of France, who had been devoted for decades to his male favourites, to join her in a passionate night of love, being the only woman to have ever performed this feat. He had paid her a visit without thinking of such a thing, simply because it was fashionable to make one's bow to very famous courtesans. Montaigne and other travellers also thought it proper to do so. But in this case the prince who believed himself immune to the charms and fascinating wiles of women succumbed to those of the shrewd Veronica.

The verses of Veronica, in contrast with those of Tullia, were wholly concerned with this world and the senses. They did not carry a reader away into higher spheres, but remained in that of her own main business, which, however, she handled with the utmost grace. It was not until the passing years and half a dozen children warned her that it was time to retire that Veronica began to spend more and more time at the estates of her friends on the Venetian mainland. At last she decided to invest her considerable fortune in a penitent's home, one of the establishments dedicated to Mary Magadalene which were founded all over Italy during the sixteenth century.

She did not live to be old. Like Imperia and Tullia she died before she could be regarded as a matron. One of the feverish infections arising from the Venetian canals in the summer carried her off at the age of forty-five. Althougy Veronese, Tintoretto and other artists undoubtedly painted her portrait, no picture survives which can be declared with certainty to show her features.

Aretino and Zaffetta

Whenever Veronica had herself rowed up the Grand Canal, she passed on the left, between the projecting quay on which the church of Santa Maria della Salute now rises and the Palazzo Manzoni Angara, the gorgeous residence of Angela Zaffetta, designated by Aretino as 'the crown of all courtesans', though doubtless she was nothing of the kind. Yet, fond as he was of lying, he must have had some reason for his statement. It may be assumed that Zaffetta was either extremely wealthy, as indeed the palace she inhabited seems to suggest, or else had very powerful friends, as again her name appears to hint, for it means nothing less than 'Angela the Police-spy'. It is possible that it was only her father who acted as one of the dreaded confidential agents of the Republic. But she herself may also have introduced, behind the Flemish arras of her bedroom, a hiding-place where other courtesans concealed Peeping Toms, certain of those living microphones that the Government of the Doges never ceased to employ.

However that may be, Angela was not only beloved but feared. Her affectation of innocence in surrounding herself with animals, musical instruments and posies could deceive very few people. The monkey-musicians and talking parrots were accompanied in her house, as was the fashion, by painters, poets and cardinals. But she was probably only really interested in cookery. Her kitchen was at least as famous as her bed. Although certain evil-minded gossips declared that Zaffetta's couch had been made to serve for no less than thirty-one clients on a certain night, the fair lady's recipes never met with anything but the highest praise.

Superiority of North Italy

The most intelligent courtesans of the period would also include Camilla da Pisa, who wrote such touching letters, and Alessandra Fiorentina, who concluded a long screed to Francesco del Nero with a sentence admirably characteristic of her trade. 'But I am not going to worry about all that. Instead I offer myself with all my heart to your Lordship.' But it is not necessary to dwell upon these ladies in order to recognize that in general the north and centre of Italy remained astonishingly superior, at any rate in civilized behaviour and the fine arts, to the section of the peninsula south of Rome.

In Rome, which its popes had once more made the navel of the world and where the world had actually been divided into two halves by a pope, the two halves of the Italian boot could be balanced against each other better than anywhere else, at any rate when it was a question of women. A stream of good-looking and well-educated girls entered the city from the north. They had all learnt foreign languages and studied art. Very often they trailed a comet's tail of more or less gifted minds behind them. But the immigrants from the south came to Rome because they had been driven in the first place to Naples from their starving villages in Sicily and Calabria and because they had reached Naples in such numbers that even the lounging soldiers of the Spanish garrison could not feed them all.

The two groups of course met. But since each immediately occupied distinct levels of society no collision occurred. The southerners passed without protest into the lower ranks of society. The northerners hired the best premises they could find and turned at once to a different type of client. Even the authorities, though the same laws were still in force for all prostitutes and a certain pride was taken in dealing with all dissolute women in the same way, silently noted that some were unlike others. The women who could not drop the bad habits they had developed in the Via Toledo at Naples, those who stole and submitted to ponces, rioted and terrorized their neighbours, had a hard time keeping out of the hands of the law. Many of them were strung up without further ceremony.

The chastisement of Isabella da Luna

The other group, strangely enough known as 'honest whores', could count on being tolerated. In fact, many of the sentences passed might be suspected of expressing appreciation of the prisoner's beauty rather than stern condemnation. The impudent Spaniard Isabella da Luna, for instance, once compromised a certain prelate in a most disgraceful manner and the eminent gentleman bellowed for vengeance. It was duly accorded him. But it proved at the same time a triumph for Isabella and her charms. Fifty strokes with the rod were decreed. But first she was paraded through the whole city, wearing only her prostitute's black coat, slit to the armpits. The chronicler reported that she gaily allowed both widths of the fabric to flutter in such a way as to expose her white body. On arrival at the place of punishment the fifty blows were duly administered, while the crowd of onlookers respectfully admired that portion of her anatomy, the beauty of which was reserved on other occasions for such secular and clerical notabilities as were prepared to pay highly for the privilege. When it was over, Isabella shook herself, stood up and paced proudly away, just as if nothing had happened.

At no time could girls of easy virtue make their fortunes so fast as in that dawn of a new age in Italy. It was not always necessary to write poetry. Brisk horse-sense would be enough, with a sufficiently pretty little face and no time wasted. Aretino's Lucrezia, who is represented in the *Dialogues* of that unique expert and son of a courtesan* as a credit to her profession, confessed quite openly:

Aretino's Lucrezia

One of my regular customers in Ferrara had an enemy whom he would gladly have helped out of this world. I offered him my services, saying I would willingly be of assistance. Thereupon he gave me two ducats, which I was also glad to have. I assured him that his adversary would be coming to see me alone the following night, two hours before dawn. I said that my friend could then make the most of his opportunity. He didn't wait for a second hint. He kept watch outside my house for the other fellow and bashed out his brains, just as he was coming away from me and hadn't yet cooled off.

[The same Lucrezia also shrewdly observed that] our trade won't stand holding on to one client the whole night long. For this reason I used to rise about twenty times, on one excuse or another, from the side of the man who had hired me. Sometimes I even used to say that I just couldn't endure the heat of the night and would pace up and down in my shift, showing myself occasionally in that state, half naked, at the window and drivelling away so long about the moon and the stars as I stood there that men started collecting in the street to stare at me. By this means I obtained instead of the one fornicator I had left in bed, three or four others, who would visit me again on future occasions, to my profit.

These glorious circumstances, the enticement from open windows and the flow of lovers in the erotic Renaissance atmosphere, did not last indefinitely. The stricter popes who followed the brilliant ecclesiastical magnates of that period forbade the use of the open window and the temper of the age was blown to shreds as the venereal disease, today called syphilis, spread from France and Italy across the Mediterranean and eventually all Europe.

Since prostitutes were automatically excluded from the normal order of society they had always been subject to a certain amount of regulation. They obeyed readily enough, in general, even in the freer epoch of the Renaissance, the rules about their clothing. They were less willing, however, to submit to prescriptions as to where they should live and reacted most obstinately of all to actual prohibitions of their trade, which in practice meant expelling them.

* It is not quite certain that Aretino's mother, who was married to a shoemaker, ever plied this trade. But she had certainly been an artist's model. See the present translator's *The Divine Aretino*, Anthony Blond, 1965 pp. 27, 30 [J.C.]

The tax on prostitutes

The most usual methods taken by the police to deal with professional prostitution were taxation and clothing regulations. The taxes were generally farmed out, not so much on theoretical as on practical grounds. In modern times the question whether the taxes paid by whores should go to Church or State funds is the subject of both public and private discussion. But neither in the medieval nor in the Renaissance period does this matter ever seem to have caused serious dispute. Even in regions where Church and State were one, as in Rome and the lands administered by clerical authority, taxes on prostitutes were collected. The farming out of the collection was due quite simply to the fact that political units, for the most part small in extent, had to keep their administrative staff within bounds, while at the same time very few trained officials were available. All kinds of state revenues, including those levied on merchandise and for the upkeep of roads, were farmed out, so taxes on prostitutes were naturally added to the list. In many places the catalogue of such lessees has been preserved and very often records the names of highly respectable families. A prince who nominated a pander to assume the duty of collecting taxes on whores would merely have been setting the fox to guard the geese.

The level of this taxation varied a great deal. But, significantly enough, scarcely any prostitute objected to it. Only at times when they could expect no clients, as in Passion Week for instance, did the whores, as a body, pay no taxes. As the fees they received were hard to assess and easy to conceal, then as now lump sums were estimated, in the first place by the lessee. He almost always had to pay the prince an amount calculated beforehand and was therefore also himself obliged to try to obtain a fixed total of tax receipts, compiled through contributions from the various brothels and free-lance harlots of his district.

A town councillor as judge of beauty

A curious exception to this rule is recorded to have prevailed at Verona, where one of the town councillors had to decide whether a whore was good-looking or not. The prettier prostitutes had to pay three *soldi* for every night during which they were professionally occupied, while the less attractive paid twelve. The reason for this difference may be that the better-looking girls would not often be unoccupied and would therefore have a great deal to pay in the course of a year. Yet it must have been particularly hard on the less popular and older whores to lose twelve *soldi* a night out of their fewer nightly receipts. Similar principles were in force at Pavia.

The prescribed clothing was reduced during the Renaissance in most places to a small red bow, ribbon or patch on the right or left shoulder. But as there were no limits to the caprices of a prince, variations were constantly being introduced. For example, at Faenza in the province of Ravenna whores had to carry a small basket in addition to the frequently enjoined yellow headscarf. At Padua a red hood was prescribed, constituting a most striking article of attire, the purchase of which invariably led to a riot of some kind, favourable or otherwise according to whether the buyer triumphantly acknowledged her trade or was ashamed of it. When the fashion for coifs reached Italy from France, Amadeus VIII of Savoy, later Pope Felix V (d. 1451), ordained that every prostitute in his dukedom must wear the horned variety, and one of excessive size at that. This decree, as Amadeus may well have intended, put the new coifs right out of fashion in Savoy.

Clothing orders with ulterior motives

So long as the items of clothing forced upon harlots were neither positively absurd nor especially conspicuous, they were in general accepted without protest. For it was an advantage to a whore not to be mistaken for a respectable woman and often saved her the trouble of taking the initiative and thus risking rejection. That would not be so bad as the experience of even wealthy courtesans who ignored the clothing prescriptions. They might legally be undressed in the open street, an enjoyable spectacle which the strollers in Italian cities never denied themselves. It was also very difficult to obtain exemption from the rules. The state archives of Florence still preserve the formal edicts of remission which Tullia was able to obtain in the end by sending her application through the Duchess, accompanied by bulky extracts from her poems. She was excused the ribbons prescribed for prostitutes but had to promise on oath to wear only plain, inconspicuous garments.

Prostitute's accommodation and districts

The problem of accommodation was much more intractable than that of clothing. Just as today references to the flats occupied by whores appear every week in police-court reports, so during the Renaissance period plenty of people objected to having such women as close neighbours. Even in noisy Naples whole stacks of complaints were filed against nocturnal disturbances and violent molestation not only by harlots and their keepers but also by their clients. For this reason, ever since the Middle Ages a leading preoccupation of all communities had been to keep the trade in question within such clearly marked limits that it could not invade other quarters of the town.

As a rule the smaller cities succeeded in this project better than the large, where the citizens were not all known to one another and separate districts were as self-contained as those, for example, in Rome. At Milan, Padua, Cremona, Piacenza, Perugia, Reggio and many other towns, however, whores were practically confined to barracks. In other words a certain building, group of buildings or even suburb had been placed at their disposal and they were not allowed to live anywhere else. If they tried to do so they risked expulsion from the town, flogging and fines. In the bigger cities prostitution spread like an epidemic from one quarter to another, whether to entire main streets as in Rome or to suitable groups of houses and farmsteads just outside Naples, which then became favourite spots for excursions.

The Spanish city of Valencia had solved its prostitution problem in remarkable fashion, described in detail by the well-known author and traveller Antoine de Lalaing. He had visited Valencia about the year 1500 and, instead of going to the brothel which his companions visited, discovered a whole complex, so to speak, of houses, streets and walls.

Valencia's exemplary town for whores

It is about the size of a small town and is similarly surrounded by walls. There is only one gate, with a high gallows erected before it as a warning to all evil-doers. The gate-keeper takes charge of all the walking-sticks and weapons carried by intending visitors and also offers to look after their money and valuables until they return. If they decline this proposal he will not be responsible for the loss or theft of any such property. There are three or four streets of small, detached houses in the town. Here the young harlots stroll up and down, dressed in silks and velvet and decidedly impudent. Others watch at the windows. Altogether there may be about four hundred of them and their little houses are pretty and well furnished. None is allowed to charge more than four deniers, the regular price so long as they practice their trade in Valencia. There are inns and taverns in the whores' town and as the climate is very mild their domestic life can be watched through the open doors and windows at almost any moment of the day or night. The city of Valencia pays two doctors to do nothing but keep an eye continually on this nest of prostitutes and immediately undertake the treatment of any who should fall ill. The cost of this service is borne by the municipal authorities and wherever a girl may wish to be sent it must not be further than her birthplace. I record these particulars because I never saw anything of the kind elsewhere nor such careful police supervision.

The scourge of venereal disease

Lalaing, who was related to the *Chevalier Sans Reproche* and came from Hennegau, could not have suspected the great practical importance of these measures and the probable reason for them. For syphilis, old as it may be, had at that time only been known in Europe for a few years. After the great plague which had begun in Naples and decimated all Italy for years the inhabitants of the peninsula were only granted a short respite. It was on 19 January 1496 that the chroniclers recorded the first case of that originally mysterious and frightful sickness. Eight weeks later the first decree dealing with it was issued in Paris. France can therefore claim a certain priority in this matter, for before any public measures were taken against the disease a year or two had passed and people were already saying that the much abused Admiral of the Atlantic, Columbus, had brought the disease back with him from the New World instead of the gold he had been expected to provide.

At any rate syphilis, coming not only from Barcelona but also from France and south Italy, was gaining more and more ground. It spoilt enjoyment of the most beautiful courtesans and had a more lasting effect than any of the enactments of the austere Popes Paul IV and Pius V, who concentrated on the regeneration of the Eternal City and all true Christians. The progress of the disease was also promoted by the close association of prostitutes and students, not only in Paris but also above all in Naples. It was the kind of malady

139

that no one could hide from and that claimed victims even in Padua, where certain professors of that far-famed university were paid out of the proceeds of the taxation of brothels. The infection raged blindly, indiscriminately and mercilessly, like an actual killjoy, and was felt to be a manifestation of divine wrath. Loose tongues fell silent, jests and quips died on men's lips. People hardly dared even to look at one another and the uninhibited pleasures known in the fifteenth century lost their popularity.

Signs of the new era

The signs of a new era were multiplying. The Peasants' War and the Anabaptists beyond the Alps, military expeditions, battles and the sacks of cities in the Mediterranean lands, reached hitherto unknown proportions. In the disastrous year 1527 the youthful beauty of Renaissance art was despoiled by the fury of Spanish and German mercenaries. Tapestries hung in shreds, paintings were slashed by blades from Toledo and Augsburg and vases only recently excavated from Italian soil flew into fragments, when on 6 May, Rome was sacked by an army under a Constable of France who bore the great name of Bourbon. No courtesan's raillery nor smiling glance was of any avail. As if the miseries of venereal disease had not been enough, war too broke over the city, which was ravaged by swarms of plundering and devastating mercenaries, though a fresh outburst of vitality had only just awakened it to a new life.

BOOK III

THE AGE OF GALLANTRY

*

Two seaports

'Women are wonderful creatures, children are
wonderful too; both of them so enjoy having their
own way with life and we mustn't do aught in return
but praise and caress them.' – GOETHE

After the centuries of the religious wars, in which once more, but
for the last time, camp-followers ruled the field, three or four
generations of Europeans experienced the delights of an era today
referred to, either with envy or with contempt, as the *ancien régime*.
During this last vigorous period of the old absolutist forms of
government a more colourful and varied vigour than had ever been
known in Christian times was also shown in the eternal youth of
relations between the sexes. The Venetian Giacomo Casanova
could exclaim, half in astonishment and half in rapture: 'There is
no need for harlots in this fortunate age! So many decent women are
as obliging as one could wish!'

The new paradise

Everyone, however, was not a Casanova. Even in this glorious
epoch prostitutes were able to sustain competition from decent
women without yielding much ground. Nevertheless, new paths
and paradises had to be opened up in order to distract males from
the obliging and decent ladies to those who were equally obliging
but not so decent. As a rule the refinements then developed proved
to be beyond the conception and imaginative powers of newcomers.
The raw country girls who had made up their minds to live by their
charms now needed education and expert guidance from feminine
specialists who differed from the bawds of the Via Toledo in Naples

141

about as much as a fine hunting-piece differed from an arquebus. Though the grand courtesans and the strolling whores naturally clung to methods which had been tested ever since the rise of the antique world, the intermediate class that frequented the brothels and houses of assignation acquired maturity and polish with surprising speed. The luxury and grandeur of these places were designed to restore to the visitor the confidence he had lost in them owing to the continued prevalence of venereal maladies. The increased supply of both ladies and service was also intended to encourage him to pay the considerably higher prices now demanded as willingly as the trifling sums of four deniers, maravedis or sous in vogue during former centuries.

Capital cities in the West

The cities in which this evolution occurred, almost uninterrupted by the tumult of war, were Georgian London and the Paris of the Sun-king and his successors. In Madrid and Rome the Church and in Vienna and Berlin the secular sovereigns laboured to preserve some shreds of the Christian principles of chastity. But the citizens of the two more internationally minded capitals of the West gave themselves up with undisguised enjoyment to the novelties contrived for them by ingenious bawds.

The mention of Paris in this connection causes no astonishment. Even before the reign of Louis XIV every imaginable pleasure had been available there. But reports of life in the city on the Thames were read with much greater excitement in fashionable Europe. For at the turn of the seventeenth and eighteenth centuries very little was yet known of the practice of the more secret vices promoted with special force in London by a combination of puritanism and bad weather.

Few continental Europeans had ever visited the island. Buckle stressed the point that 'England, owing to its insular formation, was until the middle of the [eighteenth] century, rarely visited by foreigners'. He added that it was considered a great merit in a traveller like the Comtesse de Boufflers to have gone to England merely to broaden her mind. 'The result was, that in other countries, and particularly in France and Italy, the inhabitants of the great cities became gradually accustomed to foreigners, and, like all men, were imperceptibly influenced by what they often saw. On the other hand, there were many of our cities in which none but Englishmen ever set their feet; and inhabitants, even of the metropolis, might grow old without having once seen a single foreigner, except, perhaps, some dull and pompous ambassador taking his airing on the banks of the Thames.'

The London of George III

But the English themselves did travel, returning to their populous capital to retail their adventures abroad. For six decades London's monarch had been distinguished in only one sphere, that of his primitive appetites, which had also ruled him while Prince of Wales. Such long reigns have never been conducive to progress, but in this case society could only remain what it was so long as the masses were kept waiting for reforms. The position is best explained by the excellent Buckle, George's compatriot, whose blunt precision in that capacity suits the topic.

This reactionary movement was greatly aided by the personal character of George III; for he, being despotic as well as superstitious, was equally anxious to extend the prerogative, and strengthen the church. Every liberal sentiment, everything approaching to reform, nay, even the mere mention of inquiry, was an abomination in the eyes of that narrow and ignorant prince. Without knowledge, without taste, without even a glimpse of one of the sciences, or a feeling for one of the fine arts, education had done nothing to enlarge a mind which nature had more than usually contracted.

Unimpeded by critical and enlightened ideas and protected by the instinctive patronage of a king who accepted slavery and other primitive evils of this world as ordained by nature, the British aristocracy pounced upon everything so far withheld from an island long poverty-stricken and backward. Soon it began to be rumoured in Europe that at any rate plenty of entertainment could be had in London. The city itself, though not yet the interior of the country then became attractive to those gentlemen and ladies inhabiting other capitals or belonging to the culture-hungry provincial nobility of Europe. For such people were in this century for the first time travelling with an almost modern restlessness.

What neither the great Elizabeth nor the dissolute Charles II had been able to effect now occurred under the sway of a king subject to repeated lapses into insanity. A bridge of intellectual and social intercourse began to function in both directions across the Channel.

An invasion by girls of easy virtue

But while gentlemen and ladies from the polite world of Europe sailed to England in search of information or pleasure only by dozens, free and easy young women seem to have gone the same way by hundreds. In the Netherlands particularly the new attraction of the British capital very soon became conspicuous. The distance was not great. Nor was the voyage expensive. Consequently, by about the middle of the eighteenth century the estimated number of some fifty thousand whores in London included a considerable contingent of Flemings. French and German women followed. But in this connection it has to be confessed with regret that while the French girls distinguished themselves by remarkably good manners, those of the Germans were remarkably pushful. As for the Italian women, who probably reached England as members of theatrical touring companies or as domestic servants and decided to stay in the country, no clear evidence of their behaviour is available.

The atmosphere of places in London frequented by the *demi-monde* had noticeably improved as compared with that of the seventeenth century and the dismal *bagnios* often then combined with public baths. The uninhibited gaiety reported in language of simulated innocence by Cleland's *Fanny Hill* is found again when the celebrated diaries of Samuel Pepys are contrasted with those of James Boswell. Pepys, in the sixties of the seventeenth century, is not much more candid than Boswell a hundred years later. But the former has a great deal to complain of, from the difficulties of his assignations to the formalities of parties in the country with ladies who auctioned their pretty daughters and the frequency with which maids had to serve him with favours which it was too much trouble to obtain from Mrs Pierce. The common people, moreover, were by no means disposed to allow London to be made a city of pleasure. Every year, during Lent, whole troops of apprentices stormed the best-known brothels and threw stones at the harlots in the streets. Although the fury of these young men was only directed, incomprehensibly enough, against prostitutes, it alarmed the court as much as if a revolution had broken out.

And, Lord! to see the apprehensions which this did give to all people at Court, that presently order was given for all the soldiers, horse and foot, to be in armes! and forthwith alarmes were beat by drum and trumpet through Westminster, and all to their colours, and to horse, as if the French were coming into the town! So Creed, whom I met here, and I to Lincolne's Inn-fields, thinking to have gone into the fields to have seen the 'prentices; but here we found these fields full of soldiers all in a body, and my Lord Craven commanding of them, and riding up and down to give orders, like a madman. And some young men we saw brought by soldiers to the Guard at White Hall, and overheard others that stood by say, that it was only for pulling down the bawdy-houses.

Charles II and the brothels

When the king, Charles II, was told of the popular outburst against the brothels, he answered in the remarkable phrase reported by Pepys. 'If they don't like the brothels they need not go to them.'

Times were clearly changing and it is no surprise to learn that a hundred years later under George III prostitution had become a permanent feature of daily life in London. Visits to the brothels, of which there are said to have been some two thousand, were regular items in the budget of every bachelor and those who had no budget, because their means did not run to one, as a rule gambled successfully on a general atmosphere which made many girls content with an evening meal and a bottle of wine in return for their favours.

I resolved to be merry while I could [wrote James Boswell, the author and biographer of Dr Johnson, in his *London Journal* under the date of 19 May 1763], and soon see whether the foul fiend of the genitals had again prevailed. We were plain and hearty and comfortable; much better than the people of high fashion. There was a Miss Rutherford there, a Scotch girl who had been long in America. She and I chatted very neatly.

We stayed and drank tea and coffee; and at seven, being in high glee, I called upon Miss Watts, whom I found by herself, neatly dressed and looking very well. I was free and easy with her, and begged that she would drink a glass of wine with me at the Shakespeare, which she complied with. I told her my name was Macdonald, and that I was a Scotch Highlander. She said she liked them much, as they had always spirit and generosity. We were shown into a handsome room and had a bottle of choice sherry. We sat near two hours and became very cheerful and agreeable to each other. I told her with a polite freedom, 'Madam, I tell you honestly I have no money to give you, but if you allow me favours without it, I shall be much obliged to you'. She smiled and said she would. Her maid then

145

brought her a message that a particular friend from the country was waiting for her; so that I was obliged to give her up this night, as I determined to give her no money. She left me pleased, and said she hoped to have the pleasure of my company at tea when it was convenient.

'Miss Watts' was a well-known woman of the town, who had first been recommended to Boswell a week before, and since even at their first meeting she turned out to have a prior engagement it may be assumed that she was doing well. Yet she would clearly have dispensed with a cash fee in Boswell's case, seeing that he was determined to behave as much like a Scotsman as a native of Edinburgh had every right to do. As he 'resolved to be merry while I could' he refused to be beaten and simply descended a step lower, from the girl with a place of her own down to the street-stroller.

Scottish behaviour in London

I then sallied forth to the Piazzas in rich flow of animal spirits and burning with fierce desire. I met two very pretty little girls who asked me to take them with me. 'My dear girls,' said I, 'I am a poor fellow. I can give you no money. But if you choose to have a glass of wine and my company and let us be gay and obliging to each other without money, I am your man.' They agreed with great good humour. So back to the Shakespeare I went ... We were shown into a good room and had a bottle of sherry before us in a minute. I surveyed my seraglio and found them both good subjects for amorous play. I toyed with them and drank about and sung *Youth's the Season* and thought myself Captain Macheath; and then I solaced my existence with them, one after the other, according to their seniority. I was quite *raised*, as the phrase is: thought I was in a London tavern, the Shakespeare's Head, enjoying high debauchery.

The songs from Gay's *Beggar's Opera* seem to have been as accurate in their local colour as they were popular, though it was thirty-five years since the play had been first produced. But 'merriment' of this sort was not always so easy to find. A certain amount of atmosphere was already required at that date in London, and men of fashion in the eighteenth century would only be satisfied with cheap girls if they could get nothing better.

'I had an opportunity tonight of observing the rascality of the waiters in these infamous sort of taverns. They connive with the whores, and do what they can to fleece the gentlemen. I was on my guard, and got off pretty well.'

146

In such conditions the fashionable brothels must have flourished. Nor were their exacting clients prepared to do without the setting to which they had become accustomed for their dissipations. Grand furniture and carpets, lofty and attractive rooms, chandeliers, toilet facilities and a courteous reception were demanded, to some extent no doubt because 'vulgar love', as Boswell calls it, was not altogether safe, especially in London. The common people, ignored by everyone else, scarcely ever let a strikingly well-dressed man walk the streets without abusing him. Ladies could never go out except in carriages. The wearing of masks was general, particularly in the case of ladies, even when not going to a ball. Gentlemen were accompanied by their servants even for short distances. Casanova, for example, never went out alone in London, though it is true that he was inordinately afraid of crowds and also in rather a nervous state during his stay in the city.

The court brothel

For the first time since the days of Charlemagne and the harems of the Middle Ages an undisguised court brothel was set up in the reign of George III. It is probable that no such establishment had been needed in earlier centuries because of the long-standing practice of labelling one or other of the rooms in the palace, quite openly, as 'reserved for the king's harlots'. The Georgian Court brothel comprised a group of houses near St James's Palace. They stood in a lane significantly named 'King's Place'. The inmates were well-groomed and well-dressed girls who were never allowed to walk in the town, but only in the royal parks. The women were strictly supervised and the stiff entrance fee charged for admission to the brothel kept away all the men who did not belong to the innermost circle of the court. Charles James Fox, before he became the dreaded adversary of William Pitt, frequently visited the place.

Those to whom even the most exclusive brothels were uncongenial could only go in search of courtesans at the sometimes wildly extravagant public balls. In eighteenth-century London many large ballrooms, sometimes part of a conglomeration of such halls, served the sole purpose of meeting, examining and bargaining with courtesans. Vauxhall, with its baroque and Far Eastern styles of architecture, was soon supplanted by Ranelagh, with its gigantic baroque rotunda, in the centre of which the orchestra played, while the visitors decorously sat or strolled round it.

According to Smollett, 'one half of the company are following one another's tails, in an eternal circle, like so many blind asses in an olive-mill; where they can neither discourse, distinguish, nor be distinguished; while the other half are drinking hot water, under the denomination of tea, till nine or ten o'clock at night, to keep them awake for the rest of the evening'.

At the house of Madam Cornelys

Entertainment was more lively at the house of Madam Cornelys, not, to be sure, an Englishwoman but one of the many handsome Venetians who had popularized the Italian stage first in Vienna, then in Holland, where she reached the arms of Mijnheer Cornelys, and finally in London. As Teresa Imer she had begun her career under the protection of a Venetian senator and simultaneously as one of Casanova's early loves. But her affair with the latter turned out badly for him. When they met again at Vienna he still found her irresistible and provided her with a baby. He described her establishment in the following terms:

After my presentation at Court I returned to my sedan chair and was carried by the two bipeds who bore it to Soho Square, where Dame Cornelys had invited me to a midday meal. A gentleman in Court dress cannot dare to show himself in the streets of London without running the risk of being bespattered with filth by the vulgar mob and his English friends would only laugh in his face if he tried to complain about it . . . I was admitted, with my Negro servant Jarbe, to the Cornelys establishment, where, after walking through a dozen fine, large rooms, I was shown into the *salon*, where the mistress of the house awaited me in the company of two English ladies and two English gentlemen . . . After we had risen from table and taken coffee, which was handed round in the French style, Madame Cornelys showed me a banqueting-hall which had been built at her orders. Four hundred persons could be seated there at once, at a single huge table in the form of a horseshoe. She told me, and I was very ready to believe her, that no other hall of such size existed anywhere in the whole vast extent of London. She added that the last banquet before Parliament rose would be given there in three or four days' time. She has twenty maids, all rather pretty, in her service and a dozen lackeys in grand liveries.

'The whole gang of them rob me,' said she. 'But I'm obliged to keep them. I need a man with brains and energy to help me run this place and be devoted to me. If I could find someone like that I could certainly amass a splendid fortune within a few years. For the English never count the cost of their pleasures.'

Although Teresa Cornelys presented her and Casanova's daughter, the charming Sophie, to him, the Venetian did not accept the lady's scarcely veiled offer to take charge of the festivities at her side. But his excellent head for figures must have been impressed when she told him that every year she gave twelve suppers and twelve balls for the nobility and the same number for citizens of the middle class. On each occasion between five and six hundred guests turned up, each paying two guineas, which entitled him to be served with anything he wanted.

Miss Chudleigh's dresses

The Venetian lady, after her adventurous life among actors, dancers and princes, had achieved fame in London. Among other successes the wedding of Princess Augusta, the king's sister, to the Duke of Brunswick had taken place in her apartments. When the great banqueting-hall was demolished some decades later a commemorative tablet was found indicating that the foundation stone had been laid by Elizabeth Chudleigh. As famous as she was notorious, this London woman of fashion had been one of the chief attractions at the big public balls on account of her daring modes of dress. She cannot have worn any of these confections at the wedding of Princess Augusta. But there were certain occasions when she and other ladies had been more notable for the scantiness than for the inventive detail of their costumes. Mrs Elizabeth Montagu – to be sure not a very charitable critic – reported after a masked ball held in May 1751:

'Miss Chudleigh's dress, or rather undress, was remarkable; she was Iphigenia for the sacrifice, but so naked, the high priest might easily inspect the entrails of the victim. The maids of honour (not of maids the strictest) were so offended they would not speak to her.'

On this incontestable evidence Miss Chudleigh appears to have been the real originator of the fashion for exposure which came to a climax under the French Directory and was represented in its boldest and for the time being final manifestation by the fair Countess Bagration, the 'naked angel' of the Vienna Congress.

But it was not only the more or less daring attire characteristic of such balls that favoured the production of a Dionysian atmosphere at these revels. Their architectural and decorative settings also inspired a riotous mood. Madam Cornelys and her keenest competitors, the organizers of the balls held at Almack's Club, went in for oriental pomp and also sometimes for aquatic entertainments, in which water-nymphs always provided the main attraction. Even in those days, as is still often the case in England, the supply of food was inadequate and if the guests had anything to complain of it was usually the menu.

Erotic balls given by Mrs Prendergast

There was no mystery, however, about the erotic balls given by Mrs Prendergast and the so-called meetings for billiards which took place at an establishment called De Fountein in Amsterdam. At the Fountein wealthy Englishmen, a few Dutchmen and at times also a few German connoisseurs sat quietly drinking rum or gin at small tables in the lofty, brightly lit attic of a house where the lower floors were occupied by a dance-hall and a café. The tables were ranged under the windows and a billiard-table stood in the centre of the room. But none of the gentlemen were playing. They simply sat there, sipping their liquor and critically watching the game in progress. A dozen stark naked young Dutchwomen were handling the cues. Whenever one of the regular customers at the Fountein received a card inscribed 'Billiards at half-past nine' he knew at once what to expect and had a perfect alibi to show his wife into the bargain.

The erotic balls given by Mrs Prendergast took place at her seraglio in Pall Mall and were only accessible, as might be expected in such a smart neighbourhood, for a fee of five guineas. They were therefore decidedly more expensive than the Cornelys evenings. It is true that at Mrs Prendergast's visitors were not fobbed off with even a single lady making a show of private audacity by wearing some sort of veil, for here no one had any clothes on at all except the men. The ladies appeared in narrow black masks and dancing slippers and in order to avoid any sort of embarrassment a cold buffet was available and music was supplied by a dance-band discreetly facing the wall.

South sea revels by the Thames

The celebrated Charlotte Hayes made no such concessions to polite usage. She did issue invitation cards. But they were couched in distinctly blunt language. The entertainment she offered at her 'South Sea Revels' – they were called 'Dances from Otahiti' at the time – would not be permitted so openly, before a large group of eminent spectators, anywhere in Europe today. Nor would any twentieth-century Hayes dare to style her establishment a 'convent' and her girls 'nuns'.

Charlotte Hayes catered for a fastidious circle of clients, whose money obtained what she could not herself supply. They were therefore mostly elderly gentlemen of means or rich widows, both of whom were well provided for, the gentlemen mainly with very young girls from the provinces, for whom they had to pay from five to twenty guineas, and the ladies with experienced young bachelors, who might cost anything up to fifty. As even such grandfatherly caresses as any lord might have allowed himself with members of his own staff cost four or five guineas when combined with a game of piquet, it is not to be wondered at that Charlotte Hayes retired with a fortune of at least some £250,000. She would have been able to earn about the same amount if she had ever thought of having her brothel-diary printed and published by herself. For its unvarnished narratives, full of unconscious humour and shocking frankness, noting the preferences of both male and female customers, sometimes positively touching in their innocence and sometimes quite peculiar, put the coolly arrayed statistics of Kinsey and his disciples right back in the shade. The entries, naïve as a grandmother's, can occasionally be appreciated as actual brain-teasers. For example:

Four day virgin

'9 January. Girl for Alderman Drybones. Nelly Blossom, about nineteen, unvisited now for four days and in virginal condition . . . Twenty guineas.'

The only London brothels more expensive than that of Hayes were the flagellation establishments. They reached their most flourishing period a little later, at the turn of the eighteenth and nineteenth centuries. Though often considered an English speciality, flagellation has in fact been of great importance in sexual life generally, and in prostitution particularly, ever since classical times.

In London the rod became standard equipment for whores between 1750 and 1760. A certain Miss Jenkins was the first prostitute who owed her reputation to this instrument. The 'Posture Girls', of whose performances some very powerful descriptions have been preserved, must no doubt have aimed at the same object with their displays on inn tables.

A supposed English disease

About the year 1800 the flagellation brothels had become so famous that even a Crown Prince like the later George IV made no special secret of his visits to one of them, the house of a Mrs Collett in Tavistock Court, Covent Garden. But a practitioner possibly even more celebrated was Theresa Berkley of Charlotte Street, who kept not only a unique arsenal of rods, whips, nettles and so on but also quite a number of implements of torture. As she herself indulged in the mania from which she earned her living, her profession may have been rather tiring, for she only practised it for eight years. All the same, she managed in this short time to amass a fortune of some ten thousand pounds, which her sole legatee, a brother who had turned missionary, repudiated with disgust. So the profits of all the torments and thrashings she had administered reverted to the Crown and the bequest of her voluminous and extremely outspoken correspondence, of much more value to the history of civilization, was destroyed.

On the other hand some highly instructive advertisements have survived from her stock-in-trade and the possessions of her and her successors' customers. These documents prove the direct connection between the cult of flagellation and schoolteachers and governesses fond of caning.

The great courtesans

Considering the equipment, structures, novelties and installations which all these ladies needed to make a fortune or else go bankrupt, as did poor Madam Cornelys, despite all the alleged English hunger for pleasure, the few great courtesans of Georgian London had rather better luck. Instead of dealing with greybeards or eternal schoolboys, they were friendly with educated and often very handsome men. They found life worth while, with only envy to vex them. Their whole success, moreover, was due to their personal charm and the attractive power they exercised during a few years in their lives.

Almost all were of lower-class origin, a high proportion having started life in the inns, where a good-looking staff attracted many travellers, and they often possessed in addition to their physical charms a considerable degree of intelligence. Certainly they always needed a man to release them from their service as maids or waitresses, buy them their first smart clothes and teach them a minimum of good manners. But once they had found him they soon gave him the slip and often climbed the social ladder faster than he did.

An example of this kind is afforded by the adventurous couple Ange and Sarah Goudar. The former came of a good Montpellier family. He was a cultivated ne'er-do-well, a political journalist who pressed his views on one sovereign after another and had travelled all over Europe before he came to London and caught sight of a pretty Irish girl named Sarah in one of the taverns. Soon afterwards she married Ange, who was some thirty years her senior, and thereafter shared his fortunes.

Sarah Goudar

Swindlers have always been fond of working with strikingly pretty women. Goudar was of the same opinion in this matter as Cagliostro. He meant the radiant Irish beauty to play the decoy for his gaming club and in due course sell herself to the highest bidder. The couple lived for a considerable time in this way on Count Buturlin, then for a shorter while on King Ferrante IV of Naples. This last relationship gave Sarah a place in history. Ferrante being a prize idiot, who had been taught to write for the first time by his wife Marie-Caroline, his affair with Sarah ended with the queen staging scenes of jealousy and eventually expelling the Goudars from Naples. Casanova, who knew all the details of this business at first hand, recorded the general view of Sarah's career.

Sarah Goudar was not surprised to see me, for her husband had of course told her what to expect. But her attitude was all the more disconcerting to me. She was dressed in the very height of fashion and behaved exactly like an Italian or French lady of the first rank. Her manners were easy and natural and she played her part to perfection, speaking Italian with an unaffected vivacity of Neopolitan women. Her beauty quite enraptured me and I couldn't take my eyes off her. She realized that I was silently comparing her with the young waitress in a London tavern which she had once been and laughed heartily ... In less than fifteen minutes the room had filled up. I noticed five or six ladies belonging to leading families of the city and at Court and about a dozen gentlemen, among whom were dukes, princes, a marquess and a few foreigners. Before the long table, seating some thirty persons, was laid, Madame Goudar sang an aria, accompanying herself on the harpsichord, with a voice as pure as that of a nightingale and a virtuosity of style which only surprised myself, for the other guests were clearly already familiar with her accomplishments in this line.

All this was due to Goudar's training. He had brought her up to this level in six or seven years and after wandering about Europe for some time had finally established the fair Sarah in the fashionable world of Naples. The ecclesiastical ceremony with which he began the process was, to be sure, a farce. He arranged a public conversion of the young 'Englishwoman' to Catholicism, though Sarah, being Irish, had never abjured that religion.

The character of the couple's relationship changed as they grew older. Although Sarah did not betray her Ange to the police, as the pseudo-countess Cagliostro had betrayed her pseudo-count, she began to dominate him. She actually appeared in a literary guise, perhaps because he could now offer her nothing more than the satisfaction of having graduated from the status of waitress to that of authoress. Nevertheless, both partners ended in the embittered poverty of adventurers who have lived too long, dying in Paris, the international refuge of all wrecked lives in the eighteenth century.

A whore named Charpillon

A somewhat different career was that of a woman known as Charpillon, undoubtedly one of the most alluring visions that ever walked a London street. She rose rapidly and securely from the protection of mere ambassadors to become the mistress of the Lord Mayor. Her real name was Augspurger, and she may have been a Swiss Jewess.

Charpillon had reached London in the company of a small group of relatives as aged as they were avaricious. While still only seventeen she had attracted, like Sarah, the attention of the unquestionably gifted talent-spotter Goudar. But while he retained the pretty Irish girl for training by himself, he soon procured for the much-travelled young Augspurger a financially potent initial patron in the shape of the Venetian Ambassador Francesco II, Lorenzo de' Morosini, Knight of the Golden Fleece and other orders, wealthy, arrogant and narrow-minded, in short an ideal type of being to launch the career of a young prostitute destined to go far. He took a small house for her, where their intimacy would on the whole be less liable to interruption than in an apartment, and made her an allowance of about fifty pounds a year, not very much considering how many persons expected to live on it.

Before Charpillon turned to more generous clients like the rich Lord Baltimore, Lord Grosvenor and the Portuguese Ambassador Saa, she netted a second Venetian, again with Goudar's help. This was no less a person than Giacomo Casanova, who had settled in London with his usual ostentation, which must have given Goudar the impression that he had money. But in this case Charpillon's object does not seem to have been so much the extraction of cash as victory in an obscure business matter, originating in Geneva and involving an outstanding debt owed to the Venetian by her mother, most bitterly contested by the Augspurgers. Such was the commencement of an extraordinary comedy of harlots and swindlers well up to the standard of the most fanciful novels of Renaissance times.

Casanova's defeat

The chances and changes of this cruel game cannot be particularized here. All that need be stated is that the beauty of seventeen played cat and mouse with the lady-killer of forty from Venice and that the idol of so many women, unused to acting the part of a mouse, behaved like an infatuated schoolboy. When he complained to Goudar one day of Charpillon's prim attitude, his friend offered to bring him a patent armchair equipped with spring-catches which would render Charpillon, the moment she sat in it, his helpless victim. Casanova refused the offer with indignation. He, Casanova, had never yet used that sort of stratagem, he declared. It was lucky for him that he did refuse. For at that point in Charpillon's career it would no doubt have been impossible to prove that she was a prostitute, so that the stern old magistrate Fielding would have relentlessly sentenced Casanova to be hanged for the rape of an innocent girl, unless of course she preferred to blackmail her assailant under the threat of this penalty.

Disgusted and suspecting danger ahead, he determined to retreat. But just then he received a note asking him to call at her house. On arrival he was asked to wait a few moments and then shown, as if by inadvertence, into the very room in which the girl was taking a bath.

The aunt preceded me to a door, which she opened, pushing me through it, and then closed behind me. I saw Charpillon standing naked in a small tub. Pretending to think her aunt had entered the room, she asked for a towel, at the same time assuming a posture more seductive than any lover could imagine. But no sooner had she caught sight of me than she crouched down, uttering a shriek . . .

This single instance of the technique of softening up must suffice. Its success, at least in the present case, can be gauged from the fact, among others, that the eminent psychologist Charlotte Bühler, in her analysis of Casanova's career, regards this experience as the turning-point in his hitherto fortunate, indeed all-conquering, progress. He himself recognized it as such.

She was so beautiful that it was difficult to find even the slightest fault in her. Her hair was a bright chestnut colour, her eyes blue and her skin of the purest white . . . Her breasts were not very large, but perfectly formed, her hands small and fleshy. Though she had tiny little feet, she walked steadily and proudly . . . It was on that fateful day at the beginning of September 1763 that I started dying . . .

John Wilkes victorious

She only seems to have made one man happy. He was John Wilkes, energetic member of the House of Commons, political journalist and editor of the *North Briton* newspaper. Wilkes was a tough character. Persecution, exile and imprisonment had not tamed him. At forty-six he was some twenty years older than Charpillon when she became his mistress and remained with him for five years. After 1777 nothing more is heard of her. It is uncertain whether she died young or merely fell so low that the world and society, the chroniclers and gossip-writers, ceased to take any interest in her.

The career of Amy Lyon, later to be known as Emma Hart and

finally Lady Hamilton, combines elements from those of both Sarah Goudar and the Augspurger girl. Amy was born about 1765, the child of poor parents. She worked to begin with as a domestic servant and waitress, then became lady's-maid to a rich woman in whose company she managed to acquire a smattering of education by somewhat indiscriminate reading. She learned the power of her beauty at an early age when one of her relatives was pressed into the Navy in accordance with the custom of that time and his captain would only release him in return for the possession of her person. The Goudar of her life was John Graham, a connoisseur of feminine beauty, a glib talker and a charlatan.

The cabinet of Dr Graham

Graham began with a very simple recipe for success, occasionally followed even nowadays by lecturers on drawing and photography. He confronted his mainly male audience with an exemplary specimen, feminine of course, of youth, health and beauty, completely nude as required by the 'scientific' character of the lecture. The profits which accrued to the impostor and his pretty assistant soon encouraged him to exhibit her in more and more extensive and splendid settings. The lecture-rooms were succeeded by whole temples of health, the last and best known of which stood in Pall Mall. Amy had to show herself to thousands of visitors, sometimes enthroned as Vestina, the goddess of health, sometimes lying on a bed of state, but always in tableaux which involved theatrical stripping, and led to the recognition of Graham's institute as a brothel for the pleasures of the eye.

This period had one positive and one negative consequence for the fair Amy. On the negative side, having hitherto only surrendered to individuals, she now lost all sense of shame and reserve and began to feel a positively insane reverence for her own physique. Positively, she acquired a certain familiarity with the effects of dress and picturesque attitudes, which bore fruit in later years after she had become Lady Hamilton and achieved European fame with her living reproductions of poses mostly taken from antique or later art history.

Prostituting herself psychologically rather than physically, Amy acted as both model and mistress of the eminent if also eccentric painter George Romney (1734–1802). This relationship alone would have been enough to make her famous, for Romney unquestionably owed to her the ardour of his portraits, and the thrilling sensual energy of his depictions of myth, repeatedly inspired by Amy's figure. He painted her by turns as nymph and bacchant, as Circe, as Calypso and even as Mary Magadalene, the Pythian sibyl, and St Cecilia. As the model of a man of true artistic genius and impeccable taste Amy was able to perfect her skill in representation and her instinctive understanding of decorative and plastic display.

At about this time she inevitably attracted the attention of the draughtsman Thomas Rowlandson, a dreaded caricaturist, who recorded in one of his sarcastic coloured lithographs the fact that she was by then the most famous model for the nude in London.

At any other time this reputation would have excluded her from society and relegated her to Bohemia. But in the London of George III even aristocrats paid less attention to the conventions than they did at other periods. Sir Charles Greville, to whose family the earldom of Warwick had just been transmitted, took over Amy. Thenceforward she called herself Emma Hart and passed as the aunt of the children she bore to Greville.

Amy Lyon becomes Lady Hamilton

The financing of so renowned a beauty finally proved too much for h.ɔ resources. A little family council was held and a rich uncle undertook to pay the debts to his improvident nephew Charles and carried off the fair Emma as his share of the bargain. This uncle was Sir William Hamilton, member of a junior branch of the ducal family of that name. Some thirty years older than Emma, an antiquarian and ambassador to the Neapolitan Court, he was a man, wrote Goethe, 'of taste in all things, who, after having wandered through all the realms of creation, obtained a beautiful wife, the masterpiece of the great Artist'.

For the ageing aesthete and collector Emma Hart may well have been the latest and most valuable of his acquisitions over so many years. But for her the transfer to Naples revealed a world more brilliant than she had ever known before, where Graham's many-coloured lamps were superfluous and no one knew anything about the children she had borne to Greville. In Naples she was regarded by Hamilton and his large and cultured circle of friends as a phenomenon just as far beyond good and evil as any other demanding admiration, whether antique work of art or feature of the contemporary city, which thirsty travellers in that region might encounter.

Goethe added:

Hamilton has now, after all his long devotion to art and nature, reached the climax of all delight in both fields in the person of a beautiful girl, about twenty years old and English, who lives with him. She certainly is very beautiful and well built. He has had a Greek robe made for her, which suits her remarkably well. Thus clad, she loosens her hair, picks up a scarf or two and adopts such a variety of postures, demeanours and expressions, etc., that at last one really believes one is dreaming. Effects which so many thousands of artists only wish they could produce are here to be seen in their entirety, in motion and in surprising alternations. The attitudes, standing, kneeling, sitting, lying, serious, melancholy, teasing, impudent, repentant, alluring, threatening, frightened and so on succeed one another and develop out of one another. She knows which folds of the veil to choose for each mood and how to modulate them. She can contrive a hundred different sorts of headgear from the same kerchiefs. The old knight holds the light for her and participates in the business with his whole soul . . . Early this morning Tischbein was painting her.

Although Goethe weakens this passage by continuing, 'The joke is incomparable', there can be no doubt that Emma Hart aroused genuine admiration, if naturally most of all in 'the old knight', Hamilton himself, who soon afterwards actually married her and so enabled her to be received at court.

Caroline of Naples

Queen Caroline, who had so angrily expelled Sarah Goudar from Naples, received the brand-new Lady Hamilton with open arms. England had once sent her a talented and helpful minister, Acton, who had become her lover. Now she had obtained from the same source a young and handsome companion, no longer inexperienced, to share her debaucheries. It is generally accepted as certain today that Caroline and Emma, as soon as they were tired of male company, fell into each other's arms like Greek *hetairai* and a high proportion of dissolute women to this day. Ferrante IV, hunting down his strapping peasant whores, stood no more in their way than did Hamilton, perpetually occupied with extending his collection of antiques and in this process, according to Goethe, not averse from shady transactions.

Acton, who completely dominated the lout Ferrante, manœuvred Naples, during this politically disturbed period, out of one breach of faith into another, thus exposing the kingdom to repeated French attacks. Nelson and the British fleet were consequently the only hope of so weak a state. It was due to the fair Lady Hamilton that Nelson, incidentally against the orders of the Admiralty, always cruised, with his guns, in the offing, wherever the Neapolitan Court happened to be located. When he was at last ordered back to London the Hamiltons accompanied him. The 'old knight' no doubt realized that he had no chance against the hero of Aboukir, the one-eyed, one-armed officer who bore the romantic odour of frigate-life about him.

Downhill after Nelson's death

In 1801 Emma, Lady Hamilton, gave birth to a daughter who was christened Horatia. Nelson considered himself to be the child's father. Hamilton died in 1803 and in 1805 Nelson fell after winning the Battle of Trafalgar. Although the fair Amy was now the widow of a respected and wealthy man and had been the mistress of a national hero, she began to experience hard times instead of a peaceful old age and to go downhill. In the country to which she had returned everyone knew her origins. Sunny Naples, where the king and queen themselves had participated in the wild revels among the ruins of Pompeii, seemed infinitely far away. But Lady Hamilton would of course have been enabled, with what she still had, to live on as a discreet matron if her capacity for serious application, self-discipline and resignation to her lot had been above the average. Unfortunately, at forty, though she had put on some weight, she remained beautiful and more familiar with extravagant living than most women of her time.

At first neglected and soon afterwards treated with contempt, she dropped back into the habit of casual prostitution from which she had formerly extricated herself so fast. But even so she could not earn enough to finance her expensive tastes. Debts, imprisonment for debt and flight from her creditors marked for her the years in which Europe laboriously freed itself from French dictation. She died in 1815, the year of the Hundred Days, when the fame of England's new hero, Wellington, was eclipsing that of Nelson.

Fanny Barton and Garrick

Amy Lyon, the former boarding-house maid, has remained, as Lady Hamilton, the most renowned of all English courtesans, though others may have developed their natural talents to more purpose and also possessed a stronger personality. Most of her rivals in this sense started in the theatre. For the London stage was flourishing at that time as had hardly been the case since the days of Shakespeare. Yet it may be noted that by no means all of these women finished their careers in a brothel. In Georgian London it was perfectly possible, as the example of Fanny Barton proves, to become, after some years in a bawdy-house, the star of the Haymarket Theatre, the wife of its musical director and the darling of the public. Nor was Fanny alone of her kind in rising to such heights. She must have been a remarkably capricious sort of creature, quite out of the common. For she did what she liked with Garrick, the most famous actor of the day, adored by women, just as Charpillon had infatuated Giacomo Casanova. She may not have renovated plastic art like Emma Hamilton. But she certainly gave a new impetus to the fashion of very low-cut gowns, such as are depicted in Cretan vase-paintings. She called this mode *décolleté*. But it would more accurately be referred to as topless nowadays. Fanny, whose married name was Abington, must have had an iron constitution. For in spite of her addiction to this type of garment, most unsuitable for the English climate, she reached the age of eighty-four.

A triumphant combination of beauty and intelligence is reported to have distinguished, in particular, the actress Anne Bellamy of the Covent Garden Theatre. She was the illegitimate daughter of Lord Tyrawley and no doubt had a very handsome mother, for the peer was known to be a connoisseur in that field. Anne Bellamy actually rose to run a *salon* of the kind maintained by her eminent rivals in Paris. Though she may not have had the greatest men in the country at her feet she could nevertheless number among her lovers cabinet ministers, generals, the celebrated statesman Fox, a great lover, and Philip Dormer Stanhope, the fourth Earl of Chesterfield, notable not only for his tolerant poilcy towards

Ireland but also for his letters, so refreshingly free from moral bigotry, to his natural son.

Anne's memoirs are remarkable not only for their frank statement of the kind of love conducive to a full life but also for their freedom, in this matter, from all rhetoric. She came to the conclusion that she herself had only experienced entirely satisfactory sexual pleasure after an evening of intelligent conversation had previously 'freed the soul and transported it to the Elysian Fields'. She obviously felt a real need for the company of successful and gifted men. It was not mere vanity that impelled her to seek it.

Kitty Fisher pie

Fanny Murray and Kitty Fisher, often named in the same breath with Anne Bellamy, were probably only comparable with her in their physical beauty and charm. No doubt they were her inferiors mentally, Kitty because she repeatedly sold herself in primitive fashion, even when it had long been unnecessary for her to do so, and Fanny on account of her outrageously obscene talk. Kitty was commonly said to be as prompt in honouring a bill as the Bank of England. No one would more readily redeem a note for a hundred guineas as Miss Fisher and she did not care in the least who presented it. But if an old friend, even the Duke of York, happened to offer anything less, she could be as furious as if she had been spat upon. The vengeance she took in this case became famous. She had the duke's fifty pound note baked in a pie and ate it for breakfast. All London had a new topic of conversation and the elderly duke was made to look foolish.

The original of Fanny Hill

Fanny Murray and Kitty Fisher allowed themselves to be painted together, for a rich lover, in their unadorned beauty. The picture was unfortunately either lost or destroyed by some fanatic, as were two similar paintings by Gustave Courbet. But it is easy to imagine the delight of some wealthy London rake at being able to compare two such renowned courtesans. Fanny Murray, the daughter of a musician, left no memoirs but has nevertheless entered literary history. John Wilkes, the tamer of Charpillon, who was his mistress for years, described the fair Fanny's activities in his extremely outspoken satire *An Essay on Woman*. In 1749, when she was at the height of her reputation, John Cleland gave her Christian name to the heroine of his *Memoirs of a Woman of Pleasure*. Even if it need not be assumed that Fanny Murray was the original of the celebrated Fanny Hill certain aspects of her career were certainly embodied in Cleland's novel, as popular today as it ever was.

The reports of Boswell, Casanova, the Chevalier d'Eon, the German professor Lichtenberg and other socially privileged investigators of the London of George III represent the obvious moral degradation into which the society of the metropolis had fallen as a sophisticated idyll, a harsh note, perhaps, in the brightly coloured image of the *ancien régime*, but by no means a catastrophe in the history of civilization. The destructive effects of these gay activities only became clear to the following generations, which saw a libertine take the place of a madman on the English throne.

The most unworthy squabbles over the king's private life occupied both Houses of Parliament, while George IV sought to divorce his queen and convict the unfortunate Caroline of Brunswick of adultery, though he had long ceased to cohabit with her and had a good deal to answer for himself in his liaison with his titular mistress, the temperamental Mary Anne Fitzherbert, countless other love-affairs and debaucheries of the most diverse order.

The great families suffered heavy losses in prestige and capital. Economic ruin, suicides, bastards, venereal disease and insanity corrupted the stock of a rapidly growing empire to an extent that, owing to the delicate matters of detail involved, cannot yet be fully estimated.

The nabobs

Old-established institutions and the moral basis of society were also weakened and imperilled by external influences. Members of old families who had grown extremely wealthy in India and the other colonies went on behaving, on their return to England, as if they were still dealing with natives who had no legal rights. They seemed to think they could compete with maharajahs even in London. These nabobs, as they were called, being financially independent and therefore without ambition, even though there were not very many of them, nevertheless gave a new impulse, by their example, to the pursuit of pleasure in London.

The practice of flagellation has generally been associated with

163

the English educational system and the harsh naval life of the day. But the nabobs have been held responsible for the rise of a second perversion more widespread in the England of the late eighteenth and early nineteenth centuries than anywhere else in the world, the mania for defloration. For a visitor to a brothel to demand virgins indicates not only the possession of considerable funds but in addition and in particular a degree of moral derangement amounting to definite eccentricity. As there could be no question of such a male expecting either special co-operation or any specific experience from such girls, he would be attracted merely by the prospect of destroying the innocence of a young, unsuspecting female. But however peculiar this mania may appear and however incomprehensible it may seem to a normally sensitive being, it was nevertheless rife in the London of George IV.

Defloration mania

Bawds and the police agree that a good deal of the activity of brothel-keepers consists in procuring 'fresh merchandise', so as to be always prepared. The girls must be at least sixteen, in order not to expose clients to prosecution, and must be able to produce proof of virginity in order to justify the high price charged in such cases. Many of the young women endured the medical examination and what followed it good-humouredly and for a good fee. Others had to be drugged, or, if the client objected to that, reduced to obedience by blows. An astonishingly high proportion even of those who woke up with thick heads after being anaesthetized and were therefore quite unconscious of having been deflowered remained in the house where they had been ravished, or after once escaping soon returned to the pavement. From the case of a single one of these shady gentlemen, a rich London doctor who had up to seventy virgins placed at his disposal every year, it may readily be deduced how many London girls were lured in this way on to the downward path.

White slave traffic across the Channel

As soon as the young girls from the London slums had made their first profits in the high-class brothels they were despatched to the continent, where, in their shy and terrified state, they were once more confidently put on sale as novices. In the first half of the nineteenth century the most notorious and dreaded brothels were those of Brussels and Antwerp. 'Big Business' men, those newly enriched from the Dutch possessions in Indonesia and Belgian financiers, met in the *demi-monde* centres of the Netherlands whenever transparently worded advertisements notified the arrival of a fresh batch of girls. In a first-hand account of this traffic, for which only a cross-Channel passage was needed, Alfred S. Deyer wrote:

In some houses, where the inmates are particularly harshly and violently treated, the walls and double doors are padded to prevent the shrieks of the victims and other sounds of the nightly orgies reaching the street. It is common knowledge that the patrons of these places, soon surfeited with the ordinary forms of immoral behaviour, and lusting for novel sensual stimulation, inflict upon the inmates the most inhuman, unnatural and diabolical outrages, the character of which cannot be further described here and which it would be difficult to indicate even in private conversation. In order to slake this thirst for novelties the householders take care to provide a succession of fresh victims, among whom, for a change, negresses are often included . . . The Brussels Police Commissioner himself acknowledges that the owners of the disorderly houses are ready to pay anything for new and if possible perfectly innocent victims. Hence English girls, who perhaps command the highest prices . . . are systematically tracked down, enticed and sold into a slavery which is infinitely more cruel, shocking and dastardly than the servitude imposed on Negroes, since the former is applied only to young, helpless beings, who are forced into the service of lust, not labour.

A melancholy balance-sheet

The most prominent, powerful and reckless feature of the gay life of seventeenth-century inns and the great popular amusements of balls and masked gatherings in the eighteenth century had been prostitution. 'Merry England', Ranelagh and Carlisle House had passed away. Hundreds of public and thousands of secret brothels had brought about the participation of a tenth of the London population in the prostitutes' trade, whether as inmates, attendants, managers or landlords of these houses. The times were long past in which clients ordered girls to be delivered to them in sedan chairs, one after the other, until one contrived to please the customer. Now they sat in rows, two hundred at once, like so many parrots, and the visitor chose the one he wanted. Prices had gone down. But risks had gone up. A million and a quarter people were suffering from syphilis every year in England alone. Many un-detected murders occurred, for sewage pipes led from the brothels on the banks of the Thames into the river and carried the bodies out to sea. Such was the *demi-monde* of London on the threshold of the new era.

Boswell's departure from London

On 3 August 1763, the day before he left London, James Boswell wrote in his diary: 'I should have mentioned that on Monday night, coming up the Strand, I was tapped on the shoulder by a fine fresh lass. I went home with her. She was an officer's daughter, and born at Gibraltar. I could not resist indulging myself with the enjoyment of her. Surely, in such a situation, when the woman is already abandoned, the crime must be alleviated.'

Gentlemen could at least still be considerate in those days. They could even commit their reflections to paper. Because they were so frank, their diaries can be regarded as part of the literature of gallantry.

But a comparison with conditions in London only a hundred years after Boswell and two hundred years after Pepys seems to show that since their times the fusion of *demi-monde* and under-world in the city had become more complete than anywhere else on earth. That was why British connoisseurs so often preferred to satisfy their requirements on the continent.

The freedom from moral restraint in Georgian London could only be matched in Venice. An international port like that on the Thames, it was also the seat of a sovereign power controlling a maritime empire that remained important, with its colonies and commercial interests throughout the world. Venice, moreover, was visited by more foreigners at that time than any other city except Rome, Paris not excluded.

De Brosses in Venice

James Boswell, a young provincial nobleman in London, had des-cribed the somewhat disreputable attractions of the great city at first with astonishment, then with amusement, and finally with a certain amount of sophistication. The *Confidential Letters* of Charles de Brosses, Count of Tournai, Baron de Montfaulcon and son of a Judge of the Supreme Court of Burgundy, were written from Venice to friends at home in Dijon, the French provincial town so renowned for its mustard. The friends complained repeatedly that for a young man of thirty he was writing far too much about architecture and painting and far too little about habits, good and bad. Accordingly, he pulled himself together and wrote on 14 August 1739 to M. de Blancey:

You must know that nowhere in the world do liberty and negligence prevail more unrestrictedly than here in Venice. So long as you leave the Government in peace you can do what you please. I am not referring to the activity to which we owe not only pleasure but actually our very being, the matter of matters. In this country it causes no more offence than any other natural function. That is a good custom, which ought to be universal. But here even what healthy-minded persons consider wicked goes quite unpunished. At the same time there is so little malevolence in the national character that in spite of the opportunities afforded to criminals by the wearing of masks, nocturnal habits, narrow streets and in particular bridges without parapets . . . less than four murders a year are committed and those as a rule by foreigners.

In this passage de Brosses in the first place disposes of the fear of the stiletto which was then rife throughout Europe. It was supposed that while the lutes had fallen silent daggers were still flashing as they had in the novels of the Renaissance. The heads of stay-at-homes, if not of travellers, were haunted by these glittering weapons. A second presupposition was the assumption that it was easy in Venice to seduce even ladies of good family and all the more difficult, therefore, not to be seduced by them. In this connection de Brosses had no doubt applied, as young gentlemen of rank usually did, in the first place to his ambassador, the representative of France in the Venetian Republic. He was especially well advised to do so in this case, for all of the diplomats in the city it was the French in particular who were accustomed to include the Venetian *demi-monde* in their studies of Venetian society.

Our ambassador said the other day that he did not know of more than fifty ladies in good society who slept with their admirers, the rest being too pious to do so. They have agreed with their father confessors not to indulge in the main thing but to allow anything else the fellows may require at a reasonable price.

The 'admirer' in Venice had a special function and a special name, *Cicisbeo*. As he never, apart from the fifty mentioned above, reached his objective, there was something ridiculous, even now suggested by the name, about the part he played, though it is hard to see why. In Venice it was the Admirer, not the husband, who was made to look foolish. The latter remained master in his own house, so long as he did not excite mockery by exhibiting a jealousy for which a reasonably tolerant spouse would have no cause. For no Venetian lady would ever dare to break a contract with her father confessor.

The cicisbeo had to be scented and serviceable at any moment. Doubtless he had to render such intimate assistance as fitting garters, lacing corsets and placing pins. He took care, in his capacity as a perpetually pining lover, that his lady should be properly admired when she rose from bed. Her *déshabillé* and dressing-table had no more secrets for him than for her maid. But whatever favours he received were acts of charity. He took his ardours, thus daily stimulated yet never quenched, either to common harlots or to courtesans, whichever he could afford, or possibly to one of those island convents to which he could be rowed out after buying the silence of the gondolier.

It is not impossible, with mutual agreement, to arrange a short interview in a lady's private gondola. For the gondola is sacroscant. No gondolier employed exclusively by a lady has ever yet accepted a bribe from her husband to betray her. If he ever did so he would be drowned by his colleagues the next morning. The activities of Venetian ladies nowadays have been most prejudicial to the nunneries, the inmates of which once possessed a kind of monopoly of amorous dalliance. Yet a fair number of them still contrive to hold their ground, I won't say with distinction, but at any rate in dignified competition. For at this very moment three of the city convents are engaged in a passionate struggle to decide which of them is to have the honour of providing a mistress for the newly arrived nuncio.

This passage at once recalls MM and CC, the beautiful young nuns of the Santa Maria degli Angeli convent, to whom Casanova and the French ambassador Bernis paid their respects together in 1753. Young de Brosses shared the impression made on the two great connoisseurs.

I should really stick to the nuns if I had to stay on here. All those I saw through the grating during Mass, as they chattered and laughed throughout the service, seemed to me extraordinarily pretty and very alluringly dressed. They wore charming little coifs, plain white of course, but as loose about the neck and shoulders as the stage costumes of our Roman actresses.

Although nunneries had a bad reputation at times in other cities and countries they nowhere played so important a part in the erotic concerns of a single city as they did in Venice and nowhere else were their activities so much discussed. It was no good pretending to make a secret of it. Lovely nuns were one Venetian speciality and the extraordinarily widespread practice of unnatural intercourse between men and women was another. But while the latter aberration, often somewhat inaccurately described by the one word sodomy, had originally been adopted as a precaution against venereal infection, nuns had always held an indisputable advantage over other women in a city scattered over so many large and small islands.

The convent walls towered, silent and mysterious, over the still waters of the lagoon. No street led to them. Only gondolas glided noiselessly into the darkness of the overhanging pines. Robes rustled. Then the gondolier pushed off again. Thousands of gondolas were rowed through thousands of nights. Only very rarely was anything heard of such activities, as when, for instance, two abbesses fought a duel with stilettos over the elegant abbé de Pomponne or when the beautiful Maria da Riva surrendered to the Comte de Froullay, ambassador of the King of France.

John Murray's adventure in a convent

The chastely robed and yet so enticing nuns of Venice were so renowned that the brothel-keepers catering for the polite world and the diplomatic corps often presented their merchandise as from a convent. A genuine Count Capsocefalo, for example, who had come down in the world, offered the British ambassador to Venice a girl whom he alleged to be the famous nun MM, whom everyone initiated in these affairs knew to be the mistress of the French ambassador de Bernis. It was not until a Venetian friend of both ambassadors took the Englishman to the convent where MM acted as housekeeper that he confessed he had been swindled. No doubt

169

he got over it, for he was none other than the John Murray of whom the ever crudely outspoken Lady Montagu wrote that he 'was a scandalous character in every sense of the word, a man who couldn't even be trusted to change a ducat, a diplomat who misused his position for smuggling and kept a whole retinue of brothel-keepers in his service'. Murray not only possessed an extensive collection of miniatures of his various mistresses but also formed liaisons with some of the best-known courtesans in Venice. He bequeathed his whole fortune to one of them, a certain Cattarina Pocarinolli, after adopting or rendering legitimate her four children.

The visitor to Venice would clearly be bound to fall into the hands of one or the other of these two fascinating but calamitous groups, nuns or courtesans. De Brosses' long letter went on:

> In order to complete my section on women, above all here in Venice, I had better add a word about the courtesans. They form a really remarkable corporation owing to their good manners and you must not believe people who tell you there are so many of them that one positively falls over them. That is only the case at carnival time, when you find as many women prostrate under the arcades of the Procurators' Palaces as standing or walking there. At other times there are no more than twice as many here as in Paris. For that reason they are all very busy. Every single one of them is regularly engaged from midnight or half past twelve onwards, so latecomers have no chance. The difference from Paris is that here they are all of a most captivatingly gentle and obliging disposition. You may make any request you like and they will always answer, *Sara servito, sono ai suoi commandi* ('With pleasure, at your service!'). For it would be considered rude to address anyone except in the third person. But as a matter of fact, when you realize the kind of trade they practise, the demands commonly made on them are quite reasonable. I recently found one of them so delightful that . . . What could I do? I couldn't very well still suspect her after she had sworn by the *beatissima Madonna di Loreto* that what I did would have no consequences.

Venetian women

Though both nuns and courtesans engaged in the same activities, in the first case they were thought dishonoured while in the second the charm and courtesy exercised aroused admiration. For even ladies in polite society and poor girls who only had an occasional love-affair were true Venetians, an obviously quite special type of

170

human being, a variety of womanhood under as powerful a spell as the city itself, though as everyone knows there were torture-chambers and dungeons in Venice, as well as the 'leads',* the slave-trade and an avarice never impeded throughout the centuries by the slightest moral considerations. An old-time wag once declared that he had cut up the brain of a pretty Venetian woman and found it contained a pack of cards, some miniatures of her admirers, a strip torn from a carnival costume, unpaid dressmakers' bills and a tiny alarm-clock which struck whenever it was time to eat. But another expert on Venice, Philippe Monnier, maintained that the clock could only be relied on to strike the hour for making love. It was through the courtesans, at any rate, that all Europe came to know Venice from the inside, so to speak. So many accounts have survived of the dealings of foreigners with them that one is almost tempted to assert that the city of twentieth-century honeymooners was in earlier times the favourite resort of all bachelors.

The more famous the foreigners were or were to become the more clearly it appears that the Venetian woman alleged to have carried such a remarkable load of lumber in her head proved a match for them. The bad losers held their tongues or burst into abuse like Montaigne who, after making the round of the leading courtesans, expressed himself as follows.

Montaigne disappointed

M. de Montaigne did not find among the Venetian ladies the beauty which has been so much extolled, although he saw the most eminent of those who traded their attractions. On the contrary what impressed him most was the princely display of furniture and clothing made by at least a hundred and fifty of these ladies, though it was only their trade itself that gave them the means to meet the cost.

One of the good losers, who admitted that the Venetian women had made a conquest of him, was Jean Jacques Rousseau. He did not keep a diary but wrote his *Confessions* instead. Nor did he have to rush from one spa to another in Italy because he suffered from bladder trouble and flatulence, but with the ingenuousness of a poet and the thirst for information of a philosopher let every marvel he

---

* A prison with a leaden roof, from which Casanova escaped on 1 November 1756. [J.C.]

saw have its way with him, especially the greatest of all marvels, woman.

'Common harlots have always repelled me. But in Venice all other girls were out of my reach, since on account of my standing I could only be received at very few houses in the city.'

Rousseau here refers to the fact that the entire diplomatic corps in Venice was strictly supervised, as were also, in particular, any Venetians who associated with foreign diplomats. On one occasion a young patrician encountered the Austrian ambassador, significantly enough on the staircase leading to a courtesan's apartments, thus finding himself for a time under the same roof as a foreign diplomat. He at once made a beeline for the Inquisition offices and reported the incident before it could be denounced and misconstrued. In these circumstances friendly association with native families or even an approach to one of their marriageable daughters would be practically out of the question for a diplomat coming from abroad.

Impunity after visiting the Paduan

The stout-hearted nobleman Vitali gave me my first chance . . . We had been discussing the pleasures of Venice over a meal. The gentleman present reproached me for my indifference to the most delightful of all distractions and extolled the unique charm of the Venetian courtesans. Vitali said that I simply must make the acquaintance of the most amiable of them all and offered to take me to her, assuring me that I would never regret it. I couldn't help laughing at this obliging offer and Count Peati, an elderly gentleman of venerable appearance, remarked with a frankness I should never have credited in an Italian, that he believed I had more sense than to let an enemy introduce me to girls.

More to avoid looking foolish than because he really desired it, Rousseau allowed himself to be taken to see one of the most renowned courtesans who, like most of her trade, had no proper surname but was called after her native city of Padua close by.

Padoana, whom we visited, had a pretty in fact quite beautiful face. But it was a kind of beauty I didn't care for. Vitali left me with her. I ordered sherbet, asked her to sing something for me and after half an hour rose to go, placing a ducat on the table. But with a singular display of scruple she refused to take it and with an equally singular display of folly I removed the reason for her scruples. When I returned to the Em-

172

bassy I was so certain that she had given me a dose of the French disease that I wasted no time in sending for a doctor . . . I couldn't believe that one could escape from the arms of Padoana with impunity.

A second adventure was arranged for Rousseau by a naval captain to whom the young embassy secretary had been able to render an important service. Rousseau was actually still sulking, after boarding the vessel to attend a celebration there, because the ship's guns had not saluted him, when he became aware of the surprise the captain had in store for him.

Rousseau and Zulietta

We were only about a third of the way through the meal when I saw a gondola approaching. 'Hey there, *monsieur*,' cried the captain. 'You'd better look out! The enemy's coming!' I asked him what he meant. But he answered only with jests. Meanwhile the gondola came alongside and I saw a dazzlingly beautiful, alluringly dressed and nimble little piece of goods climb aboard. With three steps she was in the cabin and in no less time seated beside me, before I'd even noticed that a place had been laid for her there. She was dark-haired, at most twenty and uncommonly charming and lively. She spoke only Italian and her intonation alone would have been enough to turn my head . . . Her big black oriental eyes shot whole firebrands into my heart and although surprise at first somewhat damped my ardour, it very soon revived and to such an extent indeed that despite the presence of onlookers my charmer soon found herself obliged to put a stop to my drunken or rather love-crazed enterprise. As soon as she saw that she had me where she wanted me, she moderated her caresses slightly, though not her vivacity . . . She took possession of me as though I were her serf, gave me her gloves, fan, sash and hat to hold, ordered me to go hither and thither, do this or that, and I obeyed her.

They were rowed in the French Embassy gondola to Murano, where Jean Jacques and a male friend had the honour of buying the beauty anything she wanted, while she flung tips about which came to just about as much. At Venice once more, the friend took leave of the pair outside her house and Rousseau was privileged to attend on her while she changed her costume for the evening. Her name was Zulietta. The presence of two pistols glittering among boxes and phials on her dressing-table was explained by her in the following characteristic terms:

'When I bestow my favours on men I don't like, I make them

173

pay for my boredom, as is only right and cheap at the price. I put up with their caresses but I won't stand any sort of roughness. The first man who misbehaves in that way will find that *I* shan't miss him!'

The real affair began as soon as she had taken off everything except the *vestito di confidenza*,

a more than frivolous nightgown, such as is only known in southern Europe. I would rather not dwell on a description of it, though I remember it only too well. Any attempt to imagine the grace and charm of that fascinating creature would always fall far short of the truth. Youthful nuns are less refreshing, seraglio beauties less vivacious and the houris of paradise less seductive. Never has so sweet a rapture been offered to the heart and senses of mortal man. Ah, if I had only been able to appreciate it for a single moment, to savour it in all its fullness!

Zanetto, leave the women alone!

But he couldn't. The most contradictory feelings surged through him. At times he felt unworthy to touch that glorious body. At times, again, her beauty seemed to him a diabolical delusion. In short, he sat down on the bed and wept. He also made a lot of other mistakes. Finally, Zulietta gave it up.

'She paced the room, fanning herself, and at last addressed me in a cold and scornful tone. "Zanetto," she said. "Leave the women alone and go and study mathematics." '

Whatever ecstasies Zulietta might have enabled Jean Jacques to enjoy, they would never have made her so famous as that phrase of dismissal. Actually, the whole of the seventh book of the *Confessions* contains no more striking portrait than that of the young Italian woman, for her mannerisms, personality, talk and general demeanour immediately convey the very essence of the charm constituting the special Venetian variety of worldwide harlotry on the courtesan level. The Venetians were certainly free and easy enough, but without a trace of vulgarity. They were not only desired. They could be the object of love. They did not yield until they had made a conquest. The preliminaries were not those of a bargain but in themselves a feast of promises. No doubt the captain had paid for everything in advance. But Zulietta meant to do more than earn her fee. She intended to fascinate, enrapture and gain the love of her partner.

The most beautiful woman in Italy

She seems indeed to have been in her prime the most beautiful of all Italian women. For de Brosses, who met her a few years before the affair with Rousseau, refers to her in similarly rhapsodical terms.

I believe that if angels and fairies united to create the human race they would never be able to model two such delightful creatures as Ancilla and Zulietta. Lacurne has gone quite mad about the first named and I about the second, at any rate since the day I saw her in the robe of the Medicean Venus and at least equally admirable in shape. She is rightly considered the most beautiful woman in Italy. It seems to me that our ambassador would be only too pleased to be loved by the first-named and that the Neapolitan ambassador is already most friendly with the second.

While diplomats and other foreigners formed the greater part of the clients of Venetian courtesans, the native citizens had their hands full either as loving husbands or obsequious *cicisbei* or else as first one and then the other. The courtesans, moreover, made things easy for the alien visitors. They showed no timidity and were not stingy with their charms, certainly not Zulietta, who, when de Brosses first met her, was probably only just eighteen. For the 'robe of the Medicean Venus' is a mere circumlocution, no doubt employed so as not to dazzle the writer's friends in Dijon with too bright a radiance, for complete nudity.

Ancilla, whom Zulietta was destined soon to surpass, did not fall behind her in this respect. When she dropped the French ambassador for the British, John Murray, who brought his friend Casanova with him to see her, she had no objection to the presence of that eminent connoisseur.

My presence did not disturb the pair in the least. He showed himself a valiant performer, while the voluptuous Ancilla obviously enjoyed displaying her beauty to my gaze. All the same, I did not contribute to their pleasure by taking an active part myself. I was in love with MM. But that was not the only reason. Ancilla's voice was always husky and she complained from time to time of pains in the throat. I suspected her, therefore, of suffering from a grave venereal malady, though Murray appeared none the worse for his intimacy with her.

Death of Ancilla

The pains in the throat were a warning of her early death. The fair Ancilla, both dancer and courtesan, succumbed to cancer in 1755, when she was not yet forty. But Casanova had been justified in his suspicions, for Ancilla had herself treated for syphilis by the fashionable Venetian doctor Licchesi. This step led to one of the most remarkable trials ever held in the sphere of medical jurisprudence. It also proves that Ancilla's audacity equalled that of her rival Zulietta. Ancilla had promised Lucchesi the high fee of a hundred sequins for his mercury treatment. But before she paid it she demanded proof in his own person that she was no longer infectious. This requirement indicates the same disillusioned attitude to her profession at that expressed by Zulietta when she laid a brace of pistols on her dressing-table. But though no one objected to the pistols Ancilla could not enforce her demand. Lucchesi, who lacked confidence in his mercury, declined the test proposed and sued for his fee in court. The magistrate upheld his petition on the ground that such a test would be contrary to morality and the doctor could not be expected to submit to it.

Zulietta outlived Ancilla by fully thirty-five years, during which first her beauty, then her charm and finally her intrigues were the talk of the rest of the century. A prominent Venetian named Muazzo had admired her looks when, while still a child, she brought him a frock-coat which her father had cleaned for him. Her next lover was a wealthy lawyer who had her taught singing. Under his patronage she made her first appearance on the stage as a eunuch in one of Metastasio's operas at, of all places, the prudish Court Theatre of Maria Theresa. The Venetian girl's charm was found so striking that she was instantly dismissed, henceforward to rate as a *sfrattata* (evicted actress). For in those days any actress with so little charm as to be allowed by Maria Theresa to perform in Vienna would be bound to fail elsewhere.

A title of honour from Vienna

With this title of honour Zulietta had free-thinking Venice at her feet. Her first lover was a nobleman named Querini. Then came the Marquess Sanvitali, who had felt himself obliged to compensate, to the tune of a hundred thousand ducats, a laundry-girl whose ears had been boxed by his marchioness. Zulietta, with a fortune of such proportions behind her, could afford to pick and choose her lovers. She no longer needed to live in the Rialto, the prostitutes' quarter, but had a smart apartment near the church of San Paterniano

Vescovo. Soon afterwards she departed to the city where in that century a good-looking woman could rise in the world more quickly than elsewhere. In Paris Louis xv did not care for her. But the Austrian ambassador, Wenzel Anton Count Kaunitz, made full amends for Maria Teresa's former treatment of the pretty Venetian. That irresistible young lady even ensnared a certain Count Zinzendorf in Paris, though this gentleman could not have been the pious founder of the Moravian Brotherhood, for he was only exiled until the year 1747, whereas Zulietta did not reach Paris until after 1750.

But Kaunitz did not quite come up to her expectations financially and finally a certain Marquis de Saint-Simon dropped her at his wife's request. Zulietta was therefore forced to sell some of her diamonds in order to be able to return home in a style suited to her position and marry Francesco Antonio Uccelli, the son of one of her patrons and three years younger than herself. This marriage officially put an end to her short but brilliant career as a courtesan. She does not seem ever to have gone to London, where Ancilla spent four whole years. Perhaps Zulietta's experiences in Paris had proved to her that her charms were best appreciated in her native land.

Courtesans as exports

Pretty girls who could sing a little, like Zulietta, or shake a leg on the stage, like Ancilla, were exported from Venice in those years all over Europe. At Stuttgart Gardella, who had not been so very expensive in Venice, became the much admired mistress of Karl Eugen of Württemberg, while another Venetian girl named Binetti had to be content with the favours of the Austrian ambassador to Karl Eugen's Court. At Barcelona one Nina held despotic sway over the elderly Governor Ricla. In Paris, London or St Petersburg gentlemen's heads were turned by positive swarms of Venetian actresses. The same thing happened at Warsaw and Antwerp, not to mention the small repertory companies which any shrewd Venetian could collect in his own city, consisting of one male professional player, two attractive 'nieces' and at most a 'chaperone'. Such parties could be let loose to worry Europe if for any reason they had made Venice too hot to hold them.

But in general the government of that small commercial republic got on very well with its courtesans. Once indeed they were all expelled from the city during a wave of moral austerity. But almost immediately they were recalled in a rueful proclamation containing the phrase, which elicited as much astonishment as laughter, *nostre benemerite meretrici,* 'our deserving harlots'.

Services rendered

The kind of services these women rendered may easily be guessed when it is realized that in the eighteenth century courtesans and diplomats came into more intimate association than ever before. At that period Venice had practically no power to influence affairs except through statecraft. It was accordingly absolutely vital for her to be better informed than either her friends or her enemies. Only if she always knew everything that was to be known could she successfully play the part of intermediary, at all times the last trump card of a weak hand. The harlots who returned to Venice were not only received with honour – a masterstroke worthy of the Grand Council – but were also compensated for the accommodation and fees they had lost. They had grown to be so essential a feature of Venetian policy as to make the secret contacts they arranged and the amount of information they picked up when alone with an admirer simply indispensable.

Much loved

This twilight world, half erotic and half political, in which so many a male adventurer of the Europe of those days basked, proved advantageous to ladies reluctant to take the final plunge into prostitution. These were beauties who travelled in the company of their mothers, were presented now and again to a prince at some tolerant court, to give him the opportunity of inspecting their *décolletage,* and regarded a reception as a suitable antechamber to their bedroom. Some of them bore great names, for instance the fair MM already mentioned, who acted as treasurer of her convent of Santa Maria degli Angeli on the island of Murano. Her secular name is known today to have been Maria Eleonora Michiel and her brother was a Procurator of St Mark's. Signora Renier-Michiel, not quite so beautiful as MM, was famous for her verses and charming 'confessions'. During her stay in Rome she was called 'the little Venetian Venus'. Cornelia Gritti too, born a Barbaro, added more grace than decorum to her families' distinction. Her poems are forgotten. But she has achieved immortality as the witty mistress of Goldini, Metastasio and Francesco Algarotti. Though the latter presented Holbein's Madonna to the Dresden Gallery, he was paradoxically made a count, not by Augustus III of Saxony, but by Frederick II of Prussia. Yet none of these three celebrated men can have pleased Cornelia by their attentions so much as did Carlo Frugoni, today entirely forgotten despite his fifteen volumes, when he wrote the line *sogno il bel fianco in suo giacer vezzoso* ('I dream her lovely flank's reposeful grace'). One can be certain that the most ambitious poetess would prefer such praise to the most well-meaning criticism of her verses.

Ugo Foscolo and Isabella

The mysterious women who bore such names, which time has almost erased, enjoyed careers of practically inexhaustible interest, as in the cases of Cecilia Tron, equally generous with her beauty and her spirit to her friends, and Marina Querini-Benzon, who survived a wild life to meet Byron and introduce him to the fair Guiccioli. It was in Venice too that others first embarked upon the careers of gallantry that the chroniclers of the age recorded, for the city furnished an incomparable point of departure for amorous experience. Greeks of both sexes found it to be the gate into Europe and many a European first encountered the fascination of Greek women there. Ugo Foscolo, the glorious fiery spirit who died so much too early, met Isabella Teotochi in Venice, the girl to whom he wrote the finest letters he ever penned. She was painted by Madame Vigée-Lebrun during the prolonged stay of that brilliant portraitist in the city.

The 'Greek' ladies were not always genuine. That had been the case too in ancient Rome, where the native girls profited from the high reputation of Athenian *hetairai*. One Venetian named Anna Gazzini received rich foreigners under her pseudonym of 'The Greek' and married the English baronet Richard Wynne, much to her advantage, just as the ambassador Murray's Venetian had provision made for her and her children by his will, whether they were his or not. Such unions between British males and Venetian women became so extraordinarily frequent as to arouse the attention of English ladies, some of whom clearly only went globe-trotting in

179

order to track down every scandalous affair of this kind to its source and to prevent, for instance, a Venetian courtesan from being accepted in London society, without protest, as Lady Wynne.

From Venice to London

I am under a sort of necessity of troubling you with an impertinent letter [wrote Lady Montagu on 3 October 1758 to her daughter]. Three fine ladies . . . set out for London a few days ago. As they have no acquaintance there I think it very possible (knowing their assurance) that some of them may try to make some by visiting you, perhaps in my name. Upon my word I never saw them except in public and at the resident's [John Murray], who, being one of their numerous passionate admirers, obliged his wife to receive them. The father's name was Wynn. Some say he had £1,200 per annum, others £2,000. He came several years since to Venice to dissipate his affliction for the loss of his lady. He was introduced by his Gondolier . . . to this Greek, who I believe was then remarkably handsome, having still great remains of beauty. He liked her well enough to take her into keeping, and had three daughters by her, before her artifices prevailed on him to marry her. Since that she produced two boys.

Giustiniana Wynne, later Countess Rosenberg

Lady Montagu does not mention the exceptional charm of the three girls. Nor could she have suspected the worthlessness of the sons, who at fourteen were infected with their first venereal maladies. Giustiniana Wynne, one of the pretty daughters, after a taste of fashionable society in her youth, became an admired authoress. Her three volumes of letters are today as valuable a source for the history and society of her time as her brief reflections and reports on Venetian life, events and conditions. Her mother kept open house, though in no sense a disorderly one, and Giustiniana's love affairs accordingly began at an early age. It is quite possible that the departure from Venice referred to in Lady Montagu's letter was due to Giustiniana's pregnancy, which could be terminated more conveniently in a cosmopolitan city like Paris than in Venice, where all the men lived who were destined to be important to the girl, such as the patrician Memmo whom she hoped to marry, the adventurer Casanova, who, in keeping the secret of her journey to Paris, nearly got himself convicted of seduction, and the Austrian ambassador Philipp Joseph Count Rosenberg, who married her in 1761.

A scene such as could only have occurred in Venice brought the three men together at an earlier date. Memmo and Casanova were visiting Ancilla, the poor woman then being within a few months of her death, though still ceaselessly active, when a gondola hove in sight. Memmo recognized its occupant as Count Orsini-Rosenberg, envoy from the Viennese Court. As no Venetian patrician was allowed to meet a foreign diplomat on familiar terms, Memmo dressed at lightning speed, bolted out of the room and just managed to encounter Rosenberg only on the stairs, instead of in the courtesan's apartment. The count, not in the least embarrassed by the place where they had met, roared with laughter at the Venetian's terror of diplomats . . . None of the three guessed that they would all be again concerned in later life with a woman of similarly dubious virtue but indisputable beauty, Giustiniana Wynne, who became Countess Orsini-Rosenberg.

Two empresses

'Far, far from us be all manner of real vice; but ten thousand times further from them, as far as from pole to pole, be the whole tribe of false, spurious, affected, counterfeit, hypocritical virtues. These are the things which are ten times more at war with real duty, than any vice known by its name, and distinguished by its proper character.' – EDMUND BURKE

The extraordinary multiplicity of the forms of debauchery did not come to light with the first publication of Krafft-Ebing's *Psychopathia Sexualis*, though before that date there may have been few people capable of surveying the whole field or, like the Marquis de Sade, imprisoned for long enough to work out such a survey. In fact the reality was at all times more various than any catalogue had anticipated. Capital cities in particular strained every nerve to cut as bizarre a figure as possible in social history. In each of them prostitution developed a special character, rakes had special preferences and special arrangements were made, as if by secret agreement, to meet them.

As compared with flagellation in London, the Black Mass in Paris, the Venetian courtesans who dressed as men and the fair nuns of Murano, Vienna had for long no marked speciality. The usual contemporary habits were in vogue. Important male visitors were made free of prostitutes' accommodation and the women were requested not to demand fees from them. Harlots were also admitted to festive processions, allowed to dance in public and encouraged to run races. On certain days of carnival, whores were also permitted to dance with young artisans in front of the city gates and as on these occasions the women wore elaborate garlands the dances had a truly bacchanalian character. In the suburbs and centre of the town, the Tiefen Graben for instance, the medieval brothels survived until well into the sixteenth century. Thereupon, in Vienna as elsewhere, the great wave of syphilis so pitifully reduced pleasure in the sexual act that after the epidemic had passed its peak no one thought of setting up 'women's quarters' again.

Woman enthroned

Nevertheless, there were obviously still plenty of harlots in so large a city, and of course also people who did not wish to admit the fact. In every century it has been popularly supposed that if one persists in ignoring something it ceases to exist. The elevation of the cult of such ignorance, for forty years, into a principle of government has been one of the few faults attributed even by the great Maria Theresa's court historians to her administration. But, frankly, such a fault was inevitable. Women in general, and in particular when sovereigns, have rarely been able to keep in the middle of the road. Where feeling is decisive extremes are apt to be followed. Many female rulers have been excessively strict in the moral field and just as many have been the very opposite. But a light hand on the rein, indulgence where that policy would be most advisable and regulation according to reason rather than morality have never been the outstanding characteristics of women on thrones or in political life.

It is a remarkable fact that in the eighteenth century the two great empires of Austria and Russia were administered by women. But while Catherine II, partly from conviction and partly from coquetry, had some sympathy with the Enlightenment, led a personally free life and only took steps against pretty women at her court when she scented ritals in them, Maria Theresa's maternally stern conduct was based on religious conviction and an intense hatred of both male and female drifters and adventurers. As in that century most travellers belonged to the educated classes or at least behaved as if they did, the Austrian empress's hostility to foreigners was felt to have tarnished some of the lustre with which the domes of Vienna had shone since the victories of Prince Eugène over the Turks.

The chastity commissions

There were several possibilities open to monarchs. Even Louis XV, so very far from an apostle of chastity, could at any time and without previous legal proceedings send a gentleman with a *lettre de cachet* to anyone whose presence in Paris he found inconvenient. In

Prussia, Württemberg, Italy and Spain such secret decrees, which seldom aroused protest, were taken as a matter of course. But Maria Theresa neither considered herself a despot nor wished others to consider her one. She drew up regulations and created an entire bureaucracy of bigots and moral snoopers. It was naturally impossible for hundreds of minor clerks, spies and informers to develop the far-seeing magnanimity exercised by their empress. Consequently the Austrian chastity commissions very soon became a far worse evil than prostitution.

If they are not to be attributed solely to Maria Theresa's feminine prejudices and fervent Catholicism, two further heavy afflictions laid upon the imperial city may be thought to afford some grounds for soul-searching and moral legislation. In 1713–14 the plague had claimed nearly nine thousand victims and on 5 June 1741 the Danube brimmed all its embankments, flooding large areas of the town, which was at the same time threatened by a hostile Bavarian army.

Yet it does seem extraordinary that a female ruler with so much else on her mind should devote herself to sexual offences alone, as they were called in those days, matters so hard to detect and harder still to judge fairly, rather than to any other section of the vast field of morality.

'It would be a dreadful thing for Palm to do'

I have been told [she wrote on 30 April 1771 to Count Christian Seilern], that Palm [Prince Karl Josef] after making certain very extravagant promises to a certain Weissin, a singer at the Deutsches Theatre, to induce her to yield to him, thereupon, when he could not achieve his object in this way, made similar promises to her husband, offering him independence for life. Send for this man [i.e. Herr Weissin] and try to find out the truth, without committing yourself in any way, by promising him protection. It would be a dreadful thing for Palm to do, if he really has acted so hypocritically. But it would also be dreadful if he has been calumniated.

Maria Theresa's daughter, Marie Antoinette, had just been married off to one of the most repulsive libertines in Europe. Another daughter, Caroline, was competing with courtesans in Naples. The Dubarry, not even a mistress of noble blood, but a veteran strumpet, had succeeded in bringing down the minister Choiseul, one of the most aristocratic men in France and in favour of the Austrian alliance. Yet Prince Palm's dealings with an actress attracted interference from the very highest quarter.

Even more characteristic is an almost desperate letter to Kaunitz from Maria Theresa when the position of her court theatres had become so hopeless that there was nothing for it but to make the impresario Affligio, a gambler with a bad reputation, their manager.

Kaunitz and a bad example

I am utterly dismayed by the affair of the theatres. Only you can help me. Draw up such a clause as you mentioned to me yesterday, providing for cancellation of the contract if he [Affligio] does not maintain perfect decency both in the performances and the persons employed therein, for whom I hold him responsible. But I have another worry which you alone can relieve me of. I want you to assure me that you will never visit or receive any of these women and girls. No doubt I can rely on your own discretion. But a bad example encourages other people less well behaved than yourself . . . In that case I will sign the agreement, though with a trembling hand.

Maria Theresa of course knew all about Kaunitz's conduct as her ambassador in Paris. The fair Venetian Zulietta was not the only Italian woman with whom he had been on intimate terms. But the empress could not allow her most trusted adviser, a man of strong personality who had rendered indisputable services to his country, to do as he pleased in wholly private matters. She had to keep a watch on everything and insist upon at least an outward show of chastity, for the sake of her own peace of mind, as she herself very characteristically says, in order to repress feelings, not on rational grounds.

A female sovereign of this sort, in a century when the ablest persons were also the most restless, was bound to have just about as bad a Press as possible. All Europe resented her behaviour or, still worse, laughed at it. The caricaturists dedicated their most obscene drawings to the austere empress and correspondents described with glee every difference of opinion which arose between her and her son Joseph on such problems, and also every love-affair upon which the powerful statesman Kaunitz ventured to embark, despite so many expressions of the imperial disapproval.

It was notorious, for example, that Kaunitz honoured the dancer Maria Theresa Fogliazzi with his protection. A marvellously beautiful woman whom, incidentally, Casanova had wooed in vain, she returned regularly, to the disgust of the empress, from tours in Milan, Turin, Petersburg and other cities to the banks of the Danube. Nor did her marriage to the gifted choreographer Angiolini separate her from Kaunitz for long.

The dangerous Fräulein von Salis

A much ridiculed quarrel with Joseph occurred when Maria Theresa considered it necessary to warn an entirely blameless Swiss lady, who happened to be travelling alone, to leave Austria within a few days. The young woman was a member of the respected family of Salis. After Joseph had called on her to apologize for his mother's behaviour, he publicly announced, with delight, that she had a good deal more intelligence than Count Schrattenbach, who had to see to her expulsion.

In view of this approval in the highest quarter and other examples forthcoming from court circles, the chastity commissions imposed arbitrary action on the lowest social level, a proceeding always the most resented of all owing to the prejudice and injustice inevitably arising in the naturally narrow minds of minor officials. The Viennese police, never particularly popular, soon came to be regarded with more suspicion than ever, since practically all the citizens sympathized with the persecuted. The police themselves, being mostly Viennese, disliked what they had to do.

The extent to which everyday life was subjected to the snoopers can hardly be imagined today and in fact is only credible by reference to the Pilgrim Fathers in Massachusetts in the preceding century, when every household was supervised, active piety was required and all deviations from the official attitude entailed oppression of every kind.

Instead of fops and adventurers it was now agents, informers, false 'friends' and other pseudo-sympathetic coevals who hunted down the girls of Vienna. They were only left alone in the street when it might be surmised that they were going to church. If they were pretty and didn't keep their eyes on the pavement, they were suspected of deliberately attracting attention, forced to undergo painful interrogations, robbed of their belongings and, until they could prove themselves innocent, locked up in a communal cell with women picked up for other offences, a much more severe trial of their virtue than a solitary shopping expedition.

Strict prohibitions always lead to blackmail. Loose-living girls, who were seriously impeded in the normal practice of their trade, found a way, with professional ingenuity, of working in with the informers. They made eyes at some prowling bachelor or even married man. This being an unusual occurrence, the chosen one immediately took advantage of it, went home with the girl and as soon as there could be no more doubt of the purpose of his visit, the police guardians of morals knocked at the door. The male fornicator was usually the most rewarding catch. Girls had little opportunity to save money in those days.

Viennese housemaids

These dangers and the lack of opportunity for prostitutes led to the triumph of the housemaid. Those of Vienna had long been a particularly attractive lot, recruited not only in the capital itself but also from the far-famed stocks of Bohemia and Hungary. A dozen such graceful figures could be met with in many a nobleman's house. They scorned the crinoline, considering that it spoiled their outlines, and in any case there could be no danger, for after all they were employed in a decent house where even the morals police couldn't come and go just as they pleased. It would of course be unfair to group all the Viennese housemaids in the army of the so-called 'coquettes'. But it was the period of the chastity commissions that laid the foundations of their frivolous reputation. A few decades later, at the Vienna Congress, it scored a unique triumph and made the whole class known throughout Europe.

The promptitude with which the housemaids sprang into the breach, when the nymphs of the *Graben* found the practice of their trade difficult, affords excellent proof of the allegedly weak sex's unconscious aptitude and adaptability. As if they were all really potential servers of Venus, they organized themselves into auxiliary troops the moment the front line was overrun or put out of action. This was the case in ancient Rome, where the actresses came to the aid of the courtesans, in the Middle Ages, when the vagrants ended the isolation of small provincial towns and above all in London, where the barmaids willingly agreed to serve in case of need.

187

Of course all these instances actually only prove that the demand for sexual satisfaction will always find ways and means to attain it and that no regulations, however strict, can abolish but at most only divert such appetites into fresh fields of femininity where, as has been said, 'the foot of man has never set its hand'.

The result of this action by the maids of Vienna was that after Joseph II had dissolved the chastity commissions new armies of dissolute young women entered the market. While trade conditions had been bad these girls had enjoyed helping out on occasion and now they wanted to go on doing so.

A new erotic model

Maria Theresa's stern measures had not abolished Viennese prostitution. They had simply introduced the erotic model of the seductive Viennese housemaid. It was perfectly natural, therefore, for Jean-Etienne Liotard, after painting the great empress, to immortalize also a pretty maid called Baldauf. He gave the picture the misleading name of *La Belle Chocolatière* – as if one could ever clap eyes on such a vision in Demel's cake-shop! Respectability was restored by the present owners, the Dresden Gallery, which lists this delightful item in its catalogue as 'Portrait of the Housemaid, N.N.'. A Prussian traveller named Nicolai expresses himself more politely. 'The housemaids, a special kind of handsome servant-girls, are quite peculiar to Vienna. They are all pretty, with delicate complexions, which they no doubt improve artificially. They have dainty little feet, wear embroidered shoes, are spotlessly clean and invariably clothed in silk.'

Housemaids in literature

It is not to be wondered at that in these circumstances a whole literature, entirely concerned with housemaids, arose and is today highly valued by collectors. There was also a special guide devoted to the maids, just as there had been lists of courtesans in Venice, London and Paris. The great popularity of Johann Rautenstrauch, a local author today forgotten, was doubtless due, in addition to his strikingly lean figure and yellow tail-coat, to his pamphlet on housemaids. It went into more editions, at Vienna, than Goethe's *Werther*.

The city swells [Rautenstrauch declared], prefer the housemaids because they can soonest make progress in that quarter. They keep lists of all the most famous in their pockets. Some of the girls are actually noted leaders of fashion . . . In many families only good-looking housemaids are accepted, probably to ensure that only pretty faces serve their regular callers.

The maids' dress was really more convenient than the prevalent fashion and was therefore soon imitated by the *Graben* nymphs. A closely fitting little bodice threw the breasts into relief. The girl herself chose whether or not to wear a neckerchief with it. The figure as a whole remained slender, the waist-line and skirt stressing grace of movement, while respectable ladies sailed stiffly, like so many frigates, through the caressing Viennese air.

Rautenstrauch testified that the more prosperous harlots of those days in fact disposed of two separate types of costume, each with its own particular appeal. They dressed either as young ladies or else as housemaids 'because at that time in Vienna lots of people were mad on maids'. The natural consequence was that soon it became impossible to tell whether one was in the presence of a maid on the loose or a whore disguised as one, a circumstance not very favourable to the reputation of domestic staffs.

The Graben *nymphs*

It does not appear that the professional charmers, the *Graben* nymphs, lost heart even in these hard times. Masks and clothing helped them to bamboozle the snoopers and the whole city often rocked with laughter when one of the 'maid-mad' fraternity considered it necessary to go through prolonged preliminary antics when a brief reference to currency would have achieved his object in no time. 'The author Blumauer used to sit drumming on the window-pane with his fingers and the moment a girl corresponding with Rautenstrauch's description of a maid went by he dashed out into the street, flourishing his lorgnette, and went tripping and skipping after her on tip-toe like a dancing-master.'

Yet actually, in these conditions, the prostitutes had nothing to laugh at. Only a few decades previously one of them had been executed. The date was 24 September 1723. The unfortunate creature, named Anna Maria, was twenty-eight years old. She 'submitted to death with an excellent grace', in other words courageously endured the sword-stroke at the Schottentor. She had never had any luck, having been twice sentenced to the pillory and three times deported prior to her death-sentence. The next generation of whores fared slightly better. They simply had their heads shaved, were furnished with brooms and ordered to sweep the streets. It was not a popular spectacle for the citizens, since it gave those brisk and far from taciturn young women a daily chance of vengeance. Woe to the client they recognized on the spot! Woe to the worthy official who unsuspectingly walked through the *Graben* when the 'charmers' were sweeping! At once they would form up, with their brooms and cropped heads, like troops on parade, and yell an only too explicit greeting in chorus.

Respectable gentlemen had of course to be protected from being exposed in this way. The original intention had been to "expose' the women by cutting off their hair and putting them to compulsory labour in public. But those who have nothing more to lose derive a certain advantage from that very circumstance. So the next expedient was to send the girls to prison, where they remained until 'the arrangements made by our admirable police' resulted in their pregnancy. Twenty 'of the younger and better looking female prisoners' found themselves in this condition owing to the attentions of two of their gaolers. After the shock of this revelation the women were transferred again, this time to the laundry trade.

Necessity the mother of invention

The few who still tried to resume their former occupation had to resort to all kinds of artificial expedients. Addresses and charges could be pinned to trees beyond the fortifications. Coloured ribbons and streamers might be seen waving, as if by chance, from a window. Certain other windows stood open all day long, affording comprehensive glimpses of the private lives of the girl tenants, who, since they were at home with no one to interfere with them, trotted about with hardly anything on. But of course these displays were only given in streets where most of the accommodation was rented by whores, as for example in the narrow Nailmakers' Lane, still so called today.

Another possibility was the pretence at employment in a trade where it seemed quite natural to see two or three pretty girls about.

This worked out well as a rule for a few years, especially at places where well-to-do customers were to be found. But sooner or later the police would be bound to intervene.

According to the Viennese *Auspurgisches Extra-Blatt*:

The French dressmaker Madame de Musset, who has had a bad reputation here for a long time, having already been deported during the lifetime of our late revered empress for her wicked conduct, especially for the permission of illegal and scandalous gatherings in her apartments, has been ordered in the highest quarters to undergo several years' imprisonment here for the offence of inciting a girl of thirteen years to lead an immoral life, thus causing the death of the innocent child concerned. The prisoner is to be kept on short rations and birched at least once a week.

Easier for the nobility

Such reports indicate the illogical behaviour of the old Austrian authorities even in their attitude to prostitution. Any male visitor to Vienna who wished to live there as in other capital cities had first of all to assume the title of Baron, a claim which no one ever troubled to investigate. He could then dispose, in aristocratic circles, of ladies who were perhaps not the most untarnished in the city but who were at any rate ready to meet his wishes and had promoted themselves to be baronesses in exactly the same nonchalant way in which he had become a baron. The milliners, mannequins and housemaids replaced the supposedly eliminated prostitutes and all went well until something happened such as the death of too young a female participant, the bankruptcy of some over-generous count or an excessive bill for a copper engraving, which the Emperor Franz could not pay, so that the empress heard about it and after a critical survey of the southern beauties therein depicted, remarked: 'Shameful! It's a crime of that engraver to want so much money! I bet the original was cheaper!'

It was suggested to Joseph II that he might allow the establishment of at least a single brothel, in a lane leading off the *Graben*. But he considered that the immorality of the times could find ways and means of satisfaction without the provision of any such thing and had in fact proved so inventive that it was no good interfering at all.

While Prince Schwarzenberg was prime minister the Vienna police commissioner, Weiss von Starkenfels, had the ill-luck to arrest a bawd who had always served the prince particularly well and never yet disappointed him. The commissioner hastened to apologize in the most abject terms, saying that a 'mistake' had been made. 'What do you mean – "mistake"?' thundered Schwarzenberg. 'Either you knew that the woman had dealings with me, in which case your arrest of her was a deliberate insult to me, or else you didn't know of any such association, in which case what sort of a police commissioner are you?'

Results of inconsistency

Since no official measures were taken except a few relating to the stage, only fifteen hundred duly registered prostitutes existed at Vienna, a city with a million inhabitants, during the early nineteenth century. This position implied that secret prostitution, with all its accompanying phenomena, prevailed on a huge scale. Citizens at every level of society remained in close contact with the corresponding underworld group. The nobility were in touch with actresses from the south or roving adventuresses, the middle classes with servant-girls and the *Graben* nymphs, and the proletariat with the staffs of the pothouses at Lerchenfeld and other extra-mural suburbs.

The empress and her son, by their reluctance to intervene officially by taking any practical steps in relation to so disreputable a feature of the life of the capital, had come to be more helpless in this field than most of the rulers of their day. They were powerless to prevent the luxuriant growth of what they wished to ignore and as half-measures are never popular even among the masses of a people the few resolute proceedings such as the hair-cropping were rendered ineffective by a flood of tearful broadsheets.

> Sisters dear, don't make a pother,
> lamentation will not aid.
> Let them cut your hair, don't bother,
> that is what the judges said.
> Many others still go proudly
> through the streets decked out most loudly.
> Ah, but sisters, hear ye me.
> They've deserved it more than we.

In such doggerel or similar pamphlets the *Graben* nymphs were assured of popular sympathy and recognized as victims of despotism.

Alfieri in Berlin

If after receiving impressions of this kind one moved north up the adventurers' road through Potsdam to Warsaw and St Petersburg, it nevertheless appeared that in spite of chastity commissions and the empress's motherly concern for morality Vienna still remained one of the more cheerful of European capitals. Not everyone expressed his surprise and disappointment so clearly as the young Italian count destined to be the great poet Vittorio Alfieri. He was then only twenty and no doubt unfair to Berlin, where he spent no more than a month. But his retrospective notes are certainly revealing.

As I crossed into the realms of the great Frederick, which seemed to me nothing but a single great barracks, I felt a doubling and trebling of my hatred of the abominable profession of arms, the most abominable, nay, the only foundation of despotic power . . . Count von Finck, the King's Minister, who introduced me to him, asked me why I had not put on uniform for the occasion, as I was, after all, in the service of my own king. I answered that I considered there were already enough uniforms to be seen at the Berlin Court. The King spoke the usual four words to me. I looked hard at him, keeping my eyes fixed respectfully on his, and thanked heaven I had not been born to become his slave.

One can't help wondering what Alfieri would probably have written if he had visited the tiny Brandenburg capital a few decades earlier. For then he would have found the inhabitants obeying rules as to when they could wear braided coats and when they couldn't and how much food they could consume at those climaxes of their monotonous lives, baptisms and weddings.

At marriage and other feasts of the most elaborate sort no more than eight dishes in all are to be served, not counting separate plates of vegetables and salad, while at banquets for the middle classes six and for the poorer sort four are permissible, though not all at once. On special occasions, however, three kinds of roast may be placed on one dish.

It is hard to believe that at such a time and in such a city there was any prostitution worth talking about. Surely every whore must have listened for the tramp of a soldier at her heels and every fashionable woman must have dreaded being hauled before a magistrate for wearing silk or having too many dishes served at a supper for two?

Regulated pleasures

But even soldiers are men and even kings cherish, as the least of their ambitions, that of not looking ridiculous to foreigners. Accordingly, a certain amount of enjoyment of life began in Berlin as elsewhere, though, like everything else in Prussia, it was subject to very special regulations.

It has recently been noticed that in the places of public resort graciously permitted to be opened in the Friedrichstrasse for the entertainment of the citizens certain persons of the lowest possible extraction have been so impudent as to appear. A circumstance of this kind is diametrically opposed to His Majesty's wishes and it is therefore hereby proclaimed that henceforward such persons shall by no means be admitted, in order that other more honest and honourable persons may not be deterred from entering these places.

The nervous citizens referred to had a monarch who was also nervous at times. Frederick II behaved under the heaviest fire as if his crook-handled cane made him invulnerable. But he had a window in the Red Eagle hostelry walled up simply because one morning as he rode past he had caught a glimpse through it of the beautiful Italian dancer La Reggiana in the nude. It was obvious, therefore, that he was not altogether unbiased in these matters, though not so blindly wrathful a persecutor of prostitutes as his predecessor and namesake, who had closed all his country's brothels in 1690. But Frederick II, throughout his reign, pursued a wavering and illogical policy in this connection, strongly contrasting with his otherwise firm handling of domestic issues.

A hundred secret brothels

After the prohibition of 1690 prostitutes, who, though flogged and harried, could not all be simply strung up, scattered all over Berlin. Instead of remaining concentrated in certain streets and buildings, as hitherto, they took up positions in taverns and coffee-houses, mingled with the ordinary life of the city and by their infiltrations made several quarters, where they had previously been unknown notorious by their presence. As a result of this decentralization about a hundred small brothels, hardly one of which had more than ten inmates, came into existence some ninety years after the drastic decrees of Friedrich I.

It was in this way that prostitution became associated with normal life to an extent scarcely to be found in any other German city. Some premises with such innocent-sounding names as *The Golden Hat*, *The Anchor* or *The White Swan* acquired a reputation as bases for the sale of sexual pleasure equal to that of places more uncompromisingly and facetiously named by the Berlin populace, such as *The Red Pump* or *The Acute Angle* near the Spandau Gate, *The Little Bride* in the Friedrichstrasse and so on.

There were marked differences, though only obvious to the initiated, between these various ports of call. Some served as billets for troops, since room had to be found for recruits somewhere, and days passed before the sturdy country boys realized where they had been quartered. Again, a traveller who put up at the so-called *Chandler's Factory* without prior notification reported with disgust his astonishment at 'the shamelessly indecent attire of these creatures, who adopted the most provocative attitudes in order to stimulate oafish familiarities. A rank stench of rut permeated the place . . . which could be smelt even if one had a severe cold'.

At 'The Shaggy Jew'

A more amusing side of this situation was of course the influence exercised by the *demi-monde* on respectable citizens and the gradual development of French conditions in Berlin, whereby the brothel lost its infamy and became a commonplace feature of everyday life. Many an elderly Berliner, whom Cupid had long ceased to plague, could sit and smoke his pipe over a table at *The Shaggy Jew* or *The Black Apron*. The first time he did so the girls would come and bother him a little. But after that he could sip his coffee as peacefully as in any quite ordinary place and watch what went on in all its colour and variety, a spectacle certainly by no means to be despised.

The chief sufferers from this fragmentation of prostitution seem to have been the harlots themselves. For the worst kind of slavery is always that imposed upon individuals. They had at all times been able to come to terms with the law. But they were as much in the power of their landlord as if no one else existed who could effectively control the management of these clandestine brothels, by this time numbering at least a hundred.

Laukhardt the schoolmaster

Friedrich Christian Laukhardt, son of a preacher, could not supply a German Boswell with much material except his honest sincerity. But he had sown his wild oats by the time he came to Berlin and investigated its brothels. We may believe him when he declares that in the notorious *Chandler's Factory* the chief conclusion he came to was to carry off thence 'a girl named Jettchen, from Schwedt, whose features I considered refined and with whom I therefore concerned myself'. After she had told him her story, one of humble origin and subsequent seduction by a 'noble debauchee', Laukhardt, who was then a soldier, arranged with some of his comrades to effect a rescue of the girl. The landlord, significantly called by Laukhardt *Meister Maquereau*, a term still in vogue in Paris for his trade, could do nothing, in view of the arms carried by the party, but shout abuse after them.

The enslavement of the women always followed the same lines. The girl would be so overcharged for her initial expenses that she could almost never get free of debt, especially as she had to pay out sums difficult to check for her lodging, maintenance and miscellaneous items. Nor were the habits of prostitutes calculated to encourage saving. They spent a lot on cosmetics, did not do their own washing, had grown used to luxuries at table and were obliged to give a percentage of what they earned to the landlord.

No doubt other establishments existed. There were certainly houses where life was more elegant and brutality to the inmates less open. There would not be much compulsion there, for the staff were regularly recruited by girls who had won their spurs in the Spandau Gate quarter and wanted to better themselves. They were women like 'Lindemann' or 'Schuwitzin', mentioned by Laukhardt with ill-concealed envy. He just hadn't enough money for high and mighty prostitutes, 'society *mamsells* who live quite by themselves and from time to time, in return for cash and compliments, allow smart young men to call'.

Madame Schuwitzin

Madame Schubitz or Schuwitz had bought and furnished a small house in the Friedrichstrasse, either to make an impression on wealthier clients who could afford twelve groschen or at any rate to offer them a familiar environment. Her girls, whom she mainly recruited from the countryside, had to learn how to express themselves decently. She does not seem to have made the slightest attempt, at first, to teach the Berliners to do so. But once the young Brandenburg whores had learnt a few poems by heart, read a few sentimental novels and had a bit of practice in what was called 'paying compliments' then, according to Laukhardt, 'the nice girl, in common parlance the whore, was ready. Practically the same methods are in use at Madame Lindemann's and a few other smart places. But the Schuwitzin is generally considered to be "the tops," as they say here.

The way in which an offended visitor literally 'made a sow' out of the entire establishment* is worth recording. On the day after his humiliation the affronted party sent a slaughterman, disguised as a wealthy old provincial character, to Madame Schuwitz. The fellow had himself served with the best in the house, both refreshments and girls, and when the time came to pay handed over a heavy gold watch, which he said he would redeem later. This form of settlement was not considered very satisfactory. But worse was to come. One fine morning a few days later the debtor turned up, this time in his true character as a knacker's yard labourer, with a dead sow on his cart, and offered the mountain of carrion in question to the manageress of the famous house in the Friedrichstrasse in return for his watch.

Whether the instigator of this affair was really 'an affronted count' or simply Madame Lindemann, the scandal put an end to her rival's prosperity more rapidly and effectively than if the police had sealed the premises.

Compulsory insurance for harlots

At the time of this incident it was no longer 'Old Fritz' who ruled Prussia but Friedrich Wilhelm II and the fair Wilhelmine. Berlin then ranked as one of the chief capitals of Europe and operated a

* In German Air Force slang to 'make a sow' out of a target is to put it out of action. [J.C.]

pensions scheme for prostitutes called, with Prussian precision, the Whores' Health Service Fund. The brothels were divided into three distinct classes. The first comprised six houses, each with sixteen inmates. Every member of this highly exclusive body had to pay the Fund one thaler a month, while the bawd in charge of each establishment paid twenty. But most of the grander prostitutes at this period preferred independence. The fund's records list ninety-three who paid in their monthly thaler without needing to be represented by a bawd, even before the golden days of the French invasion began.

The moral climate of European capitals showed throughout the eighteenth century such obvious differences and drastic variations that it is hardly possible to speak of characteristically absolutist principles in relation to prostitution. One common feature of policy in this field was its direction on moral rather than sanitary grounds. Another doubtless important consideration was the sovereigns' extreme reluctance to deal personally with problems affecting the common people, so that the police operated over a wider sphere than their training entitled them to control. In the capitals the police commissioners, nearly always of aristocratic birth and seldom adequately educated for their task, were neither intellectually nor technically capable of dealing with the questions raised by the new era that was dawning. Consequently the European police system as a whole remained essentially medieval in its operations, in other words at least three hundred years out of date.

The population being left to itself, without any support worth mentioning from the authorities, remained orderly enough in the rural districts, where patriarchal systems, labours familiar for centuries, village customs and the automatic supervision exercised by small communities had no difficulty in controlling morality, especially as neither the character nor the extent of threats to its stability increased or changed at all noticeably. But in the towns life had been transformed. The greater luxury of the courts, the interpenetration of the aristocracy and upper middle class, soaring commercial activity and the beginnings of industry had given rise to a prosperity eagerly absorbent of foreign influences and enfeebling to ancestral tradition. Spain looked to France, Austria to the Mediterranean, Scandinavia to England and Russia to the West. The big and small capitals competed with the rising health resorts where international society met in the fashioning of a new mode of life that, despite a certain tendency towards intellectual, conversational and educational ideals, nevertheless at bottom meant merely the revelation of further opportunities for enjoyment to the well-to-do and ruling strata of European peoples.

The dynastic lottery

The differences between Paris and Petersburg, Vienna and Berlin, or Dresden and Warsaw, are almost negligible when seen against these main features of social development. The dynastic lottery had more influence on the situation, for a saintly empress might succeed a Messalina and an ascetic an erotomaniac. But above all the structure of the despotically ruled state gave every chance to caprice and inconsistency. It seems as though women took more advantage of such openings than men.

Nowhere did extremes and contradictions, contrast more violently than in the new capital of Russia, St Petersburg, founded by Peter the Great at the beginning of the eighteenth century and by the end of the nineteenth containing well over a million inhabitants. The orthodox clergy had twice attempted to burn down the new metropolis, which had usurped the primacy of Moscow. But even Peter's successors clung stubbornly to the city built on the western marshes. For by then it had become an international port and closer to the western world than any other town in the huge country.

German and Dutch mechanics, together with tens of thousands of Russian peasants, had built the city. The Tsar had always much admired the Germans, enjoyed their company and spoken among his intimates an extraordinary Russo-German gibberish. The western element in the streets and palaces of St Petersburg was also strengthened from the adjacent Baltic lands, where great estates were held by Germans and Swedes. It may well be, therefore, that Casanova was right to declare that, on the banks of the Neva at any rate, German was the only language the nobility, the foreigners and the native masses had in common.

The 'Dresdenska' in Petersburg

In view of such a variety of influences it is not surprising, though it may not be exactly a matter for congratulation, that one lady from Dresden and another from Vienna share the discredit of having opened the first brothels on western lines to be established in the Russian capital. Not even the name of the Saxon lady has survived. Elisabeth I, daughter of Peter the Great, was so horrified at the existence of a brothel in her capital that the legal record mentions no name but merely refers to the 'Dresdenska', the Dresden woman.

Elisabeth's moral austerity was of relatively late growth. During a reign of twenty years she had received in bed a procession, amounting in numbers to the wartime establishment of a company, of flunkeys, butlers and grooms of the chamber. Through these she had presented Russia with some brand-new breeds of counts, fresh from the soil. She had promoted her favourite Rasumovsky, son of a Ukrainian peasant, successively to chamberlain, count and field-marshal, in order to be able, at this last stage, to marry him. According to Bernhard Stern she did not 'thereby increase in virtue, but only in piety'. It was a piety which drove her to stern measures against the 'Dresdenska'.

The Saxon lady had furnished a fine house on the straight Vosnesensky Prospect, leading from the Fontanka to the Neva. The building could hardly be called a brothel. At most it was a *maison de rendezvous*, precisely calculated to meet the needs of St Petersburg society. The gentlemen who spent the produce of their estates in the capital were by no means starved of mere contact with the other sex. Each one of them had hundreds or sometimes thousands of serfs, among whom he could choose, as often as he liked, the prettiest girls and the married women most expert in love to come and live with him. What he missed in Petersburg was a place where he could meet his equals, an elegant house in a quarter above suspicion, where the ladies could fancy themselves in a 'tea-room' – an illusion which the gentlemen did not have to share – where nothing could cause offence either outwardly or indoors and which so far from creating embarrassment removed any conceivable reason for it.

The proceeds of such arranged or casual meetings, tea-parties, so to speak, with a surprise ending, enabled the lady from Dresden to live in quite a grand style for some years. The entrance fee was kept high. For there could be no sense in extending the circle of initiates unduly. Single gentlemen, couples and eventually real ladies showed up. A small all-purpose unit of smart girls remained constantly in attendance.

Weddings of atonement

When the house was raided, a scandal ensued, if not of European at any rate of ultra-Elbe dimensions. Frederick II himself pilloried, in a good-natured lampoon, the Tsarina who had so very suddenly turned moral censor. The Dresden lady suffered only the mild penalty of exile, probably because she had presented the empress with a full list of the guests at those 'parties'. They were all now obliged to do what Elizabeth herself had done, viz. marry in order to regain their lost honour. The little squad of jolly girls were made baronesses and countesses as fast as, at the palace, the lackeys and the footmen who handed round chocolates, the ballad singer and the butlers, had become noblemen. But even this drastic measure did not appease the Tsarina. Now that general suspicion had been aroused, her minister Davidov had to head a special commission to clean up the whole city and banish hundreds of dissolute females from it.

Saxony's revenge

But the lady from Dresden obtained unexpected satisfaction some decades later. Her countryman, Counsellor of Embassy Gustav Adolf Wilhelm von Helbig, by then one of the Dresden syndics, had been in his youth a secretary at the Saxon Embassy in Petersburg, where for nine years he had enjoyed the opportunity of studying the feminine successors of the great Tsar and their activities at first hand. In his compilation on the Russian Court favourites, first published by Cotta in 1809, it is evident from his calm and lucid prose that the 'Dresdenska' was a mere phenomenon of her time, by no means outstandingly vicious.

Our readers will conclude, by the time they finish this book, that under no Russian Government were there ever so many base-born and utterly depraved favourites, with no claims to any sort of psychological merit, as under Elisabeth I. At her Court swarms of peasants, grooms, coachmen, common soldiers and domestic servants who could not be appointed to official posts on account of their limited understanding were given conspicuous Court rank, decorated and above all quite undeservedly provided with immense riches.

201

Madame Riedl

The woman who tried to emulate the Dresden lady had come to Petersburg in the capacity of companion to Baroness Goletti, wife of the Austrian ambassador. Though her name, Riedl, is German, social historians have regarded her as Hungarian and she may well have been a native of Pressburg, Raab or Odenburg. No doubt she had been trained in the seraglios of Budapest, capital of a country alleged by Dufour 'to be entitled to the status of a Great Power, at any rate so far as the history of prostitution is concerned'. But the career of Madame Riedl also illustrates the intimate relations, characteristic of the whole eighteenth century, between diplomacy and prostitution. Her reliance even in Petersburg upon this often effective combination brought her to her ruin.

When she opened her first house, competition with it was practically confined to a single establishment, the so-called 'Trilingual', a brothel occupied on the ground floor by Russian women, while the first and second floors accommodated French and German girls respectively. There were always enough inmates. It was only the porter's job that fell vacant occasionally, as it was hard to find one who understood all three languages.

But in the time of Catherine II a place of this kind, known to everyone, could not meet the requirements of the court. The 'Dresdenska' had already gambled successfully on her idea of an 'exclusive' brothel and Madame Riedl followed suit. There was plenty of money about in Petersburg. But discreet opportunities for spending it were on the whole lacking in the city. The first house she bought was accordingly not, like her predecessor's, in a long, fashionable street, but in a quiet residential quarter, the Volkonskaya. It had, moreover, three exits, so that there were always chances of a precipitate retreat. In the thirty-two rooms ladies and gentlemen met either by previous or by improvised arrangement. The ladies kept on their veils or masks and thus gave the proceedings a mysterious, fortuitous character much to the taste of many nobles who loved taking a risk. The story goes that on one occasion a count or prince handed over two hundred roubles and then found himself provided with his own wife. But as a rule clients appear to have been well satisfied, for in a short time Madame Riedl opened a second establishment, this time on the island of Vassily Ostrov in the heart of the city.

An aquarium for males

The character of this building could only have been paralleled in London. In fact it is likely that reports from that quarter inspired it. Society ladies were the target, their opportunities, unlike those of their menfolk, being so limited. Madame Riedl constructed on the island a kind of swimming-bath, with a wooden wall surrounding it, divided into forty cabins with one small window each, through which lady visitors could survey the men swimming in the bath. Subsequent events took place on a wide divan situated under the window. They were so much talked of that Catherine ɪɪ herself is said to have paid an occasional visit to the establishment, more for the sake of the window than the divan, the chronicler adds deprecatingly.

As the ladies grew more and more interested in the swimming-bath, abandoning the thirty-two rooms in the Volkonskaya, Madame Riedl decided to make a radical change. Henceforward she catered for ladies exclusively on the Vassily Ostrov island and provided the gentlemen who called at the house in the Volkonskaya with girls imported from Hungary only.

Nothing from the West could have pleased the Neva aristocrats better. The pretty creatures wiped away a tear or two when they were told on the quay that the posts for ladies' maids in the palaces of the nobility were not yet available, so that they would have to take up other work for the time being. But after all they had been consigned to the care of Madame Riedl. They could do nothing in the great foreign city, where no one understood their language, but make the best of a bad job.

The end of a procuress

It was not Madame Riedl's white slave traffic on this large scale that eventually got her into trouble, but her neglect of the police. In Russia persons whose earnings amounted to as much as hers were expected, if they wished their affairs to go on prospering steadily, to slip a few roubles into the proper channels. Smart and influential friends are only of use so long as they do not need to disclose their activities. As a result of a police plot Madame Riedl found herself in the dock on a charge of high treason. No one appeared on her behalf. For in the age of despotism the mere practicability of a trial of this kind indicated displeasure in the highest possible quarter and no one wanted to be drawn into whatever might come of it.

The girls do not seem to have been severely punished. They were recognized to have been merely victims of the scheme and most of them embarked on their homeward voyage without excessive delay. Madame Riedl, however, was sentenced to deportation. Her establishments were confiscated. She died in poverty soon afterwards, somewhere in the vast expanses of Russia.

In these same vast expanses, inhabited by so many peoples, women had suffered heavily right up to the threshold of modern times. For on the one hand Russia remained backward in comparison with the western countries, where women had naturally attained in the course of centuries to a certain degree of emancipation, and on the other hand Russian society differed from that of primitive ages when the position of women in a community was accepted as normal and beneficial. To the social historian the Russia of earlier days, traversed from north to south by a low range of hills that unites rather than separates the continents of Europe and Asia, suggests an open door that left its inhabitants a defenceless prey to all the fiercer passions.

The Riedl and 'Dresdenska' brothels were of course succeeded by similar establishments. In Moscow and Petersburg they were kept in being by the rich families. At Odessa, Baku and other ports they lived on the requirements of seamen and merchants. But to the ordinary Russian woman they remained as much a matter of indifference as was for a long time everything of foreign origin which Russia studied and imitated.

The fair serf

Why should anyone pay two hundred roubles for admission to a first-rate brothel when he could buy a pretty serf for a hundred? Even the fastidious Casanova abandoned Madame Proté, then regarded as the most beautiful woman in Petersburg, to another member of the picnic party, quite ungrudgingly, when he came upon his Zaire.

Zinoviev and I had walked a distance of about a hundred paces from the imperial manor-house when I caught sight of a peasant girl of truly startling beauty. I called the young officer's attention to her and we walked towards her. But she ran off as lightly and nimbly as a deer, disappearing into a nearby hut. We followed her in, where we found her

204

father, her mother. several children and the girl herself, who was crouching in a corner like a rabbit fearful of being torn to pieces by pursuing hounds.

Zinoviev . . . talked for a long time with the father in Russian. Naturally, I understood nothing. But I guessed that they were speaking of the girl. For the father suddenly called her over and she came across to us with an obedient and submissive air and stood with her eyes cast down. Zinoviev, after a good deal more talk, left the hut. I gave the father a rouble and followed my friend. He told me that he had asked the peasant to give him his daughter for a maid, to which the father had replied that he would be quite willing to do so but that as she was still a virgin the price would be a hundred roubles.

Although at that period Casanova had not much money to spare, he didn't hesitate a moment. Thenceforth he had a radiantly youthful mistress to bloom beside him, over whom he had every right except those of killing her or taking her abroad. If he had beaten her no one would have troubled himself about the matter. For months the Venetian enjoyed a positive springtime of love and saved a lot of money into the bargain, for any fashionable mistress would have cost him many times as much. He only put an end to the affair when the girl's jealousy became a nuisance to him. But Zaire did not return to the bosom of her family, for her father would never have been able to repay the hundred roubles. Casanova sold her, as if she had been a horse or a carriage, to a rich, elderly merchant. As she was by then well supplied with clothes and had learnt a good deal, it is to be assumed that the man from Venice made a profit on the deal.

Defenceless rustics

No doubt many good-looking Russian girls, since the days of Peter the Great, went the same way as Zaire. Many of them, too, would think themselves lucky to do so, since if they had gone on living on any estate in Russia as a serf they would have been similarly exploited, without getting to know the world or acquiring even a smattering of education. Just as for peasant boys service in the army was often the only means to any sort of improvement in their circumstances, so the pretty faces and comely figures of many Russian girls enabled them to escape the fate of lifelong agricultural labour. In such conditions it is intelligible enough that in many of the smaller provincial towns of Russia young people went to the local brothel to learn to dance and listen to music.

In that enormous country nothing was unheard of. One landowner boasted of having deflowered sixty of his maids. During one peasants' revolt the mistress of one estate was stripped to the skin and boiled in a big copper till she turned scarlet as a lobster. Night after night, during the dreadful deportations, which lasted for weeks, the most attractive of the women prisoners were outraged by the escorting troops. Some ladies of the manor tormented their own sex more cruelly than any man could. When the rural squires came to town in search of new sensations they met in private to indulge in sexual perversions. Catherine II had her own notorious 'Little Circle'. A contemporary group of nobles founded a 'Physical Club' at which, immediately after orgies of gluttony, they proceeded to arrange an undisguised lottery. Almost all eighteenth- and nineteenth-century travellers in Russia have described such scenes, taking place behind closed doors, when a single good-looking woman took on all comers and then coolly paid the bill and pocketed her profits.

The Estonians of Dorpat

It was owing to the peculiar requirements of the grossly self-indulgent or precociously depraved landowners that two substantial groups of prostitutes were able to emerge from the rank and file of their competitors in Russia. These were the gipsies, who did particularly well in Moscow, and the Estonians, who acquired special fame in Dorpat. The latter race, of Finno-Ugrian stock and only numbering a few hundreds of thousands, had been depressed after the conquest of the Baltic lands by German knights and merchants to the condition of a subordinate population, supplying their masters with serfs. In the towns they acted as messengers and finally, though very late in their history, as mechanics. On the big estates their young women had suffered just as much, in their bondage to the soil, as Russian girls in the same condition. By the eighteenth century the best looking of the Estonian female serfs had found their way to the city of Dorpat, where the Swedes, during their brief occupation of the country, had established a university for Baltic and Russian students. These young men, whose monthly allowances were often quite considerable, fell easy victims to the

Estonian prostitutes, reputed to be peculiarly vicious. There were some five hundred registered whores in Dorpat, a city of about 40,000 inhabitants, and there must have been at least another five hundred women who plied the same trade in secret. Forty per cent had previous convictions for thefts committed while so engaged. So many were infected with venereal disease that there were more cases of syphilis in Dorpat than anywhere else in Russia. A quarter of the students returned home with serious symptoms of the malady.

Stern, in his *History of Public Morals in Russia*, states correctly enough that 'prostitutes are the same all over the world, in Rowdy Lane at Riga or in the Avlabar, the whores' quarter, at Tiflis'. But the picture of conditions in this connection along the western border of Russia is one of the darkest the period can show. For Dorpat, as a university town, exercised a kind of monopoly. Its professors were famous and its lecture-rooms frequented by intellectuals from every quarter of the gigantic empire. The contamination and corruption of the best brains of the two dominant races, Russian and Baltic-German, was the terrible revenge, taken year after year, by the young women of Estonia for the crushing of their small nation.

BOOK IV

LOST ILLUSIONS

*

Two empires

> 'Let the happy, if they will, cast the first stone at me.
> They have no need of the atmosphere which has
> given me back my youth and where I have regained
> memories and former habits which have not yet lost
> their hold upon my feelings.' – LOUIS ARAGON

When Paris is called the city of love, it can hardly be domestic, but
rather mercenary, love that is meant, at any rate in the widest sense
of the term. The references may range from the mistresses of great
men to brilliant courtesans, obliging young ladies and finally the
more or less officially controlled prostitutes of the street or the
brothel. But since such forms of love exist and always have existed
in all capital cities without anywhere having exercised any special
attraction, there must be something unique about the case of Paris.
While no one would feel capable of pronouncing the word love
after sampling the Hamburg Reeperbahn or the sex markets of
Japan, the United States or Naples, similar proceedings in Paris
seem to have a charm of their own. It may be only tinsel. But there
is no trace of it even in cities not far away, such as Brussels, London
or Marseilles.

The city of love

The special connection of Paris with various forms of love is very
old, almost venerable. Many of the most famous Parisian pairs of
lovers have now become as weatherbeaten, so to speak, as the
figures carved over the main porch of Notre Dame. Their beauty

can today only be conjectured. There were, for example, Héloïse and Abélard, who were so grossly ill-used. Yet their fate does not appear to have deterred others in similar circumstances, from Ronsard and Hélène de Surgères to Marion de Lorme and Cinq-Mars, till we come to Adrienne Lecouvreur's celebrated love-affair with Count Moritz of Saxony.

The fascination of love in Paris did not therefore, of course, begin during the illustrious era of the Sun King, in whose affections a series of gorgeous mistresses were succeeded by that cross-grained, prudish widow of a poet, Madame de Maintenon. Love was not a monopoly of the court, of such glorious beings as a de la Vallière, a Montespan or even Fontanges of the graceful figure, who was poisoned because she looked so ravishing in a skin-tight hunting costume that her excessively stout rival had no option but to murder her. Love had long perfumed the air of Paris even while Louis was still young and enraptured with Marie Mancini, not particularly pretty, but very particularly charming, and while he, later so fastidious, acquired his first sexual experiences with a lady of dubious reputation from the Palais Royal quarter. The specific-ally Parisian bacillus of a love that respects no barriers and sets no bounds either to its aggressions or to its tolerance must also be held responsible for the extravagant passions of the regency in France, when all Europe first started to discuss the mysterious atmosphere of eroticism that reigned in the capital.

The French regency

This period began in 1715, after the death of the Sun King, whose heir, later Louis xv, was then only five years old. The regent, Duke Philip ii of Orléans, had married an illegitimate daughter of Louis xiv. In the eight years that elapsed before his early death in 1723 Philip showed himself a capable statesman, reducing by about 400,000 livres the load of debt incurred by the only too brilliant royal household, cutting down the army, expelling the Jesuits and initiating friendlier relations with Britain. Yet it was precisely his alert intelligence that prevented him from being content with merely keeping mistresses like his predecessor Louis xiv and his successor Louis xv. With his equally famous and infamous private supper-parties he set the fashion of stopping at nothing in intimate revels. It was imitated by the most luxurious brothels of the day and remained characteristic of the specifically Parisian establishment of this kind.

Ever since the regent, at the auspicious moment when the fair Parabère at last yielded to him, had clapped his hands to summon all his friends to behold the countess lying naked on his bed and wondering what was wrong, free love among the French had been notable for its entire lack of inhibitions, as then manifested by Philip of Orléans. Although he had been born of a German mother, the beautiful Liselotte of the Palatinate, his casual attitude in matters of love has never taken root east of the Rhine. The key word for the French is still *l'amour*. But among the Germans innumerable compounds with the word 'sin' take its place as a symbol of enticement and they call the city of love by the Seine, pleonastically, 'the Babel of Sin'.

Rococo morals

Franz Blei, who brought together a number of eighteenth-century chronicles under the title of *Rococo Morals*, felt obliged to find excuses for the writers. Yet he must have known that vice is a constant element in history, prevalent in all centuries, in some secretly, in others openly, accompanied at different periods by either cruelty or amiability. It was the latter quality, so evident amidst all the corruption of the *ancien régime*, that attracted such quantities of memoralists. What went on behind closed doors in Paris was no doubt essentially identical with contemporary proceedings in Georgian London, in the Württemberg of Karl Eugen and in the Naples of Caroline. Evil tongues even asserted that Troppau was no better. But in Paris it was not only a question of ordinary native seuxal debauchery but also of a continuous seasoning of the atmosphere by members of Italian stage companies in addition to ladies in French society, tourists from Italy, England, Germany and Spain and a few imposters from Holland, Scotland and Sicily. It was this fact which allured the facile pens of anonymous, pseudonymous or Bastille-obsessed authors to pour out such an abundance of testimony as smothers rather than revives the true character of the age.

Two whores from the Palais Royal were persuaded to believe that the Sultan had sent plenipotentiaries to Paris on a recruiting mission for his harem. The women were told that each candidate selected would be paid a considerable fortune after only three years' service . . . The two beauties approached, named Dumoulin and Viriville, arrived punctually at the rendezvous, where two of the most renowned wags in Paris, MM. Husson and Dugazon, awaited them in suitable disguise. They introduced themselves as Examiners-in-chief to the Sultan and, as may be imagined, were attended by quite a numerous staff of sub-examiners . . .

It was not until the next day that the two dupes, during a morning walk in the Palais Royal, were enlightened by their female friends and a horde of guffawing young men . . .

Chronicles of scandal and their writers

Such is one of the hundreds of anecdotes in the *Chronique Scandaleuse*, a title which developed into an idea so strikingly descriptive in itself that the collector and compiler of the valuable information thus designated, a former Benedictine monk named Guillaume Imbert, is no longer remembered. He was indeed only one of a multitude of more or less gifted men interested in the kind of adventures reported. The writers' personal participation was their chief reward. The necessary small change was provided by the rumours and gossip they heard in any case. Some of the stories were invented. But they were always arresting and amusing, though their details could rarely be checked. And all Europe kept an eye on the quarter from which they came.

A few of such chronicles appeared in Paris, printed under fictitious names. But the majority were published in neighbouring countries, for example in London or Neuwied, the authors using such pseudonyms as *English Spy*, *Chinese Spy*, *Aretino*, etc., though this device seldom saved them from the Bastille. Imprisonment there, however, did not prove a very terrible experience, for no French ruler cared to quarrel seriously with these loose fish about town, who could rely on the sympathy of all the rest of the continent. Some months in the Bastille, therefore, for one of these pamphleteers, were meant as little more than a warning to him. Longer sentences were passed only on the few who had revealed important secrets or been guilty of exceptionally malicious slander.

The Palais Royal

The most conspicuous focus, quantitatively at least, of these erotic activities was the Palais Royal. No doubt more elegant quarters existed. But these were all to some extent exclusive, while every

Parisian, high or low, had access to the Palais Royal, unrivalled at any stage of the capital's development as a general rendezvous.

A unique tradition of amorous behaviour, which means a good deal in Paris, was attached to both the buildings and the site. The latter was long owned by Cardinals Richelieu and Mazarin, who succeeded to territory formerly occupied by a few small brothels and larger medieval houses, which was later to become so celebrated. Mazarin's nieces and Richelieu's great-nephews led the erotic revels. The spacious colonnades and halls, the public and private apartments and corridors, soon all became Crown property, constituting, as the Palais Royal, a city within a city, the headquarters of light theatrical entertainment, gambling, eating and drinking to excess and, last but not least, harlotry. By then it had been forgotten that Louis xiv had played in the area as a child when a miniature fort had been constructed for him to study, and where he had nearly been drowned in a pond. It had been forgotten, too, that Mademoiselle de la Vallière had given clandestine birth to her bastards here. Nor was the glorious collection of Venetian paintings remembered which the much abused regent, the Duke of Orléans, had assembled in this quarter of Paris. It was now given over entirely to pleasure in all its forms. Every corner of the vast complex of buildings was occupied by some branch of the discreetly organized and powerful industries that served that object.

From the moment when the Palais Royal, which had come into the possession of the Dukes of Orléans, was thrown open to the public and the industrialists, it continued to flourish until the great fire of 1828. Meanwhile, what went on there had provided enough material to furnish a most lively chronicle. Though princes of the blood had never hitherto appeared in the character of landlords, the area was so favourably situated that it developed with surprising speed. In 1805 it comprised no fewer than fifteen restaurants, twenty coffee-houses and eighteen gambling establishments. Véry's Restaurant, where Fragonard died, and the Café du Cavau, where the local nymphs arranged to meet their swains under the eyes of the secret police, both stood here.

Colonnades and avenues

The next most attractive features of the Palais Royal were its gardens, with their straight rows of trees, today deserted to their slumbers. People came there at daybreak to shoot one another. Duelling pistols or swords were always in stock at the cafés, though duellists who arrived unannounced might occasionally have to be patient, on being informed by the waiter that the weapons were just then required by others. Later in the morning the nymphs paraded and made their appointments. At noon meals were taken and the events of the day discussed. Afternoons were spent in the cafés and the evenings, until far into the night, in gambling and making love.

The repeatedly mentioned strictly tripartite division of the Palais Royal whores came rather late, after the Revolution had done away with the old careless atmosphere. Until then everything had been in a cheerful state of flux, with actresses in search of a permanent patron or desirous of changing over to a richer one mingling with wretched creatures brutally referred to as *castors finis* and only in luck if darkness or a drunken client came to their aid. To these unfortunate women the illumination of the gardens by more than two hundred lamps may have seemed at times far too splendid. Restif de la Bretonne, in the first part of his account of the Palais Royal (*The Girls of the Avenue of Sighs*) expressed the common but cruel attitude in this connection as follows: 'The Palais Royal prostitutes are really very pretty, especially the young ones. As to the old, their position is the same as it has always been everywhere. An aged animal is never pleasing.'

Expulsion of the whores and decline of the quarter

The prostitutes lived by dozens, perhaps by hundreds, in the small rooms on the upper floors or beneath the stone or wooden galleries. But, not satisfied with this accommodation, more and more of them began taking over the little shops that sold all sorts of trinkets, tobacco, cosmetics and so on, pretending to be occupied with this trade, whereas in reality they continued in the old one. At last, in 1836, the genuine retailers had them all expelled from the Palais Royal quarter.

But this step proved to be bad business. The colonnades, gardens and places of public resort, formerly so crowded, grew so quiet that the whole district came to be regarded as ideal for writers to live in. Henri de Régnier, Edmond Jaloux, Colette and Jean Cocteau all settled there at various times. No doubt they heard only disembodied voices. The various types of *castors* had long since departed to other regions of the great city. Not even the early morning duellists, who would have felt so lonely in surroundings once festive, now joyless and abandoned, could bring themselves to breathe their last in such an environment.

The fact that the Palais Royal, though the most renowned and longest-lived pleasure resort of its kind, was by no means the only one in Paris, proves the precise acquaintance of an amazingly large number of citizens with the details of the entertainment profession and the careers of those concerned with it. Despite immigration swarms of tourists and foreign actors and actresses, the outward constitution of society was far more stable than it is today. At the famous Foire Saint-Germain, for instance, a permanent place of amusement, a farce could be staged in which the personal vices and peculiarities of leading courtesans were represented by actors disguised in the skins of animals. This fancy dress was probably adopted in order to evade interference by the court. But every spectator understood the underlying intention as well as if he had actually been himself entertained in private by members of the small group of outstanding priestesses of Venus.

Consideration of the Palais Royal, the Coliseum, an enormous resort somewhat Britannically referred to as a 'summer Vauxhall', and other similar places of assembly is bound to arouse admiration of the women who became so eminent among the unquestionably huge horde of harlots that all Paris talked about them. It is true that some of them were also popular actresses and singers. But there were only a few of these. The rest, hardly less celebrated, owed their fame exclusively to their liaisons, if also of course to the traditional delight of Parisians in the wit, anecdotes and characteristic personal traits of their heroines, which they related for years on end.

A dumb blonde

It is clear that the beautiful courtesan Mademoiselle du Thé must have been a vacuous creature. She had developed a special technique of her own, that of pregnant silences, and as the result of a number of other advantages had made a considerable fortune by the time the programme of the Saint-Germain des Prés fair listed her as a robot:

MACHINE. A very beautiful and extremely curious contrivance representing a handsome woman. It performs all the actions of a living creature, eating, drinking, dancing and singing as if it were endowed with a mind. This mechanical woman can actually strip a foreigner to his shirt in a matter of seconds. Its only difficulty is with speech. Experts have already given up hope of curing this defect and admirers prefer to study the machine's movements.

Mademoiselle du Thé was actually the key figure in a piece by one Landrin, a playwright now forgotten, which was put on at Audinot's Theatre. Like all the other prominent courtesans Mlle du Thé, who had no idea what the comedy was about, did not fail to appear at the first night. Dressed up to kill, bedecked with feathers and sparkling with diamonds, she was obliged to watch, from her box, a representation of her own person on the stage. Almost fainting, she persuaded her protector, the Duke of Durfort, to complain to Audinot. But the bold manager refused to take action. Nor would he reveal the dramatist's name. For some weeks Landrin's play kept everyone laughing.

Proceedings by Mademoiselle Granville

While Mlle du Thé's rise was due to her introduction of a duke, in his boyhood, to his first steps in love, then considered of vital importance, Mlle Granville went all out for money. Her lessee, a certain M. de Jonville, made up for a rather weak solution of blue blood with a tightly-packed wallet. Nevertheless, she betrayed him with a young army officer. When de Jonville surprised the lovers together, his mistress, instead of being overwhelmed with remorse and begging for forgiveness, turned the tables on the intruder, assisted by her spirited companion. They locked the door, tied up de Jonville and then forced him to witness the conclusion, with every imaginable elaboration, of the scene he had interrupted. In his rage and shame at this treatment he conceived a terrible revenge. He deliberately infected himself with syphilis, which was easier in Paris at that time than avoiding it, the idea being to pass the disease on to his former mistress and her new lover, who would then be obliged, for this reason, to quit the service in disgrace.

But in spite of all the rivalry among courtesans they retained a certain professional solidarity. Mlle Granville soon found out what de Jonville meant to do and kept out of his way, leaving him to stew, so to speak, in his own syphilitic juice. An ill-advised action he brought against her for the return of 20,000 livres exposed his misfortune to all Paris and made him look ridiculous. In the event, though Mlle Granville was locked up, de Jonville himself was banished from the capital without having got his money back.

The Duke of Richelieu

The higher nobility and the diplomats treated fickle beauties, it is clear, with a good deal more skill and probably also longer experience. Armand Duplessis de Richelieu (1696–1788) was only twenty-three when he was imprisoned in the Bastille for the third time. But he already held other records, especially where women were concerned. If he had not been the great-nephew of a famous cardinal and statesman, a fact which might have led to confusing the two, one might talk today of a Richelieu instead of a Casanova, when referring to a man credited with a specially large number of love-affairs. Some three thousand are attributed to the later Richelieu, a man both good-looking, gifted, a Marshal of France and rich into the bargain. Nearly all his mistresses were more or less pretty female employees of the French National Theatre, which was directed, with the utmost enthusiasm, by the duke.

According to the French secret police, the only body which to some extent supervised the erotic activities of that bustling era, Marshal Richelieu's record was only endangered by one other Marshal of France, namely Charles de Rohan, Prince de Soubise (1715–87). The police calculated that he had some 2,500 affairs, a figure which it must have been rather difficult to arrive at. For while Richelieu dashed into his liaisons like a knight errant, fighting duels, facing perils and shrinking from no kind of trouble when a conquest was in view, Soubise collected, in the oriental style, a harem.

A harem in Paris

In this establishment, which was very tastefully furnished, Soubise enjoyed the company of some of the best-looking prostitutes in Paris. Even the more renowned of them, such as Mlles La Prairie, Guimard, Costé and others, had to conform with the custom of the house, which prescribed complete nudity on all occasions. But this idea, remarkably logical though it was, had not occurred to Soubise himself. He had borrowed it from the Abbé Terray.

It may be noted incidentally that Richelieu was the better general. He had distinguished himself in the Genoa campaign of 1748, deprived the British of Minorca in 1756 and a year later defeated the Duke of Cumberland. Soubise, on the other hand, went down before Frederiok the Great at Rossbach, despite a threefold superiority in strength, and was also repeatedly and most ignominiously beaten by Ferdinand of Brunswick. Richelieu's tough physique enabled him, though nineteen years older than Soubise, to outlive his rival. He contrived to reach the age of ninety-two, for all his debaucheries. The caricaturists of the revolutionary period loved to depict the sharp-featured old marshal being pushed in his wheeled chair from one keyhole to another, so that he could still keep half an eye at least on social activities. But that was about all the fun they got out of him, for he cheated Robespierre's executioners by giving up the ghost before they could hurry him to the guillotine.

Both Soubise and Richelieu, in spite of their strenuous erotic industry, were obliged to leave two of the most celebrated courtesans of their day to the attentions of foreigners who, as was so often the case in Venice, happened to be influential diplomats. One of these ladies was called Levasseur or alternatively 'Mademoiselle Rosalie'. The other, named Cléophile, though not an outstanding beauty, had a distinctly lively personality.

Mademoiselle Levasseur

Marie-Claude-Josèphe Levasseur had already acquired a big reputation as a singer in Gluck's operas when the Austrian Count Florimund Mercy d'Argenteau, a gifted diplomat patronized by the all-powerful Kaunitz, was appointed to the coveted post of imperial ambassador in Paris. At first his mistress, she later became his wife. While the liaison remained secret she used an entrance to the count's quarters which was normally reserved for spies. She could thus obtain access to him at any time and it was well known that he would never allow anyone else to be admitted while she was with him. In the case of a woman approaching forty this chivalry on the part of the ambassador was remarkable. But it also revealed a dangerous nonchalance in the representative of the strongest nation in conservative Europe during the first revolutionary disorders in Paris.

The explosively vivacious Mademoiselle Cléophile had captivated one of the most notable and powerful political personalities of the century, the Spanish Count Aranda, who might be called the Pombal of Spain.* Aranda's domestic policy, directed to the rejuvenation of the decadent, old-fashioned Spain of the Bourbons, succeeded in projects which no one had hitherto believed practicable. He limited the power of the Inquisition, expelled the Jesuits, assisted in the promotion of certain ideas of the Enlightenment and set bounds to the activities of the monastic clergy. But his foreign policy, which involved hostility to Britain, caused him to be transferred to the Spanish Embassy in Paris. Cléophile consoled him when the news from Madrid exasperated the once potent minister. But she also wore him out both mentally and physically. An energetic man in the prime of life when he arrived in Paris, he appeared on his return to Spain in 1787 to have grown feeble, even senile, and could no more resist the reckless upstart Godoy than he could the crafty and dissolute Queen Maria Louisa.

The change in Aranda, however, cannot be attributed solely to Cléophile. The case of Richelieu noted above proves the preservative effect that a persistent inclination for women can have on genuinely adventurous natures. It was Paris that was primarily responsible for Aranda's decline.

The stage, the aristocracy and the diplomats

These three worlds, in which the same personalities again and again came to the fore, brought polite society into alarming intimacy with the *demi-monde*. The situation was made worse by the names sometimes chosen by the courtesans. They were not all content, like Cléophile, with an obvious pseudonym. Many, who were constantly haunted by the idea of owning castles, assumed high-sounding appellations for their theatrical appearances, when they were bombastically announced on programmes as Mlle Châteauneuf, Mlle Châteauvieux, Mlle Châteaufort and so on. This habit caused the impudent courtesan called Arnoult to proclaim '*Tous ces*

---

* The Marquess of Pombal (1699–1782), a Portuguese statesman, carried out many far-reaching administrative reforms in his country. [J.C.]

châteaux sont des châteaux branlants'. The play upon words (*branlants* = quivering) needs no translation. But the obscene pun suggests more insight into the future fate of castles than might be expected from a common harlot.

Incidentally, it was the same Mlle Arnoult who consoled the actress Vestris for her frequent pregnancies by remarking, 'Can't be helped, my dear. A mouse with only one hole is soon caught.' This sally kept Paris laughing for a long while, Vestris herself being well known for her boasted familiarity with infallible Italian quack remedies against conception. They were obviously not quite so infallible as she of all people had assumed, for the famous family increased at a terrifying rate, not only in the numbers of miniature Vestris progeny running about, but also in girth. The reason was that the great male dancer Vestris had a brother who cooked for the whole tribe and had developed into a first-class gourmet in Paris.

The Vestris breed

An amazing family! Anyone thinking of writing a novel concerned with the eighteenth century could entitle it simply *The Vestris Family* and could then be sure that no feature of the *ancien régime* worth mentioning would be absent from the scene. The fact that a Count Mercy served as ambassador first in Russia, then in France and finally in England could not be compared with the existence of that hydra-headed monster of genius comprising Angiolo, Francesco, Giovanni Battista and Gaetano, all issuing from the bodies of Teresina and Violante.

Baron Grimm wrote in his *Correspondence Littéraire*:

The Vestris family is a most affectionately united one. While the beauteous Teresina earns money by sleeping with her lover, her mother tells her beads in the next room as piously as any saint. Meanwhile her brother Giovanni Battista prepares a meal which Gaetano, Angiolo and Francesco, together with Teresina herself and her lover and Violante with hers, consume in the utmost mutual harmony.

The cook returned his brother's compliments on the menu by roaring at the top of his voice in the theatre – always attended by the whole family, either in the orchestra stalls, where they applauded in unison, or else on the stage itself – '*Gaetano est le dieu de la danse!*' He pronounced the word *dieu* as *diou*. But the main point was that Parisians thenceforth regarded Gaetano as, if not the, at any rate a, god of the dance. His offhand style on the stage once went so far as to offer an enraptured pupil his leg to kiss. Neither Nijinsky nor Serge Lifar would have been ashamed to imitate his casual grace. For the rest, Gaetano also used to say that there were only three great men alive in Europe, Frederick II of Prussia, M. de Voltaire and, of course, he himself, Gaetano Vestris.

Anna Friederike Heinel

No male rival of the god of the dance appeared. But a female competitor, Anna Friederike Heinel of Bayreuth, was soon given the title of 'Queen of the Dance', a dangerous approximation to Gaetano's. After years of struggle and intrigues against this challenger Vestris determined to put an end to the contest by marrying her. The consequence was that today one has to look up the once world-famous name of Heinel under Vestris. Friederike, incidentally, was in no position to reproach the Vestris ladies, her new sisters-in-law, for their private lives. She was for years the mistress of the renowned Prince Conti, who made love to her, through fear of venereal infection, as if she were a boy. She complained loudly of this situation to anyone who cared to listen. Vestris, when he heard of it, called her a whore. She dashed in tears to Mlle Arnoult, bewailing her husband's rudeness. The other, sharp-tongued as ever, commented with a smile: 'Can't be helped, dearie. People are so ill-mannered nowadays that they call things by their right names.'

If Friederike, as slow in the uptake as nimble with her legs, realized what her friend meant to say, she would not have been in the least offended by the blunt word 'whore'. Those who lived in that delightful twilight reigning between bed and boards felt themselves to be, far more than in modern times, members of one great family. It was not only the Vestris clan which was scattered all over Europe and its courts. Plenty of other persons connected with the theatre and living on their wits roamed the continent at that period. Most of them, if not all, were of Italian origin. Wherever they met, embraces, kisses, vows of eternal fidelity, intrigues, jealousy and tearful farewells were the order of the day.

Something of this affable and casual friendliness, characteristic of professional impostors, was caught by the French actresses from their Italian colleagues. Paris was a great city, full of potential lovers and foreigners. It was not difficult to earn a living there. And as they all influenced one another in their modes of life and the large- or small-scale frauds they practised, and possessed lovers, go-betweens and confidential agents in common, it would be pointless even to attempt to draw up a complete list of those who acquired celebrity. It would be preferable to deal with them in a series of short stories, which might begin with the career of the beautiful opera singer Marie Le Fel, the darling of all Paris. She lived quite openly with her three brilliant sons, telling everyone that the eldest had been fathered by the Duke of Ancenis, the youngest by M. de Maisonrouge and the middle one by Count Egmont, the son-in-law of Marshal Richelieu. Another stage star, named La Guerre, was adored by the Duke of Bouillon, a liaison which gave rise to the harmless pun *Bouillon aime La Guerre* ('loves war'). But it was not such a harmless proceeding when the lady in question, who was mad on jewellery, relieved her lover within three months of no less than 300,000 livres, a vast sum when it is realized that although the livre under Louis XVI was only worth a fraction of its former value it nevertheless represented about that of a gold franc today.

Others were not so lucky as Mlle La Guerre. Mlle Guimard, for example, was so thin that she was said to crawl about in Prince Soubise's menagerie in the form of a spider, while Mlle Arnoult compared her with a silkworm, an astonishingly lean insect when you remember what a nice fat leaf it feeds on. The fat leaf in this case, however, was not Soubise but his predecessor in the favours of Mlle Guimard, viz. M. de Jarente, Bishop of Orléans. Mlle Dubois must have been still more unfortunate than the skinny Mlle Guimard. For the former counted her lovers until she reached the figure of 16,527, whereupon she stopped counting but didn't stop making love.

Famous bawds

Such statistics approach those of the humbler walks of love. They too had prospered in eighteenth-century Paris to an extent previously deemed incredible. How far this development was stimulated by British example cannot now be estimated in view of the brisk cross-Channel traffic of those days. It is only certain that well-heeled travellers from the Thames found all in Paris which they had been used to at home and a bit extra. Nor could the emigrants of the years of revolution, when they had to make do with British establishments, find any fault, at any rate after a short period of acclimatization, with this aspect, at least, of their new existence.

Three women are repeatedly mentioned in all the memoirs of the time, above all in police reports, tales of scandal, confidential letters and consequently also in social histories. They were Mesdames Gourdan, Justine Pâris, whose real name was Bienfait ('Welldone'), and Dupuis, alias Montigny, not quite so celebrated as the other two, but possibly the cleverest of the three and certainly the wealthiest.

Madame Gourdan at home

Madame Gourdan's house stood west of the present Boulevard de Sebastopol, at a very convenient spot between two streets, only one of which remains today. Visitors indifferent to gossip could use the main entrance in the rue des Deux Portes. Others first entered the shop of a dealer in antiquities in the rue Saint-Sauveur, then vanished into a built-in cupboard, negotiated a short passage and then another similar cupboard, to find themselves at last in a dressing-room where prelates changed their robes for ordinary civilian clothing, while army officers could be metamorphosed into prelates and citizens into uniformed holders of commissions.

The distribution and purpose of the other rooms were planned just as carefully, in a manner which has now become classic. The largest apartment, to which the main entrance gave access, was the so-called seraglio. Here the unsuspecting caller was greeted by a swarm of detestable creatures, since it was the room which every Parisian brothel was obliged to maintain at certain times for the use, at cheap rates, of soldiers and other impecunious persons, so as to keep down the occurrence of unpleasant incidents in the streets, the violation of respectable women, indecent assaults on children and the importuning of servant girls on shopping expeditions. First-class brothels like that of Mme Gourdan fulfilled this obligation, which gave the others enough to live on, by the expedient to which famous lawyers resort when engaged on behalf of poor persons, i.e. by employing substitutes. These were, in Mme Gourdan's case, older and worn out women or simple peasants who had been found unfit to serve refined clients.

A second room was also used, in a sense, as an antechamber. Here the girls from the country were cleaned up, a task which in the eighteenth century required a certain amount of energy. The unsophisticated village beauties had not only to be subjected to soap and water but also to have their skins rendered soft and white, their body odours reduced and all the hardened surfaces in evidence smoothed out. During this process certain clandestine examinations were also made by selected clients, who were enabled to observe the splashing novices in a perfect state of nature by looking through gauze-covered peepholes, and thereafter issued their first directions.

Secrets of a first-class brothel

As soon as the heading under which the new girl was to be classified had been determined in this way she was given systematic treatment. The effect of the bathing was reinforced in a make-up cubicle and all the resources of the century, from powder to patches, were applied in accordance with a preconceived plan. The next apartment, called the ballroom, generally elicited shrieks of delight from the new arrivals. Their rags had been left behind in the bathroom. Perfumes hitherto undreamed of caressed their flesh and they were confronted, already almost wholly renovated, by a unique collection of gowns of every description. The collection was unique because it was neither such as was kept in any theatre or loan establishment nor did it correspond with the wardrobe of a wealthy woman. It consisted of innumerable items of special equipment for the conquest of the male. Their multiplicity would have made the pretence at costume prevalent in the harem of the Prince de Soubise look quite insignificant. The question was considered whether the newcomer would look better in antique robes or as a shepherdess, as a stage star in a low-cut gown or mysteriously austere in a high-necked one, producing her effect solely by silent promise. Others could be dressed as fairies or festooned with flowers that framed rather than veiled a nudity recalling that of nymphs. Mme Gourdan and her right-hand assistant, Mme Brisson, no doubt spent hours on such experiments.

The next apartment must have been familiar to many visitors from London. Only its name would be new to them. It was called in Paris the 'infirmary' and contained specifics for the revival of powers weakened in the struggle for money or position. There were scented rods, 'Richelieu' pastilles – though of course he never took such things – and in particular walls covered with a choice collection of engravings and paintings of the most lascivious character. It must be stated, to the credit of Mme Gourdan and her patrons, that they read as much as they gaped. For a certainly very one-sided selection of extracts from erotic works, calligraphically inscribed and neatly framed, hung between the pictures. Furthermore, a series of carefully adjusted mirrors ensured that a client's ardour, after his first expenditure of energy, would be slow to flag.

The Fronsac scandal

Two smaller rooms were reserved for more sinister purposes. The first was called the 'Salon of Vulcan', referring to the smith of heaven in antique legend, who caught his disloyal spouse in a net of wire at the very moment when she was enjoying herself with the mighty war-god. The story had long been a favourite with European painters. But by Mme Gourdan's time it does not seem to have been quite correctly related, for the Vulcan Salon contained neither bed nor net. In their place stood an innocent-looking leather armchair, which only developed its terrifying activity when some unsuspecting person sat in it. How often it may have been used to seize recalcitrant girls in its grips and render them helpless probably only Mme Gourdan knew. But once a scandal was caused, when the Duke of Fronsac, only son of Marshal Richelieu, outraged a modest young woman who had been lured into the chair and remained imprisoned in it for days on end, till she was freed by mere chance. Fronsac was banished from the court for just so long as proved necessary to hush the matter up by bribery.

The room called *La Question* ('Interrogation') was put to no less infamous a purpose. Here, too, interested visitors had the opportunity to watch and listen. They were exclusively members of the secret police. Why it was considered necessary for them to look as well as hear behind the gauzed-over peep-holes is not quite clear. In any case this room was frequently in use and provided sinister evidence in many an official prosecution as well as, no doubt, in certain private intrigues of which the full details were never published. Sometimes people were actually arrested in the Interrogation Room, as was, for instance, Madame d'Oppy. In short, that eighteenth-century institution worked as effectively as any which in modern times employs built-in microphones, counterfeit mirrors and television cameras. It is certain that Madame Gourdan purchased by this means the police protection which was not accorded, for example, to her colleague in Petersburg, Madame Riedl.

Justine Pâris

A more amiable resort, less like a panoptikon,* the Hôtel du Roule, was kept by Justine Pâris in a suburb just outside the boundaries of the city proper, where the village of Roule had been famous for its goose-market as early as the thirteenth century. During the eighteenth century the place had expanded to suburban dimensions. Under the first Napoleon the Chaussée du Roule came to be a favourite residential quarter. The beautiful Pauline Borghese, one of the emperor's sisters, settled there between 1803 and 1814, perhaps attracted by its reputation for gaiety in the time of Justine Pâris. Today the Chaussée forms the greater part of the fashionable rue du Faubourg St Honoré.

J. M. Moreau the younger (1741–1814) painted a picture of one of the rooms in the establishment of Justine Pâris and Voltaire chose a motto for the house. But it has been immortalized by another person who had at one time boasted that he could do without prostitutes and brothels, viz. Giacomo Casanova. He had just been rebuffed by the fair Anna Maria Veronese, an Italian actress, quoted as Coraline in the market-list of courtesans. On her way to the heights of her profession she had recently acquired the protection of the Prince of Monaco and had dropped the bogus Chevalier de Seingalt (Casanova's self-invented title) as soon as a real prince hove in sight. The discarded suitor could not then have anticipated that even the prince represented no more than a stage in the rise of Coraline, who was destined one day to figure in the

---

* The name given to the prison system devised by the English philosopher and jurist Jeremy Bentham (1748–1832), based on cellular separation and hard labour. Safe custody and diligence were guaranteed by close observation from a central standpoint. [J.C.]

Almanach de Gotha as a Marquise de Silly. Meanwhile, disconcerted by his repulse, he took the advice of his friend Patu, who had suggested the Hôtel du Roule as a consolation for his bereavement.

The Hôtel du Roule

The female proprietor of the establishment had furnished it with taste [Casanova wrote in Book III of his Memoirs]. She maintained between twelve and fourteen exquisitely pretty girls there, as well as a good cook, choice wines and excellent beds. She greeted every visitor personally. Her name was Madame Pâris and she enjoyed police protection. As her house could only be reached from Paris by carriage, she could be certain that all her clients would be persons of rank or fortune. Within the premises the strictest order prevailed. Every pleasure had its prearranged price, which was not high. A charge of six francs was made for a meal in the company of a girl and twelve if one wished to dine. A louis d'or would cover supper and a bed. It was a house in which one ran no risks and of which everyone spoke with admiration.

Justine knew exactly what educated patrons required, as appears from the brief speech of welcome she addressed to Casanova and Patu, and probably to everyone else who called. This greeting preceded her presentation of the fourteen or so muslin-clad young women and the visitors' first choice of partners.

'You can take a stroll in my gardens whenever you please, gentlemen. You will enjoy their fresh air and the peace and quiet of my premises. You can also be sure that each one of my girls is perfectly healthy.'

This was plain, but not too plain, speaking, calculated to relax rather than importune, and to invite sauntering among bushes and shrubs rather than an immediate introduction to interiors, which always have an oppressive effect. It is clear that Justine had no need to attend lectures on the psychological causes of impotence or anything else connected with her trade, of which she was past mistress. The fixed prices which she notified to begin with also relieved her of disagreeable arguments about fees and any suspicion by her clients that they might be cheated. She only economized on one aspect of the transaction, that of time. Whenever Casanova and Patu had reached the stage of being about to devote themselves to the special merits of their partners, Justine would turn up, watch in hand, to pocket the sum required for the ensuing performance. The two friends soon found this habit absurdly annoying.

I took Patu aside and we exchanged a few philosophic reflections on the well-known circumstance that interrupted pleasures leave one dissatisfied. 'Let's pay a third visit to the seraglio,' I suggested, 'choose a third girl each and make Madame promise that we shall then remain undisturbed till morning.'

Patu agreed. We proposed my plan to the lady of the house, who replied that she now perceived we were men of spirit. When we entered the seraglio for the third time and abandoned the girls we had hitherto partnered, the rest laughed at the four unlucky ones, who for their part revenged themselves on us by calling us all sorts of embarrassingly rude names.

Gabrielle Siberre

I took no further notice of them after I had found my third girl, for she was a decided beauty. I thanked heaven that she had escaped me so far, since I was now sure that I could devote myself to her for a whole fourteen hours . . . She surveyed me arrogantly, even scornfully, and it took me a good hour to make a conquest of her. The trouble was that she regarded me as not having deserved to sleep with her, because I had been so discourteous as not to have chosen her the first or even the second time. I tried to make her see that the very inadvertence of which I had been guilty would now be of benefit to us both.

It is obvious that these young women had their professional pride and were well aware of their respective values. Patu's third choice had actually fallen upon a girl who had already enjoyed the favour of Voltaire. Casanova's expert eye had picked out Mlle Saint-Hilaire, whose real name was Gabrielle Siberre. She eventually rose to become a well-known figure in the fashionable world of Paris. The fastidious Venetian found her so fascinating that he undertook the long journey to the Hôtel du Roule another ten times at least.

The d'Oppy case

It may have been true at the time when Casanova visited the establishment of Justine Pâris that she was in good odour with the police. But shortly after this period all three of the great procuresses got into trouble, almost simultaneously. M. d'Oppy had set a trap for his wife in Mme Gourdan's house. She was caught in the Interrogation Room, in the act of adultery, and arrested there on that charge. In her insatiable craving for sexual enjoyment she had not been content with the services of a single bawd. The unbridled rage of the provincial cuckold upset the entire balance of the metropolitan network of pleasure.

The high level of protection extended to Mme Gourdan prevented her being sentenced. But the secret of her 'Interrogation Room' was now out, so that no one could henceforth feel safe or even unobserved on her premises. Justine Pâris was forced to sell her establishment to a certain Mme Carlier and was never mentioned again in the chronicles of the period. Mme Montigny, who had not only possessed a whole string of brothels but also the best-looking young women in Paris, was ordered to suffer the ancient penalty prescribed by law for procuresses and so often imposed in medieval Paris. Mounted on a donkey so as to face its tail, with a placard on her breast inscribed *Maquerelle* ('bawd'), she was condemned to be led through the city by two of her girl-employees.

All Paris looked forward with delight to the revival of this old-time spectacle. It was recalled that in former days the younger women had worn nothing but a straw hat on such occasions. But Mme Montigny still had money. She paid no less than 300,000 livres to escape the disgrace of the ride to which she had been sentenced and was thought to have been ruined by this disbursement. at that date the Revolution, which was to do away with all the other amenities of the *ancien régime*, being still some decades ahead, the undisputed mistresses of their profession were long lamented, especially in polite society. In November 1773, at one of Prince Conti's smart evening parties, which only the discourteous called orgies, a long funeral oration was pronounced in praise of Mme Justine Pâris 'in the presence of all the nymphs of the goddess Venus'.

Activities of the police

The presence of all the nymphs of the goddess Venus would then as now have overflowed any one of the halls of assembly in Paris. Nor was there in the eighteenth century as yet any such thing as a sports arena. Consequently it would have been utterly impossible to stage a review of the thirty thousand prostitutes of the metropolis. All that could be done was to draw up lists. These were prepared by the so-called Chief Inspector, whose duty it was to remove between three and four hundred girls from the trade every month and deport them either to hospitals or out of the city altogether. But a monthly percentage came to the same thing as an instalment on hire purchase with no definite date of termination. At any rate the quantity of young women concerned remained constant.

The post of Chief Inspector was at that time at least as coveted as that of Staff Manager at the Lido today. For it lay within the power of the single police officer in question to decide which of the thirty thousand lights of love would be allowed to carry on in business and which would have to retire from their vocation. He would of course be guided to some extent by considerations of a practical character, such as the incidence of venereal disease. But as at least ten thousand of the girls were always infected at any one time it remained repeatedly the inspector's prerogative to determine which of them he would arrest or leave alone. Accordingly, he needed only to issue a summons to a prostitute in order to blackmail her indefinitely.

The unlucky three hundred who could neither pay nor exert influence to escape their fate were packed into carts and driven through the streets to the Châtelet prison for examination by the Police Lieutenant. The citizens of course knew when this procession would take place. They lined the route, crowded the steps to the prison entrance and even filled the courtroom where the cases were decided. The whores, after being unloaded from the carts, had to proceed one by one through the throng to the dock. By the time they got there their fate had usually been already determined. For the spectators would generally forestall the Police Lieutenant by yelling 'To the hospital!', with the same ferocity as they would soon afterwards be yelling 'To the street-lamp!', 'To the guillotine!' or 'Off with her head!', whenever one of the women looked too old or worn out to be likely to attract them later on in the Palais Royal.

The farce of public administration

It is perfectly clear that the authorities, instead of exercising duly organized control and treatment of these women and giving them good advice, merely staged a spectacle for the amusement of the masses. The police officer might pronounce his decrees of spells in hospital or gaol, or of banishment, from personal observation or sympathy with an individual case. But in practice nothing at all was changed, either in detail or on any extensive scale. The number of prostitutes remained about the same, though the bawds in charge of brothels might occasionally be different, as when, for example, Mme Carlier followed Mme Pâris. It is doubtful whether the former improved on the latter's management, for she had originally made her fortune by collecting a swarm of women volunteers to follow the French army invading Flanders and thereafter opening a big brothel for the use of priests.

When Louis XVI, married to a Habsburg princess and occasionally subject to fits of moral austerity, decided to take the energetic step of forbidding prostitution, his action came far too late. The people were in any case already restless. Then the king suddenly found himself faced with thirty thousand hostile females. The danger they represented would soon become evident.

Whores as shock-troops of the Revolution

The new police orders, which in particular announced that heavy fines would be imposed on any tavern proprietor or other person harbouring prostitutes, considerably increased the difficulties of following this trade in Paris. Police raids on the Palais Royal and adjacent streets scared even the most loyal temptresses away from that quarter and only a slight incentive was needed to cause the smouldering discontent to burst into flame. As the women's earnings had dropped so catastrophically, the Duke of Orléans (later Philippe Egalité) did not have to spend much in order to use them to further his ambitious plans. These aimed at his own coronation as head of a constitutional monarchy after the abdication of Louis XVI. When the latter was tactless enough, on 1 October 1789, to give a full-dress supper party at Versailles while Paris itself was half-starved, a procession of some eight thousand female citizens set out for the royal residence a few days later.

It is possible that the expedition included a few hundred housewives who really intended to demand bread for their children from the king. It is certain however that, in addition to some hundreds of disguised males forming the spearhead of the demonstration, three thousand girls from the Palais Royal and similar quarters went along. When Louison Chabry, a young woman of the labouring class who had been chosen to make a speech, fainted after uttering her first few words to the king, the enraged termagants who accompanied her would have strung her up to the nearest tree in the park if they had not been prevented by the Versailles Guard. These furies, after their return to Paris, had reached such a pitch of exasperation that they burst into the Constituent Assembly. The benches and tables of the hall occupied by this advisory body then became the scene of a mass-orgy which put even the receptions of Mme Guimard far into the shade.

Death to the king!

This sudden intimacy with some hundreds of politicians reinforced the whores' conviction that they constituted the shock troops of the Revolution. Thenceforth they were always present wherever the masses and the soldiers clashed. In July of the following year an encounter, the obscene details of which became legendary, took place near the Hôtel du Roule, which had once belonged to Justine Pâris. That evening a detachment of cavalry was slowly riding towards the city when a number of prostitutes, some of whom had pistols in their belts, barred the way. They called upon the soldiers to shout, 'Death to the king!' The troopers refused. Thereupon some of the women seized the bridles of the horses, while others confronted the riders with raised skirts, screaming: 'That's all yours if you join the Revolution!' The detachment halted, but still declined to utter the threatening words demanded. A fair-haired girl of at most seventeen then began dancing in the road. An eyewitness named J. B. Prérion described the sequel in his memoirs:

She had bared her breasts and was holding them in the palms of her hands while she deliberately waggled her posterior like a duck. The other women immediately made a rush at her and lifted up her clothing, revealing to the blushing cavalrymen the prettiest figure imaginable, at the same time exclaiming, 'If you'd like a taste of that, just shout "Death to the king" first!'

What happened next need not be related here. But the result was that the commanding officer of the detachment, purple in the face and on the verge of apoplexy, stuttered out the required slogan, whereupon the whole troop, retaining their arms, deserted to the revolutionaries.

231

The name of the blonde prodigy of the Chaussée du Roule has unfortunately not survived. But the revolutionary achievements of another prostitute, named Théroigne de Méricourt (1762–97), are recorded in the full glare of history. Born Anne-Josèphe Terwagné, in the little village of Marcourt in Luxembourg, she became at an early age the mistress of a wealthy young Englishman, who had directed an only too penetrating glance into the opening of her low-cut blouse while she was washing clothes in the river Maas. In London she soon became familiar with every aspect of her new profession and was even alleged to have been a member for a time of the notorious household of Mrs Hayes. Soon afterwards Lord Spinster took her to Paris, where she bestowed her favours upon the Marquis de Persan, two well-known singers and other gentlemen of fashion. In 1789 she was living in Naples as one of its most famous courtesans when the news from Paris caused her to sell her jewellery and make for the banks of the Seine with all speed. She had found her true vocation.

Her first triumphs were scored in the *Club des Cordeliers*, in the presence of Camille Desmoulins. Her enthusiasm, her eloquence and probably also her figure in a close-fitting green riding-habit, brought all the members to their feet. But that was only the beginning. During the next few years, she became the mistress of Danton, Desmoulins, Barnaves, Mirabeau and other leading lights of the Revolution. On 20 June 1792 she marched at the head of her battalion of Amazons to the Tuileries. The Guards were cut down with a ferocity that foreshadows the mania which overtook Théroigne de Méricourt some years later. Then came the celebrated scene when Louis xvi was compelled by the raging pack of she-wolves, led by the whore in question, to cover his costly periwig with the red Phrygian cap of the Revolution. Wedged in the half-amused, half-bewildered crowd of spectators in the palace grounds stood a young officer, muttering, with an Italian oath, the first of the many sayings for which he was to become famous in the history of mankind: 'How could that rabble ever have been allowed to get so far? A few guns, four or five hundred casualties and the rest would have bolted in a panic.' The young officer's name was Bonaparte.

Pathology of a maenad

While Bonaparte's star began to rise, Théroigne's began to sink. In the turmoil of those days her former services seemed to have been forgotten, when after her revolutionary activities in Belgium she had been imprisoned by the imperial police in Vienna and on her release dashed back to Paris, to take so prominent a part in the Septembrist agitation that many contemporary chroniclers believed her responsible for the dreadful massacres of that month in 1792. It was then, no doubt, that numbers of her former subordinates began to detest her. Others considered that the mistress of the new men in power was putting on too many airs. In any case one day the fishwives of the Halles seized her and gave her a public thrashing. Once extolled as the Amazon of freedom, then abused as the Messalina of the Revolution, she at last went out of her mind and died in the Salpêtrière Asylum.

Her biography should be rewritten today, in the light of modern psychopathology. For the case of this woman, regarded by her contemporaries as half goddess and half she-devil, is undoubtedly one of the most interesting examples in history of that hatred of males which so often comes to a head among prostitutes but as a rule simply makes them turn to Lesbianism. Théroigne on the other hand showed symptoms of nymphomania so long as she was obliged to live as a harlot but suddenly, at a moment which can be precisely defined, took to murderous persecution of men, as when she had the journalist Sulau executed merely for having made fun of her outbursts of fury. Again, one of her last murders was that of a young Fleming, allegedly her first seducer. She recognized him as she was hurrying from prison to prison, so as not to miss any of the massacres then being perpetrated, and struck off his head with her own hand. The mob cheered her. But she then fell into a kind of maniacal ecstasy and started singing a revolutionary ballad while she danced among the pools of blood.

So many girls and women, not all of whom were prostitutes, imitated her during the revolutionary period that serious commentators have ascribed its degeneration into cruelty and terror to the women who ruled the streets. If it were not for the many bloodthirsty proclamations concocted by Marat and his meek-mannered mistress Simone Evrard in their quiet little office, there would really be little to object to in this theory. A century which saw its women

simultaneously worshipped and exploited as never before drowned
in a blood-bath brought about by Amazons.

The goddess of reason

Thérèse Angélique Aubry was a decent girl and that meant something special, for she belonged to the chorus of the Paris opera, from which the fashionable world was wont to recruit its supplies of kept mistresses. She was twenty-one years old when the extraordinary spectacle was staged, at Notre Dame of all places, in honour of the Goddess of Reason. It was November, the weather was damp and cold and the eminent Mme Maillard refused pointblank to expose her famous voice to the perils of such a murderous atmosphere. Accordingly, Paris was delighted to see a slim, beautiful chorus-girl acting the part of the goddess, composed by a renegade priest. The men who carried her on their shoulders from Notre Dame to the Tuileries thanked God that they had not to perform this office with the still young but already terribly stout Mme Maillard.

The whole opera staff, led by the chorus and ballet girls wearing garlands of flowers, marched pluckily, in their dancing-shoes and short, gauze ballet-skirts, through the November drizzle. It was with pleasure that the citizens beheld their venerable institution transferred to the service of the New Order.

Napoleon and the theatre

But soon still closer relations were to be established between the new leaders of France and the stage. For Napoleon Bonaparte, as First Consul, immediately showed a decided taste for members of that profession. Although, compared with his predecessors on the French throne, he did not keep a very large number of mistresses in the strict sense of the term, he was a true soldier all his life in preferring what the emigrants disdainfully called 'transitory affairs'. His adjutants in the field became very familiar with his often abrupt and feverishly impatient demands for some woman or other. Sometimes the young women hurriedly brought into his presence were so unprepared for the honour about to be conferred on them that they didn't even understand, as happened in the case of a pretty Viennese of a good middle-class family, the order '*Déshabillé-toi!*'

Ladies from the theatrical world were more used to being directed to undress. Both as General and as Consul Bonaparte was always at one understood, whether he was dealing with Mme Branchu, who was alleged to have begun his series of *comédiennes*, or Mme Grassini, the renowned contralto of the Scala at Milan and one of the most beautiful women of her time. In Paris at this date it was Mlle Rolandeau, the Favart theatre charmer, whom Napoleon, after a performance at Malmaison of the *Noces de Dorine*, escorted without much ceremony into his bedroom.

Mlle Rolandeau

It was already clear in her case that it was the sexual style of the *soubrette*, the frivolous but not vulgar appeal of a pretty and unremittingly flirtatious little creature, that put the great man in the best of tempers. The brisk Corsican could never wholly relax except with these 'columbines', who were less suited to straightforward drama than to the farces that in those days regularly preceded, as curtain-raisers, the evening performance at a theatre.

He delighted in also calling a 'curtain-raiser' his pursuit of the charming Mlle Rolandeau across the lawn at Malmaison, by way of appetizer, and coolly pulling up her skirts when he caught her. At that date he could not foresee that soon afterwards Joséphine Beauharnais would be ringing down an iron curtain between him and the actress. Yet five months later her successor appeared on the scene. This was the still very young but wonderfully attractive Mlle Georges, picked out of a repertory company by the famous Lesbian Mme Raucourt and launched in Paris at the age of fifteen. The daughter of an actor, she began her metropolitan career at the Théâtre Français.

In the short time that elapsed before Napoleon discovered her she had already embarked on an affair with Lucien Bonaparte, one of his brothers, and was being kept by a certain Prince Sapieha. On 19 Brumaire (10 November 1799) Lucien had rendered Napoleon decisive aid* and at a later date came to be the one representative of the family who would not submit to the emperor. His anticipation of the latter in the favours of Mlle Georges was not in

* On that date Lucien, a deputy for Corsica to the Council of Five Hundred in Paris and its acting President, had refused to put the vote of outlawry which the majority of the Council demanded in consequence of Napoleon's overthrow of the national councils at the palace of St Cloud. Lucien, by closing the sitting and appealing to the soldiers outside to disperse the members, turned the scale in favour of his brother. [J.C.]

the least resented by Napoleon and soon afterwards she was on her way to St Cloud.

Mademoiselle Georges

The effects upon the future emperor which Mlle Rolandeau had barely been able to stimulate reached an unexpected development in the case of this delightful adolescent. Napoleon was not yet thirty-three. He found the way back to his youthful vigour and high spirits through his affair with the girl, whom he called Georgina, though their diversions at St Cloud were far from innocent. A fair amount is known about them, for Mlle Georges at a later date not only wrote her memoirs but also conducted a correspondence with Mme Desbordes-Valmore, the poetess, with a view to their revision by that lady. At times these letters reveal more than the memoirs themselves. At any rate, according to Guy Breton, 'the meetings between Bonaparte and Mlle Georges assumed such an extravagant character that during the evenings she spent at the palace not a single keyhole remained vacant'.

Despite this uninterrupted vigilance on the part of the domestic staff an untoward incident occurred in the politically critical year 1803. Napoleon never forgave his Georgina for it and it put an end to their association. After he had undertaken a brief and hurried visit to Boulogne, which had clearly overtaxed his strength, he fainted away in the girl's arms. Georgina, who had never experienced any such thing before and already saw herself mounting the steps of the guillotine as the murderess of the First Consul, could think only of rescue from her own predicament. She rang the bell so loudly as to arouse every occupant of the palace. Doctors and servants were followed into the chamber by Joséphine herself, Bonaparte's legitimate wife, in her dressing-gown. She found, at the centre of a circle of silently attentive males, the First Consul lying, white to the lips, in the arms of a young woman whose beauty could not be doubted, since she was stark naked.

The ensuing matrimonial dispute must have been violent, for the consul not only dropped Georgina but also actually endeavoured to have her succeeded by her keenest competitor, Cathérine-Joséphine Raffin, known as Mme Duchesnois. The rivalry between them had divided Paris into two camps. The adherents of Mlle Georges were called Georgians, with an additional play on the word *gorge* ('bosom'), a feature of the actress's figure renowned for its beauty. The 'Carcassians', who backed Mme Duchesnois, as well as sounding like 'Circassians', carried a reference to the *carcasse* ('skeleton'), which was all the austerely slender frame of their heroine could oppose to the shimmering epidermis and robust development of Georgina's physique.

Mme Duchesnois waits in vain

The apparent humiliation of Mlle Georges was followed by a fiasco in the case of Mme Duchesnois. For after all there were now other claims upon Napoleon's time than those of his actresses. When Mme Duchesnois arrived at the Tuileries the consul sent a message to tell her to wait. After a while she timidly notified him, through a servant of her continued presence. The order came back that she was to undress. She spent another half-hour, nude and shivering, in an antechamber through which couriers and servants continually passed. Then she heard, with relief, the command: 'She can go to bed now.'

But there were no more developments that evening. Napoleon worked all through the night. Mme Duchesnois, half crazy with rage and shame, was obliged to slip into her carefully chosen underwear without having achieved her purpose and return home.

Bonaparte did not always decide in favour of his official work in such cases. On one occasion he had been greatly struck by the youth and abundant gaiety of another Théâtre Français actress named Bourgoin and sent her an invitation to call on him, though he had been told that she was then the mistress of his Minister of the Interior, the outstanding statesman and chemist Jean Antoine Chaptal, aged forty-eight. The two men happened to be working in the same room when the consul was informed that Mlle Bourgoin was waiting for him in his bedroom.

'Tell her to undress. I'll join her in a moment,' the ever busy Head of the State replied. The brutality of this answer was no worse than tactless. But it lost him a colleague who had carried through a vast modernization of the French economic and traffic systems in four years.

The list of Mlle Bourgoin's successors is too long to be discussed here. But the later career of the fair Georgina deserves a few more lines. She had the luck to gain the favour of a monarch whom

Napoleon himself courted, the Tsar Alexander. In 1812, on her journey back from Russia through Germany, she also became the mistress of Jerome Bonaparte, King of Westphalia. She died in Paris at the age of eighty.

But her last years were spent in distress, poverty and unhappiness. She may often have envied her predecessor Thérèse Rolandeau who in 1808, while still a young woman, came too near an open fire in her own house and was burnt to death. The gods frequently showed more mercy to such females than the civil authorities did, as when the aged Georgina's humble request for employment in the capacity of a cloak-room attendant at the Paris Exhibition of 1855 was bluntly refused.

Change in attitude to women

The worthy Georgina's application for this post showed Napoleonic insight. For between 1 May and 30 September 1855 no fewer than five million persons visited the Exhibition in the hideous building of stone, steel and glass which had been erected in Paris under the supervision of Plonplon, a cousin of Napoleon III. In that year the first British sovereign to venture upon French soil since the Hundred Years War, Queen Victoria, gave Parisians a chance to sun themselves in the brilliance of this reconciliation, which only had one drawback. It failed to rejuvenate old men.

Between the two French Empires, between the date of Waterloo and the Exhibitions of 1855 and 1867, social developments included a lasting change in the position, both private and public, of women in Europe. Théroigne de Méricourt had briefly and cruelly dreamed of feminine domination, and the plays of another *demimondaine*, Olympe de Gouges, had not only been derided by Marie Antoinette but even imperilled the intrepid authoress, who must be credited with complete sincerity and true heroism, under the Revolutionary Government, to such an extent that she ended her life under the guillotine.

After Marat's assassination by Charlotte Corday Olympe had commented: 'To close the roads to honours, public office and financial profit against women is to open to them the road to crime.' Even the new men who achieved power in 1793 could only retort by the official prohibition of all associations and groups composed exclusively of women and the trial of Olympe de Gouges before the

Revolutionary Court ended with ignominious defeats for her judges.

The Second Empire

Napoleon III, French Pretender, President and finally Emperor, might have been expected, as a descendant of the light-hearted Joséphine Beauharnais and as having been born in the Palais Royal quarter, to show some sympathy for the world of ladies who lived by their charms. But his reforms in this direction were limited to an atmosphere in his drawing-rooms which was disdainfully described as only too democratic. Social developments in Paris and the other European capitals owed nothing to established authority. The process of change was effected by stronger forces than still remained at the disposal of nineteenth-century rulers.

The first rockets of future economic power had been discharged in the middle of the century of adventurers. The wily Casanova, spy for Louis XV, loan negotiator and director of state lotteries, had failed lamentably as a manufacturer of printed silks in Paris and been imprisoned for debt because he had slept with his factory girls instead of leaving them to perform their tasks at his apparatus. A hundred years later it was no longer men of genius, artists in mystification and charlatans who set up factories here and there, promising potentates enormous profits, but busy citizens who had learnt their trade and kept all its parts running smoothly.

The nobility was no longer all-powerful. The new manufacturing classes enforced a new distribution of activities even in the world of pleasure-seeking. The close association between noblemen's boxes and actresses' dressing-rooms had not yet entirely ceased. But it was not now such an absolute rule as it had been under the First Empire. The actress henceforth played to a wide audience of impartial admirers who did not watch every one of her movements on the stage with a view to escorting her at once to a princely bed. She could assume often enough from this reserve on the part of the new public that she would not in future necessarily have to submit to the favour or disfavour of the fashionable set.

The regrouping of society, which took place most rapidly in England, more advanced industrially than the rest of Europe, rather more slowly in France and decentralized Germany, achieved all that the clearest thinkers of the French Revolution had anticipated. Under the new economic system, based on industry, individuals of both sexes acquired a significance which they had hitherto enjoyed only in exceptional cases. In both western and eastern Europe the institutions of serfdom and a landed aristocracy had divided mankind into two sections, one large and deprived of legal rights and one small and privileged. But now, although the equality proclaimed in theory was still far from operative in practice, the authorities were obliged to take account of persons formerly not deemed worthy of consideration.

In France such nameless citizens had carried Napoleon III to power, on the first occasion with five million votes and on the second with seven and a half million. It was the nameless ones who set the wheels whirring which produced the new prosperity. But the nameless were as much exposed in their factories to exploitation, against which they had no remedy, as they had been in the old days to their landlords. Their miserably-paid labours now facilitated the rise of a new, widely-dispersed class, well supplied with funds, which influenced taste, demanded entertainment and visited the theatres, restaurants, gambling establishments and brothels which had formerly been reserved exclusively for the aristocracy.

The middle class and the half-world

Accordingly, the half-world, with its ancient traditions of luxury, came into contact with a middle class which was just taking its first timid steps into high metropolitan society. Eager for pleasures hitherto known only from hearsay and wavering between the pride of newly-acquired wealth and middle-class respectability, a new consumer on a large scale entered the market. He was received as affectionately by the oldest profession as once it had welcomed powdered dandies with buckled shoes and periwigs. Unsure of himself in his environment and inexperienced in the technique of erotic conquest, the new man was not particularly attracted by the habit of strolling under colonnades or making signs from one coach to another. Consequently, the brothel now assumed the aspect of a citizens' sexual paradise.

It operated on the principle still recognized today in many first-rate French restaurants, simply because the modern customer is no longer capable of ordering a first-rate meal without assistance. One just has to do what one is told. And to do what they were told enraptured the newcomers, whose mentality was that of servants. They were the tyrants of the factory floor but the slaves of their overweight wives. It was all very well for M. de Nieuwerkerke, Director of the Louvre, calmly to plan his embrace of the fair Countess Castiglione on the roof of his museum at midnight, to the pealing of all the church bells in Paris. But M. Dupont or Mr Smith or Herr Müller, the businessmen, preferred to visit one of those places where, according to Léon Bopp, one 'could choose any of sixty girls in rank and file, all parading bare as ungloved hands, so that one could take in every detail of their persons, from red-ringed eyes to ingrown toenails'.

No one had time any longer for such little supper-parties as Alexandrine Gourdan had once arranged nor for strolling among the bushes of Justine Pâris's garden, in an atmosphere of pastorals and compliments. One simply wanted to be served with as much as possible at agreed prices. The menu reigned supreme.

In 1840 two hundred brothels, now called *maisons de tolérance*, existed in Paris. These 'tolerated' establishments, since they were open to all, very soon expanded beyond the former boundaries imposed upon prostitution by tradition and law. The small, quiet residential area of the Ile de la Cité at the centre of the capital remained as free from harlotry as ever and the environs of the Palais Royal quarter were still as crowded with whores as they had always been. But on the whole it was the same in Paris as in London, Berlin or Vienna. With the multiplication of classes of citizens the districts merged into one another and the new circular roads which had arisen on the site of the former walls proved more attractive than the narrow old streets they surrounded to an exuberant society untroubled by misgivings in its promiscuity.

Regiments become divisions

Louis-Philippe had indeed cleared the bare-breasted female frequenters of the Palais Royal out of that long-lived Augean stable. In particular he had closed the Galerie Orléans, where the foul weeds of previous dynasties had proliferated so rankly, to the nocturnal priestesses of love who roamed there. But his police then drove the entire swarm on to the boulevards, which were invaded at certain hours by vast columns of prostitutes.

The quantities of free and easy girls in the streets of Paris and its conspicuously numbered houses had really grown from regiments to divisions. There had been thirty thousand of them under Louis xv, who not only accepted the title of 'well-beloved' from his subjects but also allowed them a fair consumption of love themselves. After Waterloo twenty thousand still lived on the presence of allied troops in Paris and the excitement of the returning emigrants. But in 1840 Paris had no less than 42,700 registered prostitutes in a city of 900,000 inhabitants. Allowing for the numbers of these who were women and children, the proportion appears higher than had ever existed in Paris before. The fresh wave of consumers had necessitated an increased supply. The old profession, with an adaptability matured over millennia, had met the challenge within a few years, adjusting itself more rapidly than other branches of the national economy, traffic and public life, to the new conditions. Love was now mass-produced. Standardization had taken place of refinement and instead of prostitution being concentrated in certain quarters of a town, the modern capital city had become saturated with supporting bases and communicating arteries of harlotry. The artificial network of the contemporary amusement industry, almost invisible and yet sparkling in all directions, like the snare of the heavenly blacksmith Vulcan, had caught the new world in its own shame.

Two world wars

'Indeed I have long since learnt that vice is really nothing
but disorder and lack of due proportion.' – MONTAIGNE

The statement that it is not the prostitute but the decent woman
who is a product of civilization is one of those apparent paradoxes
popular at the end of the last century. Creative minds, however,
declined to accept it and set about a thorough investigation of the
truth.

As a result of the German victory of 1870–71 France had ceased
to be a monarchy and thus rather suddenly outstripped both
Germany under the Emperor William I and Victorian England by
about half a century. Among the new themes in favour with artists
and writers in quest of reality that of the prostitute soon came to be
preferred. While ordinary citizens and the boulevard Press concentrated uncritically and unprofitably upon the fashionable
cocottes, even those of the fallen empire, the new generation of intellectuals sought out degraded women in their own environments,
not for sensational reasons, but almost in a spirit of brotherly love.

Zola's Nana

While it was being rumoured that Bismarck was cultivating Mme
Paiva, who had married first a Portuguese marquess and then a
Count Donnersmarck, Zola chose the gay Blanche d'Antigny to be
the model for his *Nana*. Blanche had once gone for a stroll along the
boulevards naked under her cloak for a bet, and also performed a
number of other foolish but charming exploits. The conduct of the
young women of the old aristocracy of Europe in its various capitals was such that one could hardly blame the liaisons maintained
by young lords and counts with well-known courtesans. On the
other hand artists and writers found that the humbly-born girls
who made things so easy for them had souls and also that their
mode of life exerted a fascination all its own.

There were some exceptions to this rule, such as Picasso, who did not want collectors to feel that they had to have pictures of brothel interiors hanging on their walls. But others openly visited these despised establishments, even when, like Degas, they stood the resultant canvases back to front against the walls of their studios. The first scientific investigations of the problem of prostitution began to be published, full of statistics and data which had to be altered from decade to decade. At the same time a dozen eminent painters started puzzling out, with their own eyes, the details of the mysterious lives of harlots.

Theme of the prostitute

The artists turned to this subject, of course unpopular at the time and thus making it hard for them to get their pictures accepted at any exhibition, not because they wished to produce a sensation, but because they were conscious of a secret community of interests between women who had always been barred from decent society and 'bohemians' who had chosen to live at its margin for the sake of their art. Eventually paintings and drawings of this sort became familiar to everyone and consequently the world took to the study, in an intellectual sense, of the outcasts from its ordinary social intercourse. In this way the prostitute, first treated as object and soon afterwards as subject, came to be a favourite theme for speculation by intelligent people and has remained so to this day.

The existence of painters and sculptors of animals is no surprise to anyone. But that Constantin Guys, who lived to be ninety, should have descended to the lifelong depiction of thousands of prostitutes was felt to be inexcusable by all but a small group of his friends, including, to be sure, such deathless names as those of Gavarni and Baudelaire. Guys, who had fought at the barricades in 1848 and reported events in crayon sketches, as was still done by correspondents during the Crimea War, had been fascinated by the strange association of naïve fancies with relentless tragedy, as exemplified by the animated puppets of soldiers' brothels. 'But if anyone wanted to satisfy his unhealthy curiosity by studying the drawings of Constantin Guys, he would find nothing there to lend a spice to his diseased imagination, only inevitable vice.'

Guys and Van Gogh

It was Baudelaire who coined the phrase *le vice inévitable* and there were few who understood its meaning as well as he. Reality for them meant something which had never before been seen in its natural atmosphere, the glare of the footlights being as deceptive as the darkness of night. The level below which it was impossible to fall, since it was already rock-bottom, exercised the attraction of a refuge upon imperilled minds, those threatened by madness, or those more numerous persons whose struggle for normal happiness had been impeded by some infirmity.

Vincent van Gogh lived for years with a Flemish prostitute whom he repeatedly painted. Even in the crises which marked his later life at Arles he still took refuge in the local brothel of the little town, until the day in 1888 when he cut off his ear and sent it, carefully packed, to one of the girls there, whom lack of money had so often prevented him from visiting.

Toulouse-Lautrec

Henri Marie Raymond de Toulouse-Lautrec-Monfa, the son of a count, had been crippled while still a boy as the result of two accidents. He had therefore been obliged to give up riding and hunting. It was not until he was just twenty, when he took a studio in the rue Tourlaque, Montmartre, that he resumed an active life. It is prudently described in the catalogue of his works at the Albi Museum as having been motivated by a 'thirst for hard work and alcohol'. But in reality he was becoming more and more closely acquainted with the world of prostitutes. At first he simply painted in studios near various small cafés, dance-halls and brothels. Then he began to work in the brothel itself, the house in the rue d'Amboise for instance, and even to live at No. 6, rue des Moulins, a brothel as famous in those days as the *Perroquet Gris*, with its big No. 2, in the rue de Steinkerque, where he was no less stimulated.

It is easy to understand the distress of provincial dignitaries at having to deal with an artist of this kind, whose fame they did not wish to repudiate but who at the same time, though he occasionally painted somewhat disreputable female singers and dancers, returned again and again with special preference, even showing a kind of nostalgia and tenderness in this connection, to the depiction of the interiors of brothels. It always happens in such cases that an artificial distinction is made between the artist and his subject, whereby he is reduced to the status of a critic and it is alleged that he meant his pictures to be a condemnation of vice. But in the case of Toulouse-Lautrec the question of vice did not arise at all. When he lived, as François Villon had once lived, in a brothel, he did so because he was unhappy and homeless, not because he wished to sleep with any of the girls. For that purpose no one needed to go to the rue des Moulins, still less to take his crayons with him. His wallet would have been sufficient. Life in the brothel, alternating between alcoholic stupor and those sudden intervals of lucidity which afflict all unfortunate persons, came to acquire the same dimensions, for the thousands of students of the paintings and drawings of Toulouse-Lautrec, as, for example, the *Maison Tellier* in Maupassant's memorable novel of that name. Such an establishment seemed thus to be one of the very rare places in a pitiless world where human beings, deprived by fate of everything except a little money, could purchase the illusion of a transitory happiness, the mirage of comradeship for a few hours and the deceptive appearance of affection and security.

Montmartre and Montparnasse

So it may always have been. But when the new century began, people felt that it would bring both overcrowding and isolation in its train, at any rate in the more advanced countries and their capitals. Even in the swirling days of the *belle époque* in the nineties the artists, as they looked down from their two hills, Montmartre and Montparnasse, had been the first to realize that no one could be lonelier than in a city of millions of inhabitants. They appreciated any port in the storm of their anguish, whether for a short or a long stay. They included such men as Foujita, Chas Laborde, Kees van Dongen, Kisling, Degas, Brayer, Vertès, Pascin, Schiele, Klimt, Pechstein, Kirchner, Masereel, Bayros, Willy Geiger, Zille and many others. As they did not frequent brothels merely to satisfy primitive appetites, that singular world was revealed to them more completely than it had ever been or ever will be to ordinary clients.

According to Dignimont:

We had found a cosy little brothel at the end of the rue du Pélican. One of the girls there, a tall blonde, was splendid. She had everything I needed, but I could never make a decent drawing of her because she was always busy ... One evening I gave her my card, since the woman in charge insisted on it, and arranged with the girl for an appointment at my studio on the following Tuesday, her day off. At the appointed time the bell rang. When I opened the door the girl was standing there all dolled up, wearing a tailor-made costume and a fox fur, quite the lady. She glanced through some of my drawings and on discovering some nudes demanded: 'Do some women really pose like that, stark naked? They ought to be ashamed of themselves!' I naturally assumed that she was joking. But when I asked her to undress she turned her back on me with indignation and banged the door in a rage. Some days later I learned that she had complained to the boss of her establishment. 'That painter asked me to do something I couldn't possibly agree to!'

Rouault, Brayer, Pascin

Perhaps this story explains why Rouault, probably the greatest religious painter of the present age, portrayed so many prostitutes in their professional environment, why Yves Brayer, who illustrated Paul Claudel's 'Satin Slipper' (*Le Soulier de Satin*, 1930), appears in many of his works to have been enraptured by the brothels of southern France, and why Pascin, born Jules Pinkas, who left first Prague and then Vienna for Paris, always had half a dozen nude girls strolling about in his studio, till eventually even this expedient ceased to be effective and he saw death approaching him through their bodies.

In such company the brothel, depicted by the great painters of the day, described by such outstanding writers as Zola, Maupassant, Carco, MacOrlan and Lenormand, as well as by Werfel, Schnitzler, Kaltnecker, Roth, Frank Harris, Pirandello and others, celebrated in verse by Aristide Bruant and dramatized by such playwrights as Courteline and Feydeau, entered upon the last stage of its development. But no one yet suspected that it would be the last, that political and social freedom under republican and democratic governments would end an institution which had lasted for centuries even in territories controlled by popes and princes of the Church.

The Chabanais

No one, certainly, who came to know it in this final phase could have guessed that its glitter was that of a museum piece. The word 'garish' might have risen to the lips of an exceptionally clear-sighted visitor to the Chabanais. But he would never have uttered it. For such an epithet has always been considered inapplicable to spectacles of real interest and the Chabanais unquestionably merited that description.

Aristide Bruant, the great singer, poet and cabaret-philosopher of Montmartre, wrote:

The rue Colbert and the rue Chabanais enjoy a European reputation. One might even say that their fame is global, considering that African and Asian monarchs have honoured the houses situated there with their presence and used to have special arrangements made for their reception. It is a fact that the programme for distinguished visitors provided, after the towers of Notre Dame, the Catacombs, the Louvre, the Vendôme column, the Panthéon, Napoleon's tomb and other sights of the city had been dutifully inspected, for a call at the temple of visual delights, even if princes had to take the risk of sharing them in the company of an enriched pig-dealer.

The place really had something of the atmosphere of a temple. It was run by a highly-cultivated woman. Men of national importance paid it flying visits. Many intellectual giants set up a kind of second home there, including Ernest Renan, author of *The Life of Jesus*, who could only puff his way up the ornate staircase with the help of the manageress, Anatole France and Guy de Maupassant, who had reproduced the Moorish Room of the Chabanais in his sumptuous seaside villa, so as to continue his enjoyment of the decorations in question even while on holiday.

Félicien Rops

It was a type of luxury which is probably only now, in retrospect, judged to be degenerate. The ingredients were depicted by the lasciviously minded caricaturists of the day, especially by Félicien Rops. He was far less concerned with humanity, even the humanity of the prostitute, than with various symbols of eroticism. Perhaps no Parisien would have tried to conjure up such forms of sexual mysticism in a drawing. But no aspect of Eros could remain superficial in the view of the Flemish artist. The more playfully he handled his pencil, the more disconcerting appeared the changes he rang, with the effect of monomania, on half a dozen constantly diversified motives, a method which turns an art into a cult.

248

Rops had illustrated Sade, de Nerciat, Barbey d'Aurévilly and other writers specializing in the dark side of love. The pomp of his drawings, with their melancholy nudes, has a touch of the funereal, like that at the Chabanais, where a mass of white figures paraded against a background of faded plush. Yet this setting for women and for male spectators was the best that the period – sometimes called the Makartian, after the Austrian painter Hans Makart (1840–84) – had to offer. The gilded legend, *House of All Nations*, displayed in the entrance hall of the Chabanais, the premises of which adjoined those of the National Library, was no exaggeration.

The Japanese Room – the Far East had lately come into fashion – was awarded a first prize at an international exhibition. The atmosphere of the Louis XVI Room obliterated a revolution and two empires. The bath-tub of gleaming red copper, owing to the exciting aquatic feats performed there by the charming Mlle Kelly, had become, according to Lanoux, 'a clandestine base for the Jockey Club'.

At the Chabanais, where the hedonists of two hemispheres met, and wealth, whatever its origin, held all the trumps, the lords of the turn of the century could be deluded into fancying themselves victorious over women who had meanwhile, without having acquired decorations, capital or any illusions at all, entered, by purely feminine methods, upon their dominion. They were the great courtesans of the *belle époque* and the enchanting female apaches of Montmartre. There were half a dozen famous beauties in each group. But in summary retrospect only two contrasted rivals stand out, La Belle Otéro and Casque d'Or.

Caroline Otéro

The former reached such a great age that she was not only able to cash in on the filming of her life-story but also to enjoy the proceeds. When she died at Nice in May 1965 obituarists were amazed to find that she had lived so long. The temperamental Andalusian had however retired as early as 1914, when she was just forty-five and still regarded as one of the most beautiful women of her time. She wanted the climax of her career to be remembered as its end. It was in fact a climax, despite her rival Cléo de Mérode, known as Cléopold from the favour of King Leopold II of Belgium. Mlle Otéro was the child of a Spanish gipsy mother and a Greek army

249

officer. It was no wonder that her flamenco dancing caused a sensation wherever she went. At fourteen she had already become the mistress of a Portuguese banker. Her next lover was an Italian count, whom she married and then proceeded to use the scanty remains of his fortune as gambling capital. At first she was very lucky, amassing large sums. Then her losses began to arouse comment. The fact that a Russian count whom she had ruined, shot himself after being abandoned by her, counted for little in her set. No doubt she was more admired for holding her position in the top flight of society, despite her numerous scandalous exploits and love affairs, with the assurance of a great lady, thus enabling the monarchs of powerful nations to associate with her on friendly terms.

The woman with the 'gold headpiece', on the other hand, stood at the summit of a pyramid based on the Paris underworld. Her friendship with one or two artists is not enough to allow one to forget the fact. She was a child of the East End of Paris. The duels fought on her account were not supervised by umpires or doctors, but were shot out as wild fusillades at a street-corner.

Casque d'Or

Amélie Hélie, born in 1878, a dance-hall beauty with a temperament like that of Lautrec's Goulue at the Moulin Rouge, wore her red hair piled up in a style now familiar from the personification of her by Simone Signoret. But Amélie was shorter than Simone and for all her solid build slender and agile. Her childishly plump cheeks contrasted with the bold glance of her slit eyes, which instantly set the 'Corsicans' of the various gangs alight. All Paris followed the warfare between Leca, who really was a Corsican, and Manda, his rival, not to mention other gang-leaders. The subsequent proceedings in court, where confrontation with the suburban charms of Casque d'Or caused the hard-boiled protagonists to confess in public that they loved her, founded the apache type of poetry without which no Parisian revue or music-hall can score a success even today. Manda himself, also known simply as 'L'homme', the 'Man', became immortal in consequence of this scene, when he retorted to the magistrate's rebuke:

'Yes, we did fight, the Corsican and I, because we love the same woman. We'd got her under the skin. If you don't understand that, then you don't know what it means to love a girl.'

Madame Otéro published her memoirs at the age of thirty-five. Almost at the same time a volume appeared entitled *My Days and Nights*, constituting the reminiscences of Casque d'Or. In one passage she describes, with her own peculiar blend of impudence and poetic feeling, her application to a *maison* for seasonal employment.

My days and nights

As soon as autumn comes to an end one goes down into the heart of Paris and knocks at one of those doors which hasn't got a sign over it but displays instead an absolutely unmistakable number. Tap, tap. What can I do for you? Well, I say. December's here already and January, February and March are waiting for us and I'm one of those plants which can't stand the cold of winter. Would you like to see my legs?

Then they say, Come along in. And indoors it's so snug and warm that one immediately wants to strip to one's chemise and stay like that. A fortnight later one's so completely forgotten the draughty street-corners up our way that the mere sight of a wet overcoat is enough to astonish us.

Those were two different worlds. So it is easy to understand that in a house near the Gare Saint-Lazare the auburn-haired queen of the apaches, in a child's frock, with her 'gold headpiece' restyled as a pigtail, was perched on the cash-desk as if she were the proprietress's niece. A well-groomed old gentleman, who came every Tuesday and Saturday, brought her a spade and pail and other playthings, asked her whether she had learnt her catechism yet and finally enquired in a low voice about the price.

Two worlds

Listen [Casque d'Or wrote]. I've often asked myself what the real reason can be for the superiority of the so-called 'great' world. But I've never yet found an answer. No doubt it gives one an agreeable feeling to wear smart underclothing, pass the kind of laws that suit one and preach endless sermons about virtuous behaviour. But it would be a decidedly better plan not to be so presumptuous, for that's in fact what's wrong with the world in question. They sit in court and sentence the rest of us without mercy. Their police are always after us. Their Prefects order our men to be executed. Their priests tell us we will go to hell and their capitalists gamble on our hunger. But no sooner have the street-lamps been turned low than off they go to pay us a visit. And once they've got us stripped to our chemises they stop their gabble, their delusions of

251

grandeur collapse and their arrogance disappears. They all start stammering like little boys who want twopence to buy sweets.

By the time Casque d'Or was approaching forty and had at last resolved to get married, the lights had long since gone out over Europe. On the banks of the Somme and at Verdun the proud and the humble, the great world and the apaches, had been united in the millions who died in the First World War.

The First World War

But before they fell they had all undergone training in the communications zone and many had later been admitted to hospital. Hundreds of thousands on both sides had found a second home in reserve cadres. These male millions, who ate relatively better than those who had stayed behind and as a rule worked less hard than those in the armament industries or the women, had been provided with thousands of new brothels, since it was no longer practicable in modern armies to allow whores as camp-followers.

On the eve of the First World War Parent-Duchatelet had lamented, in a study which later became famous, the passing of the brothel, due to middle-class preference for clandestine prostitution and 'appointment houses', as being more discreet. 'The number of brothels diminishes from year to year, to the great regret of the authorities', he wrote. Carlier agreed with the sentiments of the police when he declared: 'All the efforts of the Prefecture of Police unfortunately come to nothing. They are unable even to ensure the continued existence of such brothels as there are.' The apostles of conventional morality no doubt welcomed the decrease of the numbers of brothels in Paris and Petersburg to a quarter of the previous figure, in Brussels to a sixth and even in Lyons and Antwerp to a half. But the men who knew the position at first hand were worried.

New wartime laws were passed affecting this sphere as well as others and its free development was subjected to regulation. Roaming girls or women could not be tolerated in the communications zone. It was impermissible for whole armies to be exposed to infection by venereal disease. In the face of such considerations all the usual objections to the brothel were dismissed – for instance the inability of an inmate to decline, as her street colleague could, the attentions of a client, and the tendency of the resident harlot to take less care of herself than the freelance, since the former could rely on a constant stream of customers.

Soldiers' brothels

In addition to numbers of improvised brothels in both large and small towns within communications zones and supporting garrisons, a speciality of this war was the new motorized field service brothel, the vehicles for officers or men being carefully distinguished by a blue light for the former and a red for the latter. The rush for them was so great that many prostitutes withdrew from the front line with substantial savings after only three weeks' attendance.

PRICE LIST

A. *Beverages*

Champagne, Henkell, Dry, per bottle ...	18 marks
Bordeaux Château Lafitte	6 ,,
Hungarian Wine	8 ,,
Beer, large bottle	1.50 ,,
Coffee per cup	1 ,,
,, per small jug containing 6 cups ...	6 ,,
,, per large jug containing 12 cups ..	12 ,,
Tea per glass	.60 ,,
Sodawater, small bottle	.30 ,,

B. *Intercourse*

All night	30 marks
Two to three hours evening or night ...	20 ,,
One hour	10 ,,
Any period between 9 a.m. and 6 p.m. ...	10 ,,

Lodz, March 1917.

Social Discipline Police

The brothels of the Belgian communications zone are the subject of drawings by Zille and George Grosz and have been described by Vogel, Henel, Plivier, Koeppen, Remarque, Destevsky and others.

According to Ernst Jirgal:

Only the brutish side of love, no, less than that, remained. The female merely acted as a fast and automatic deflector of lust. Consequently all family feeling was destroyed, both its germ in the younger men and its flowering in their seniors. Neither well intentioned 'Mother's Days' nor strict marriage laws were of any avail against this hidden plague-spot. For the strange thing is that evil once learned is never forgotten.

If anything could justify this traffic it was the deplorable incidents which occurred wherever no brothels existed or were not numerous enough to meet demand. All the belligerent nations had to deal with the assaults made by battalions at war strength on pleasure resorts, as happened at Cairo in 1915, or on individual brothels, as at Sedan, Ghent, Lodz and other places. But the control of mere contacts between soldiers and women gave the organizing authorities just as much trouble. During the First World War it only proved possible to impose complete abstinence on servicemen so long as hostilities were expected to be short. In the Second World War the idea was given up from the start. The soldiers were therefore allowed to meet a rapidly changing succession of women who came from environments impracticable to supervise, a large proportion being of hostile nationality or natives of occupied regions. After venereal disease the betrayal of secret information was the worst danger associated with wartime prostitution. It was for this reason also that freelance whores were only seldom tolerated in towns within communications zones.

Prostitution and espionage

As nothing much has ever been learnt from the rank and file, none of the nations at war seems to have made any special efforts to pass female agents through the brothels for common soldiers. But *demimondaines* of all complexions were launched on the trail of officers.

According to Joseph Roth:

The proprietor of the hotel where the officers were billeted, a Silesian named Brodnitzer, who had somehow or other found his way to the frontier, opened a casino. He hung a large placard from the window-frame of the café announcing that he stocked the equipment for games of all kinds, that a band would play every evening until the small hours and that he had engaged 'well known female singers from the popular halls'. The novelties began with pieces rendered by a miscellaneous collection of eight muscians. Later on the so-called 'Nightingale from Mariahilf' appeared, in the shape of a fair-haired Oderberg girl. She sang waltzes by Lehar, then the daring ditty entitled *When in the Night*

254

of Love I Turn to the Grey Dawn and as an encore gave us *Under My Little Skirt I Wear Pink Frilly Undies*. Such was the way in which Brodnitzer raised the expectations of his customers.

Roth, Rasputin and Redl

Those who wished to see more than the undies had to embark upon very much closer relations with the more or less renowned singers, dancers and plain bed-companions available, thus giving chances to the various secret services which only strike us as toylike dummies in retrospect and when reading about James Bond. In those days their activities were really a matter of life or death, especially for the female spies concerned. The main arena for these long traditional practices had been eastern Europe, partly because Rasputin was not the only Russian out of whom women could get anything they liked, and partly because the homosexual Austrian Colonel Redl was only one of many officers who had made a remarkable mess of their sexual book-keeping even before the war.

A more complicated case, though less important in its outcome, was that of another homosexual, the Rumanian attaché Trajan Starcea, who had formed a relationship in Vienna with a student named Jorga. When the evidence obtained permitted Jorga's arrest, it turned out that the Rumanians had quite simply forced him to spy on Austria because homosexuality was severely punished in those days, under the old empire. At the trial it was further revealed that a certain Rumanian had put his pretty mistress at the disposal of several Austrian officers in succession and passed the information gained in this way on to Bucharest.

A serious turn of events

The simplicity of such proceedings was not realized until the game took a serious turn. It looked as though the fashionable world of the *belle époque* after such a gay display of fireworks for so long between Madrid and Petersburg, Paris and Rome, had elected to take its departure against an appropriate background of thunder and lightning constituted by the war. Now that the events of those years have been half forgotten, they may be regarded as exemplifying the interaction between espionage and prostitution, now briefly to be considered, more effectively than the similar phenomena of the Second World War, still being used to a large extent as illustrative material.

The names of Mata Hari and Gaby Deslys continue to be remembered. Gaby Deslys had the luck, thanks to King Manuel II of Portugal (1908–10), to join the ranks of highly-placed mistresses. The funds put at her disposal by the British Secret Service should probably be regarded as more in the nature of an honorarium than anything else. She can hardly be said to have performed the true office of a spy from her position at the side of her dethroned protector. But there was of course a great deal of gossip in the circles about the exiled monarch.

Mata Hari and Liane de Pougy

Mata Hari was perhaps the boldest dealer in the sex market who had been known since the shameless young Liane de Pougy had forced her way into polite society from the provinces. Liane had taken the line of least resistance by hurling herself at the head of the Prince of Wales. It took a conceited fool like D'Annunzio to lay down positive vestments at her feet before she could pass into history. Mata Hari on the other hand, born Margarete Zelle and of mixed Dutch and Indonesian blood, used up and burned out the matter of a dozen adventurous careers in her forty-two years of life. At nineteen she set out in the company of a colonial army officer for Asia, where she found herself attached to one of those groups of Europeans devoted to slaking their tropical ardours in a round of orgies. She may not have learnt there, as she later boasted, the entire lore of the Kamasutra. But she did become familiar with debauchery in several forms and probably she did not have to overcome many scruples after the failure of her marriage, when she turned to earn her living on the Paris pavements.

She was saved from the worst that might have happened by an institution that had come into being in Paris shortly before the war. This was a marginal phenomenon of the world of prostitution in the shape of the *maison de rendezvous*, a 'house of appointment', where there were no prostitutes. The proprietresses of these establishments limited themselves to assisting females who occasionally practised free love to find partners of substantial means, who in their turn were averse from the services of professionals. Madame Zelle-Leod, a nestling recently tumbled from her refuge, but only after undergoing an extensive education there, accordingly found the very vocation to which she was best suited.

Sacrificed to the bureaucracy

One of her admirers arranged for her first appearance on the stage, beginning in a small way, at such exclusive clubs as she had been only too familiar with in Java, and later in public, on the crest of the current wave of enthusiasm for everything Asian. She toured Europe. Men ruined themselves for her sake, a circumstance from which she could hardly fail to draw profit, and important personalities fell into her lap like ripe apples. They included Holland's Prime Minister, French statesmen and German princes. The first items of information such circles imparted to her facilitated the remunerative sale of her Neuilly villa, with all its furniture. Then it became her turn to provide information. But it is very doubtful if she ever learnt any secrets of special military value. She never seems to have done anything more than was absolutely necessary to go on drawing the generous annuity paid her by the Central Powers. Her execution as a German spy in 1917 led to further exaggeration of her already overestimated services. She did not therefore fall a victim to any particular daring on her part, but to the boundless bureaucratic self-conceit of those who administered the German espionage system of those days, by which every agent was given an unalterable cover-number, preceded by a letter indicative of his or her country of origin. Mata Hari's number, H 21 (H standing for Holland), was picked up from a telegram in cipher and decoded. This event practically sealed the fate of the beauteous lady in question.

Some authors, unwilling to believe in such amateurish proceedings, have stated that the Germans wanted to get rid of Mata Hari, since she was costing too much and doing too little. Their opinion is supported by the fact that some German women agents worked so desperately hard that doubtless no such bureaucratic stab in the back would have been tolerated.

The Fräulein Doktor

One of these was the legendary 'Fräulein Doktor', according to J. R. Spinner, 'a female with nerves of steel, a cutting edge to her intellect, a sensuality under perfect control, a fascinating exterior and the eyes of a demon'. She was therefore clearly a predecessor of the type of woman which cropped up in the middle of the twentieth century during the 'cold war'. She carried far too many guns for the usually still aristocratic officer of 1914–18, whose monocle already tended to cloud over under the influence of considerably less steam than she generated. She must be held responsible for the preparation of the sensational surprise attack on the Lüttich fortress, for the twice-repeated reconstruction of the German espionage network in France at the height of hostilities and for the unmasking of the Greek double agent Cudoanninis. She escaped from a Paris hotel occupied almost exclusively by secret service men, which she had penetrated in the disguise of a chambermaid. There-after, in the possession of highly important documents which she had stolen, she literally shot her way into Switzerland.

It was not until 1918 that fate caught up with her, simply because she had impressed more men than she could herself remember. During a tour of inspection behind the French lines, which she had undertaken in the disguise of a South American hospital nurse, a Belgian officer recognized the fair and faithless one. A desperate series of improvisations saved her from denunciation. But the shock had been too great for her equanimity and the declaration of the armistice in November added its weight to her change of mind. She first covered her traces by burning all the evidence of her employment and then had the sense to renounce all further service in this line for ever. If it had turned out otherwise Fräulein Dr Annemarie Lesser would have faced Heinrich Himmler with one of the most difficult decisions of his life, viz. whether to let her go as he did Lise Meitner, use her as he used Canaris or destroy her as he destroyed so many other Jewesses.

Her virtuosity in espionage outstripped that of any of her rivals, including even the once-renowned Gertrud von Oppeln, Countess of Nys by marriage and a close friend of the Kaiser. Yet in the interests of spying Gertrud had sunk to the status of a communications zone harlot. By the time her husband mercifully put an end to her life she had become syphilitic, a drug addict and a mere ruin of her former self. He was not only acting symbolically when he laid her corpse, marked with the signs of all she had undergone, in the bed of her chief in the secret service. If all the victims of such officers were to be treated in like manner, their beds would have to be stretched pretty wide.

Curiosities of espionage

Three curious cases remain to be mentioned. The Belgian hat-shop girl, Gabrielle Petit, the sort of person whom gossiping agents at the Vienna Congress used to call a 'little milliner', was a smart, resolute young woman who managed to prowl around all over the place, wherever there might be something important to learn, disguised as a German lieutenant. Hers was a rare instance of male impersonation behind the enemy's lines, for the mere discovery of her sex would be bound to arouse suspicion.

Then there was actually a pair of Lesbian lovers, Louise and Léonie. It would be indiscreet to identify these ladies more closely, since the names of both appear on war memorials and in the roll of the Legion of Honour. They set up a whole network of dozens of spies, crossed the front lines on countless occasions with the utmost daring and passed on all sorts of small details of information only of interest during positional warfare but in such a situation particularly valuable. Last but not least they accomplished, in their fanatical patriotism, a feat usually deemed impossible to bring about. They suppressed what is doubtless the strongest of the many forms of jealousy, namely that directed against the whole of the opposite sex. Each allowed the other, if the act could not be avoided, to have dealings with men.

War in the brothels

In comparison with this dedicated severity, the activities of those who frequented the almost official meeting-places of spies, such hotels as the Savoy in Lodz, the Bristol in Warsaw and the *Fledermaus* ('bat') in Zurich, resembled a farce appended to a tragedy. Probably the wildest scenes took place at Salonica, where the Allies and the Central Powers engaged in mutual espionage through the inmates of one and the same brothel. The British General Cory had enrolled on his side one after another of these alluring little creatures, without realizing, in his inordinate zeal, that they were already working for a certain Herr Schenk. As soon as the Greek charmers had heard enough from Cory, they made a business trip to Larissa, where Herr Schenk not only learned what Cory had wanted to know but also briefed his corps of *hetairai* in what they were to tell Cory. This idyllic situation came to an abrupt end when the first professional, a representative of the Intelligence Service from Malta, took a hand. One of the naughty little creatures was shot, while General Cory was transferred to a different branch of the Army.

Women secret agents

The subject of the female spy, for all its popularity, leads to considerable differences of opinion. Talkative spies are inconceivable. So long as they are active they are forbidden to give their views on professional matters and after retirement they are seldom in a position to do so. Consequently, verdicts as to the suitability or otherwise of women for secret service work are few and far between. The former argument that women know too little about military affairs to be effective in the job has long been obsolete. It is only in the rarest cases that an agent decides what information is required and only experts can judge what it may be worth. Accordingly, it seems clear that there may still be room for women to operate somewhere along the line between Pontecorvo and James Bond. Again, attention has been called to the 'difficulty of finding a woman who, in addition to all the other qualities needed, such as beauty, worldly sophistication, refinement and intelligence, possesses the ruthless temperament which alone can ensure lasting success'. This passage is taken from an anonymous secret service memorandum. Actually, so far as ruthlessness is concerned, there can be no harder school for developing such a disposition than any sort of prostitution, from that of a street-walker to that of the highly-paid 'call-girl'. Many women have in fact embarked upon the dangerous path of espionage in order to retrieve the capacity for sentiment that they have lost. Surely the German Naval Codebook acquired as the result of an hour's flirtation aboard the pocket battleship *Kronprinzessin Cäcilie* must have meant a hundred times more to 'Red Amy' than the tariff of twenty thousand gold francs recorded as that of such outstanding celebrities as Léonide Leblanc, Cora Pearl or Anne Deslion!

Only sheer physical violence, which does sometimes unexpectedly occur even during scenes of erotic entertainment, puts women out of action more easily and faster than would be the case with their male colleagues.

The cock and the blonde

This happened at Aix-les-Bains during the First World War at a time when the French were making promises to the Italians at the expense of British interests. For that reason the latter were not admitted to a conference between the French Foreign Minister Pichon and an elderly Italian marquess. The British Intelligence Service investigated the participants. Pichon, a shrewd politician, formerly a journalist, was judged unassailable. But the Italian was reputed highly sexed and addicted to the most peculiar practices.

A certain charmer, with whom the marquess was still infatuated, duly arrived in Aix, accompanied by two male secret agents. A bargain was soon struck with the young woman, a blonde somewhat on the stout side. She was to celebrate the end of the conference by staging an orgy in the suite occupied by the Italian at his hotel. More precisely, she was to appear in a white gown cut excessively low and strangle a cock in the marquess's presence.

It turned out that gallic cocks had been underestimated by the British Secret Service. The bird fought so fiercely as literally to mangle his blonde executioner. Her gown was torn to shreds and she panicked. Her screams brought a number of people into the room. They found the old man in a trance, the girl half naked and covered with blood and the cock still no more than half dead. It was only due to the deft action of a British agent who had rushed in with the local police that the minutes of the conference could be stealthily extracted from the pocket of the unnerved marquess.

Lessons of the war

The lessons which the authorities considered they had learnt from five years of an exceptional situation were more significant than the interaction of war and prostitution. Millions of men, in fact almost the entire male populations of the most highly civilized nations in Europe, had been taught to obey. They had all been obliged to have the duration, environment and date of the satisfaction of their erotic requirements prescribed for them and to undergo, after their visit to a brothel, procedure to which no one would ever have dared to subject a human being at liberty. It seemed perfectly natural, therefore, to retain a dictatorship so convenient to governments, to exercise the strictest control over prostitution in future, to close the brothels and, for the rest, to act in accordance with the principle that nothing which is prohibited can exist.

This development, in direct opposition to public opinion and the general relaxation of standards of behaviour, came as a surprise. Its causes were not recognized until its triumph had been assured. For the policy of 'abolition' had already been heard of before the war. No less a personage than Queen Victoria had supplied its slogan with her announcement that 'Her Majesty is affronted by the existence of slaves who belong to the same sex as the Queen'.

Had the Prince Consort formulated a similar expression of the modesty prevailing at the highest social level, a humanity purified of all sexual immorality might have been able to enter upon the return journey to Paradise. But the world had ceased to evolve in accordance with the conceptions of crowned heads.

The abolitionists

A strange race began between illusion and reality, in which the abolitionists had a monopoly of the former. The best one can say of them is that they were sincere in their beliefs. Josephine Butler (1828–1906) may really have been convinced that she was doing the world good by tirelessly proclaiming at meetings and in her writings, throughout her life, that all hygienic measures were merely excuses for the further degradation of women. It was not tolerable, she declared, to set up a double moral standard for men and women respectively by obliging prostitutes to be registered, medically examined, restricted for their accommodation to communal dwelling in certain quarters or houses and subject to surveillance by the police.

If anyone serving today in an administrative department of the police concerned with morals were to read what Josephine Butler wrote, no doubt the sweat would come out on his brow. Modern experts are all agreed that the police, as the guardians of public order, are taking every possible step, in accordance with the above principles, to limit the forms and effects of the permanent evil of prostitution to endurable proportions. On the other hand a British politician named James Stuart declared on behalf of Mrs Butler that, 'The world has become a better place as a result of her life.

262

The seed she sowed can never perish.' The facts that in this better world some thousands more syphilitics than ever before were soon at large and that the seeds which they sowed in their turn, so far from perishing, produced syphilitic children with the most frightful hereditary taints, are of course due in the first place to the behaviour of debauchees. But the unrealistic demands made in order to counteract such lapses must be blamed on the abolitionists.

German female champions of morality

After the First World War Katharina Schenken and Anna von Pappritz, in Germany, continued Mrs Butler's campaign. In France, Italy, Austria and other countries, similarly minded women, supported by lawyers, doctors and in particular the clergy, joined in. In the Berlin parliament a unique event took place. All the feminine deputies, whatever party they might belong to, voted for the abolitionist measure providing for the prohibition of prostitution under legal penalties for offenders. Only the Federal Council, by refusing its agreement, prevented the mistakes of St Louis the crusader from being repeated in twentieth-century Germany.

The isolation of these champions, who saw no further than their own ranks, is proved not only by the promulgation of such laws at the beginning of the 'gay twenties', of all periods, but also by the effects the abolitionists themselves exercised, by pressing through a modified form of their Bill, which at least managed to get brothels forbidden, on the look of the streets and the unrestrained pleasure-seeking in the clandestine prostitutes' districts. According to Bauer, 'As anticipated, street prostitution became more obvious than ever after 1 October 1927, when the new law came into force.'

Strange to say, opposition organized by the prostitutes themselves did not improve matters, either because, as many experts maintain even today, no less than eighty per cent of them were imbeciles, or else because the invariably masculine treasurers of such organizations absconded time after time with their members' subscriptions, thus rendering action by the associations impracticable.

Matron and whore

The male world was accordingly deprived of the spectacle which would otherwise have been the only phenomenon to bring the twentieth century into prominence above all its predecessors and successors. This would have been the final battle between matron and whore, the two female prototypes, which have been locked in conflict for millennia in an unremitting, embittered and often secret duel.

The years of inflation and the aftermath of war had of course so widely undermined ideas of honesty that the girls who sold no more than their bodies and often found their earnings only too rapidly devalued seemed to some observers the most reliable traders of that era. Heinrich Mann, for instance, in 1931 wrote in one of his sarcastic essays:

There has been a shift in moral standards. There is now not much to choose between those of the underworld and ordinary society. Members of the latter prostitute themselves more often and venal women have more respect for sincerity. Nothing seems to stand in the way of peaceful communication between them.

Once this shift in moral standards had been brought out into the open it continued quite publicly and consequently exercised more influence on everyday life – such phenomena as the entertainment industry and its supply of diversions in the cinema, the theatre and literature – than ever before. Officially there were no more brothels. But as they had not ceased to exist, life could be full of surprises, and one had to be a pretty cool customer not to yield to the temptation of such unexpected adventures.

An arrival in Berlin

Willy Haas wrote in the section of his reminiscences descriptive of his first contact with the ferment of post-war Berlin:

The lights had gone out in our compartment before we reached Berlin. The terminus was pitch-dark. Machine-gun fire could be heard a long way off. There was not a soul about in the Potsdamer Platz. No underground trains or omnibuses were running. The hotels near the station were either full up or else no one wanted to let a room to a newly-married couple. At ʃast one of the hotel porters took pity on us. 'Over there,' he said, 'on the first floor, there's a small boarding establishment still functioning. You might enquire there perhaps.'

We went over to the place. Inside we could hear laughter, shouting and the clinking of glasses. We rang. After a while the door was opened.

The girl who had opened it was stark naked. My wife didn't know where to look. The girl asked, without the slightest embarrassment, what we wanted.

'Could we have room for one or two nights?' I enquired. She looked us up and down for a moment, then nodded.

'All right, come on in.'

That was our introduction to Berlin.

The twenties

They began with the rattle of machine-guns, manned by people who still could not forget the war. But indoors everything had changed. It was not the naked girl who was embarrassed, but Frau Haas. Nor was it the former who was regarded with contempt. It was she who gave the respectable couple at the door a cool stare. They were outside, the rest were indoors. The 'twenties' cannot be understood by anyone who did not personally undergo their weird fascination.

It was not only in Berlin that the abolitionists had triumphed. The brothels of Austria and Hungary were also closed, as though any claim to that particular form of entertainment had been forfeited by losing the war. In Vienna these establishments closed their doors in 1921, at Graz in 1926 and at Budapest in 1927. But what followed looked very much like the situation in Berlin. Bruno Vogel in his study of post-war prostitution gives statistics according to which every third house in Budapest contained accommodation for assignations or for a temporary night's lodging or let rooms by the hour.

Franz Werfel devoted a masterly obituary notice in his novel *The House of Mourning* to an imaginary building in an imaginary street, the Gamsgasse, at Vienna. There can be no doubt that this establishment, which automatically disintegrated, so to speak, after the death of the proprietor, Maxl Stein, presented all the features anticipated in a feudal brothel by visitors to the metropolis on the Danube from the many countries owing allegiance to the imperial crown. The house maintained a tradition reaching back to the reign of Karl IV of Luxembourg, an unmistakable atmosphere to which the furniture, the walls, the inmates and the mysterious perfumes all contributed, together with that air of slightly somnolent indifference characteristic of the men and women of the epoch of Franz Josef as they drifted to their downfall.

The house is still standing [Werfel wrote]. But it has been taken over by the local leather trade and even the unique, once irresistible fragrance of the antechamber has been completely dissipated, according to reliable reports, by that of Russia-leather.

For the rest, every death is decreed by fate and nothing perishes before its time. Wandering at night through streets clamorous with illuminated advertisements, the modern citizen reads at every corner the names of resorts dedicated not to pleasure but to dancing. The Negro's saxophone wails. Real ladies pass in and out through the dazzling doorways. Their delightful, unencumbered legs issue a clearer invitation than was once the rule in the Gamsgasse.

The woebegone street-walker, brought to this pass by the struggle, unrecorded and positively unending, to earn a living, shuffles wearily along the forsaken pavement. Perhaps there are no more brothels left at all now.

In the victorious countries such evasions of the real issue were plainly considered superfluous. The liberal outlook of the Allies had proved itself so convincingly superior to the puritanical conventions of society under William II and the widower's austerity of Franz Josef that in Paris the campaign for abolition at first fell on deaf ears or was actually greeted with loudly expressed derision. Women had also become emancipated in the French capital. But instead of demanding laws against brothels people turned to visit the abodes of free love, the more expensive bawdy-houses and the Bois de Boulogne, taking their families with them or making up such parties of both sexes as Victor Margueritte described in his *La Garçonne* ('The Bachelor Girl').

Literature of the new attitude to life

Zabeth and Monique took no interest in the selection but immediately dropped on to the sofa, clasping their hands behind their heads in the attitude of amused spectators. Lady Springfield dug her elbows into the bolster, so that she could look over Monique's shoulder and not miss anything. Assuming the air of an expert, she examined closely Irma's sturdy figure and Carmen's restless elegance, as they entered in their dressing-gowns, nodded politely to the visitors and, displaying perfect self-assurance, without being asked, each instantly slipped out of her single garment. Now that they were nude they showed no further trace of their origin or profession. They had been restored to a state of animal simplicity, like primitive beings before the dawn of consciousness.

Ginette, Michelle and that handsome male, Max, had undressed at the same time as Irma and Carmen, so that apart from Zabeth and Monique, who still remained clothed, the Turkish Room now contained simply a little flock of white beasts.

Margueritte's *Garçonne*, from a purely literary point of view, had gone rather far. But this author, the son of a general, was by no means alone in his daring. The main stream of release from inhibition took the same direction, which may be credited, thanks to Pierre Louys, André Gide and the young Montherlant, with carrying the most significant evidence of the recognition of equality of rights between the sexes. Male tutelage was the last thing contemplated by this attitude. On the contrary, it emphasized female emancipation equal to the man's in every respect and the participation of women in all the pleasures cultivated between the end of the war and the economic crisis. Painters, who had still been setting the fashion at the turn of the century, could now only ride on the crest of the wave. While Colette gave the inarticulate girls of the Parisian lower classes a voice and Barbusse, Céline, Octave Mirbeau and Maurice Sachs presented 'Eros Set Free', the graphic arts, formerly so eloquent, were reduced to staging charades like those of van Dongen and Foujita. The talented Japanese may in fact have suspected what was going on when, as a particularly hard-pressed victim of the French revenue authorities, he took a bamboo cage with him to a ball in Montparnasse. Inside the cage sat his beautiful mistress Fernande, 'dressed only', according to Lanoux, 'in a strip of ribbon. A placard hung on the cage announcing, "Woman for sale. Not guaranteed. The State accepts no responsibility." '

Kiki of Montparnasse

The queen of that era herself, Kiki of Montparnasse, who posed in the nude and magnanimously distributed her favours to all the regular customers of the Dôme and Coupole cafés, transferred her services to another kind of art when she became the model of a photographer of genius, Man Ray. The first time he saw her stripped he exclaimed, 'Don't look at me like that, Kiki, you confuse me!' But later on he invented the automatic shutter release, to enable him to produce a print of himself and his charming model on the same plate.

A good deal had to happen in France before the taste of its citizens for intimacy with the underworld could be vitiated. The first of the apocalyptic events required for this process was the economic crisis.

The following passage is taken from one of Scott Fitzgerald's short stories, 'Babylon Revisited':

Paul came over to say hello. 'It's a great change,' he said sadly. 'We do about half the business we did. So many fellows I hear about back in the States lost everything, maybe not in the first crash, but then in the second.'

Again the memory of those days swept over him like a nightmare – the people they had met travelling; then people who couldn't add a row of figures or speak a coherent sentence . . . The women and girls carried screaming with drink or drugs out of public places. The men who locked their wives out in the snow, because the snow of twenty-nine wasn't real snow. If you didn't want it to be snow, you just paid some money.

To take leave of the past by quoting 'Where are the snows of yesteryear?' was the most delicate way of expressing the situation. Far more drastic language was used by Wolfe, Hemingway, Gertrude Stein, Maurice Sachs, Tristan Tzara and others, as though they guessed what the world was in for.

The German High Command and the Paris brothels

The second of these events was the Second World War or, keeping to the limits of the present study, the decree by which houses of such long-standing fame as No. 12 rue Chabanais and No. 6 rue des Moulins were degraded to the status of 'Lodgings for Officers in Transit'. This phrase was explained for the benefit of young officers not yet familiar with the prudish circumlocutions of Hitler's Germany by a note to the effect that the hotels in question were under German sanitary control. With truly German thoroughness the address was followed by the name of the local underground station and directions to the nearest clinic. The leaflet also included the remarkable information that '99.5 per cent of all venereally infected cases have caught their disease from uncontrolled prostitutes', viz. not inmates of a brothel.

As Parisians were not deeply concerned with the health of German officers, the billeting of the conquerors in houses where the brilliant paintings of Toulouse-Lautrec still decorated the walls was not popular. The citizens had silently tolerated the preference for negresses shown by German visitors to the brothels before 1933, either by way of revenge for the occupation of the Rhineland by black troops or to smooth down the waves of enthusiasm aroused in unprepared spectators by Josephine Baker's banana plantation dances. But that leaflet issued by the German High Command was really the limit.

Marthe Richard

The third great event was the Liberation. It was found that the far-famed brothels of Paris were threatened by an even worse danger than 'German officers in transit' in the person of Madame Marthe Richard, renowned for her work as a spy for France and an acknowledged expert in all matters relating to prostitution.

The occasional collaboration of certain brothel owners with the Gestapo was of assistance to her. It turned out that even these outlawed French subjects, who paid over fifty-two per cent of their income to the State, had been expected by the whole country to prove their patriotism. The citizens at large were disappointed at not being allowed to decorate them like other people.

The most embittered conflicts in the parliamentary history of France ensued. Both the apostles of moral decency and the defenders of the brothels revealed a surprisingly close acquaintance with the intricacies and centres of the trade. It was actually suggested that the brothels, in order to prevent their being closed, should be nationalized, and that doctors should be appointed to manage them, the dangerous experiment of closing every such establishment in the country being abandoned altogether. But every argument in support of these proposals was met by Marthe Richard with the naming of another brothel-keeper who had collaborated with the Gestapo.

A flea-market in illusions

On 13 April 1946 the closure of the brothels, paradoxically enough already known as *maisons closes*, was decided upon. A most extraordinary kind of clearance sale, constituting a flea-market, so to speak, of outworn illusions, then took place. During the six months' grace allowed to establishments in the larger cities one hundred and ninety brothels sold off their contents. The highest prices were naturally obtained by the Chabanais, where the fittings and furnishings were associated with countless scandalous memories. The Chinese, Indian and Moorish Rooms had been visited by Pierre Louys, Oscar Wilde and very many other distinguished people. Marlene Dietrich had been there in the company of Erich Maria Remarque, though no one knew which of the two had suggested the idea.

The copper bath-tub

The ingenious apparatus supposed to have been first devised by Edward VII while Prince of Wales and the subject of contradictory explanations as to its purpose, found a purchaser at the price of 32,000 francs. The famous copper tub, in which innumerable champagne baths had been taken, was bought for 130,000 francs by a dealer in antiques and placed in the window of his shop in the rue Jacob.

According to the invaluable Romi two old ladies in black stopped one day in front of the window in question and after a while timidly unlatched the door and begged to be allowed a closer look at the show-piece. The shorter of the two explained: 'We ought to tell you, *monsieur*, that tub of yours, well, it brings back memories of our whole youth We used to be on the staff of the Chabanais in those days. We started there in 1896.'

Awkward consequences

The serious aspect of the new state of affairs became evident only a few years after the brothels had been closed. Senator Jean Durand, representing the Gironde Department, was the first to collect data significant for other countries as well as France. The number of prostitutes in Paris had risen from 10,000 to 20,000. Homosexuality had increased to an alarming extent. Cases of syphilis had doubled. Forty per cent of clandestine prostitutes had been found to be suffering from venereal disease as compared with 1.5 per cent of the inmates of brothels in former times. It might also be regretted that the hundred milliards of old francs previously paid in taxes every year by brothel-keepers were no longer available to the

Government. For the freelance whores now engaged in the same activities paid no taxes.

As Italy and even Japan had also prohibited brothels or brought former prohibitions of them into force, the civilized world now found itself in an entirely novel situation. The pressure of a rapid succession of political catastrophes and the influence of hitherto unknown political lobbies, such as that represented by the women deputies, had overcome more reasonable arguments and more penetrating intuitions as precipitately as the actual experiences of the authorities. It had been recognized before the new prohibitive laws had been passed that they could never be carried out to the letter. Consequently, so far from a new social order coming into being, an atmosphere of increased legal uncertainty arose and a dangerous rift between professional jurists and police practice permitted the prostitution rings, always quick off the mark, shrewdly advised and well supplied with funds, to exploit the unprecedented circumstances by organizing international collaboration.

Prostitution in the Third Reich

Merely for the sake of rounding off the picture, it may be noted that ever since the passing of the first abolition measure in 1927 only one European government, that of the National Socialists in Germany, had succeeded in solving the problem of prostitution, in this case by methods as simple as they were brutal. As people in that country had long since given up worrying about arbitrary arrests and behaviour of that kind, *souteneurs* and unpopular whores were packed off to the concentration camps. The rest were directed by various decrees to proceed wherever it suited the authorities. Fear of the notorious penalties involved prevented the victims from grumbling. The universal oppression of the dictatorship, which affected the entire nation, together with undernourishment, overwork and anxiety both for relatives and for personal fate, an anxiety which soon became general, all contributed to limiting the desire for sexual pleasure to a small official class. Members of the latter did not need professional harlots. As a rule they helped themselves by direct application to the various Leagues of women and girls.

The 'Arrangements' policy

As soon as the nations had been relieved from the burden of the war, and after the first years of reconstruction a certain level of prosperity began to be reached, it nevertheless appeared that the zealous women deputies had not affected prostitution in general but only certain conspicuous centres of it. Instead of a single brothel the police now had to control twenty or thirty freely operating whores, though they were given no actual orders to do so. This was the period of so-called 'arrangements', which has not yet come to an end. It involves both squabbles and compromises; nor have all countries proved equally adroit in dealing with improvisation on such a great scale. In Paris, for example, female welfare workers (*assistantes sociales*) were instituted to make preliminary contacts with individual prostitutes who had achieved notoriety and see that they did not transgress the law. In Vienna, on the other hand, a corps of women police soon made itself unpopular and is less successful today than its male rival, since the nymphs of the *Graben* had already got used to masculine police.

Positive action could neither be carried out nor was it expected, since no legal sanctions existed for any conceivable plan. The police could only raid criminal zones on the margins of prostitution and gradually build up a system for protecting young people. Meanwhile the campaign against infection remained so ineffectual that most European nations would today be threatened by a catastrophe in public health if since the Second World War new drugs had not come into play against the most serious venereal diseases.

Integration of the underworld

Decentralized prostitution, in Adorno's fashionable but very pertinent phrase, is now fully integrated and it may be added that society has facilitated this development by the very process of decentralizing the trade. In earlier centuries the bawdy-houses had been erected beyond the city boundaries or outside, though close to, the walls. They had therefore been isolated, cut off from communal, everyday life. But at present the decentralized structure of prostitution permeates the whole community. The countless tiny footholds gained in this way could be much more easily adapted to the general activities round them than the old brothels, not only because forty freelance whores could change their ground faster

272

than a single establishment with all its traditions, but also because such women were now themselves all members of the social order. Never has the prostitute been so little of a different being, so inconspicuous and on such intimate terms with the upholders of decorum as is the case today. Her skill in adapting herself to new modes of life has been repeatedly proved and may be regarded, perhaps, as one of the most cogent arguments against the imbecility so often asserted to characterize a large proportion of her colleagues.

Brothels might be closed. Prostitutes might even be chased off the streets or forcibly banished to the suburbs. But the actual trade in sex itself has been found unassailable. It has even been able to hold advanced positions, as is proved by the case of a Basel harlot, reported in a highly significant work by the Chief Commissioner of the Stuttgart Criminal Police, Willi Bauer. The woman had aroused the special resentment of her neighbours by beating her pet spaniel with a shoe. They were therefore all the more amazed when after herself confessing in court that she earned 60,000 francs a year by consorting with men the prisoner was discharged. She had taken advantage of the uncertain legal situation which prevails in Switzerland as everywhere else with regard to prostitution, which in itself incurs no penalty. It is only solicitation to immorality which is punishable.

Sexual promiscuity

This case indicates the tight-rope exercises, so to speak, which the police and the legal profession have to perform almost daily. Their task is so delicate that it hardly seems worth while. Women and girls who 'frequently change their partners', as the phrase goes, can only with difficulty be supervised in their drift to actual prostitution. Action by the authorities is therefore limited to intervention in untoward incidents, the sort of thing which more or less organized prostitution terms 'engine trouble'. If no such accidents occur, neither the French nor the Italian nor the German nor the British police have any chances worth mentioning of even exercising sanitary control over the women in question. The vast army of prostitutes at every social level, from that of the smart 'good time girl' who sends her parents affectionate postcards right down to the ranks of those who infest railway stations and barrack gates, enjoys a freedom, under the protection of democratic institutions, civic rights and its own lawyers, such as was not even accorded to the 'respectable' courtesans of Renaissance Rome. Prostitution as an abject and disreputable trade, repellently illustrated in so many books on the subject only ten years ago, has lost all meaning, if it ever had any worth mentioning.

Travelling potentates and ministers, even the grander sort of buyer or negotiator, are treated in every capital city to a supply of extremely attractive ladies, often including the most admired in the metropolis, as well as various 'beauty queens' and 'starlets' and no doubt also, depending on the rank of the guest, some representatives of even higher social stations, who might be supposed to have no longer any need of such introductions. Even in the prudish realms beyond the Iron Curtain, where dictatorial brooms had once swept so clean, a faultless service is maintained in the hotels reserved for foreigners to mobilize the feminine leaders of local society. East Berlin and Prague are at present outstripped in this field by Warsaw and Budapest. In Hungary particularly it is considered necessary to titivate the airline hostesses, who are pretty enough already, with every species of allurement. But within the next few years prostitution will undoubtedly have proved that it respects neither frontiers nor curtains – not even iron ones – and that it will always defeat even allegedly perfect systems of police control.

Supervision by taboo

At bottom this development is probably to be ascribed to the initiative in the abolition campaign having been taken by a vociferous but restricted group, which no one dared to oppose openly, and to the incessant cropping up of further groups, some quite small, each with its taboos. This agitation, however, is resisted not only by, in Willi Bauer's phrase, 'the primitive force of the sex instinct that slumbers in all normally disposed people' but also by the equally natural desire of society to enjoy its prosperity and the successful outcome of its struggle for peace. Every nation felt the post-war period to be a liberation from the oppressive years of war, whether these had been experienced as an occupied country, a dictatorship or merely as a critical emergency. Consequently the new freedom was widely interpreted as freedom to enjoy life.

274

It had scarcely been won before more or less voluntarily accepted supervisory organizations arose. Their functions turned out to be totalitarian in the sense that there could be no appeal from their decisions, and undemocratic for the reason that the members of such committees had not been elected by the masses but arbitrarily appointed. Adorno commented: 'It may be concluded, however, and contemporary neuroses support the conclusion, that the existing sexual taboos did not, in point of fact, cease to operate. All that happened was that a new type of suppression, working at a lower level, came into being, with all its destructive potential.'

Sexual taboos in Germany

The ensuing situation had never been conceived possible in a democracy nor had anyone expected the post-war period to give rise to it. Healthy and civically free adults found themselves engaged in an incessant conflict with the dictatorial pretensions of the clergy and those in charge of the young, in other words authorities, whether men or women, representative of special group interests and bent on influencing the normal development of society from such standpoints. Their efforts, which still continue, involve the imposition of new taboos at the very moment when class and race prejudices have at last been abandoned after a tiresome struggle accompanied by many reverses. The background of these exertions could only be illuminated by the insight of the judicious Adorno, who wrote: 'German sexual taboos fall into the category of the ideological and psychological syndrome of prejudice which helped to provide mass support for National Socialism and lives on in a form which its content clearly shows to be deprived of political connotation.'

The capital city is outlawed and the identity, or at any rate natural affinity, between the literature of the pavement and prostitution is covertly suggested. Private love-affairs, psychoanalysis, homosexuality and similar practices are defined as decadent without examination, their treatment in art and literature is condemned out of hand and the distribution of such productions is obstructed.

Dolce Vita

This suppression of the sex instinct has led, just as in the case of the prohibition of brothels, to a reaction which can only be compared

with an underground atomic explosion. No doubt the more grue-
some or seductive passages in books or films dealing with crime
could have been expurgated, though this action was never taken,
since the committees which might have been concerned all concentrated on the sexual element. That feature, suppressed as it was,
naturally combined with the similarly suppressed world of prostitution to create *la dolce vita*, in other words a recourse to the intimacy of a private circle, the last refuge of the allegedly free
twentieth-century citizen. In the domestic residence and the flat –
with the only danger an occasional resort by the police to tapped
telephone wires – homemade films and the meetings of exclusive
clubs, sexual interests and prostitution entered upon a new domain,
the most extensive, dangerous, inaccessible and indestructible
which had been known since the sumptuary laws of Augustus.

Public authorities in most European countries have always
talked in one way or another about the need to protect young
people, though the latter would have been bored to death by everything that was so sedulously withheld from them and have long
since turned to providing their own sets of stimuli for the sex instinct. Not only were the protests of the majority – much too
timid, to be sure – overridden in the pursuit of this policy, but the
interests of the so-called sexual minorities, which unquestionably
deserve to be taken just as seriously, were also ignored.

Sexual minorities

The existence of sexual minorities was first recognized in socio-
logical theory and debates on sexual conduct some years ago. The
persons concerned vary from the comparatively small group of
those addicted to perversion in the narrower sense of the word to
the incalculable multitude of human beings who can no longer take
pleasure in simple sexual intercourse or can only do so if it is
accompanied by circumstances of a special character. Even the
most renowned investigators in this field, so densely occupied since
the time of Freud, cannot agree as to what constitutes 'definitely
normal' or 'definitely perverse' behaviour, what in other words is
merely such a caress as even Roman Catholic priests, in their
advice to married couples, declare to be permissible, and what no
wife or even husband should tolerate. Kinsey's statistics prove
that the bedroom light is kept on more often in Greenwich Village,

the artists' quarter of New York, than it is, for example in Brooklyn, the working-class district. This fact alone shows how hopeless it is to attempt to obtain a comprehensive view of these most private of all private actions.

The consequences of this uncertainty are perhaps even more serious than those of the confusion prevailing in the sphere of prostitution with regard to the legal position and the practical measures to be taken. The least harmful result, because usually leading to rapid relief, is perplexity and resort to psychotherapy. More damage can be caused by both partners holding their tongues, deciding to live apart or putting up with a joyless marriage or suing for a divorce on account of erotic misunderstandings – in themselves of no importance and matters of utter indifference to outsiders. It is worst of all when feelings of guilt ensue, involving neurosis, psychosis, anti-social acts, a comparatively lonely life or complete isolation, exploding finally in the desperate commission of a sexual crime.

Reason and excess of zeal

The Roman Catholic Church repeatedly proves how wisely it can act as an institution, however often narrow-minded zealots may complain that they have not benefited overmuch from the enlightened behaviour in question. The policy of reassuring beforehand those about to marry, of preventing feelings of guilt from the very start, of warning a bride at once that her future experiences may not perhaps be exactly the same as can be observed among butterflies, is a proceeding today, in the twentieth century, involving precisely the opposite attitude to that which pious Christian women at earlier epochs believed themselves obliged to cultivate. For they often regarded the pleasures of natural sexual intercourse, even in marriage, as a sin and only surrendered to their husbands because they wished to have children.

The proscription of the entire sexual field for centuries has been mainly responsible for the imposition of that solid weight of guilt and inhibition under which modern society still labours. The only new development is that of many complications which would have been inconceivable in earlier times. These factors include the constant flood of sexual irritants in films, magazines and advertisements, close contact with the opposite sex in factories and offices with large staffs, increased sexual vitality among men who now only work a forty-hour week and housewives relieved of their former toil by today's domestic equipment, and finally the enhanced demand for a life of pleasure due to the incessant contemplation of fortunate, wealthy, handsome and admired individuals.

Males unprovided for

It was therefore by no means in any spirit of frivolity that in debates on the legal control of prostitution mention was repeatedly made of sexual minorities, in other words that numerous class of males unprovided for in the usual way. Discussion took place at two very different levels. But while the whores made up for their limited outlook by their professional experience, the politicians politely played down what otherwise might have appeared a somewhat singular subject in the grave surroundings of the various national assemblies.

The story may begin, for example, with a certain anonymous inmate of a *maison de tolérance* who, according to Romi, had been listening for a long time, with some of her colleagues, to the bragging of a client, who eventually announced that he had detached the wife of a friend from her conjugal duties for a single night. 'Why, that's most improper,' cried the girl indignantly. 'Fancy doing that to a friend! Next time you feel uppish, kindly come to us. That's what we're for, after all.'

One of the ladies compelled in 1956 to evacuate a prosperous establishment within six months expressed herself more pointedly.

There is as little to say about those whom I should describe as good customers as there is about those who are fortunate in life. I need say no more about them than would be enough to show my appreciation of their decent behaviour, tact and frank amiability. But there weren't many of them, unfortunately. The majority of our clients, mostly middle-class citizens, were unbalanced, obsessed or vicious . . . According to my own experience and that of my colleagues at least forty per cent of all visitors to brothels are sexually abnormal . . . A few days after our place closed we were asking one another, not without a certain amount of malicious amusement, to which of all those honourable ladies who had voted for closing down the brothels the various sadists, flagellants, chain-maniacs and ludicrous masochists who came to us would now go. While we were packing we kept thinking of our incestuously-given clients whom we always had to call 'Dad', unless they happened to be characters who called us 'Mother' or by the name of one of their sisters, not to mention the frequent visitors who, not daring to approach boys, forced us women to play Adonis to them.

All those prosperous citizens, respectfully saluted all over the district, tender husbands and affectionate fathers, arrogant lawyers, famous doctors and eloquent members of parliament, turned out to be mentally sick. As a rule their wives had no idea of the type and degree of their aberrations. It was only on us that they ventured to make their often appalling demands.

Reality can be appalling

This brief passage from Anne Salva's autobiography, *It Doesn't Make Me Blush*, is supported by examples as grotesque as they are dismal to read. But they are also highly significant, proving beyond doubt that everything is possible in this connection and above all that nothing is unimportant. Outside the walls of a brothel it is more difficult to obtain confessions and information of this sort, though it is only in ordinary society, among so-called healthy people, a region still insufficiently explored, that there is any chance of coming to their rescue in time.

In these cases accidental outbursts often throw a sudden light on critical states of mind, with effects no less grotesque than in the details reported from environments where as a rule narrators are less inhibited. A burglar, for instance, once forgot his original purpose, wasted valuable time and risked arrest because his mind was unexpectedly distracted and overwhelmed by the onset of a particular perversity.

A young couple getting ready for bed in their modest West Side apartment were disturbed by a masked burglar. He forced the wife, at gunpoint, to tie her husband to the bedpost with belts, then to strip, put on shoes with high heels which the intruder had found in the wardrobe and walk up and down in the room in that state. A series of brutal assaults followed. The husband was obliged to look on helplessly.

In this case, reported by McPartland, the husband may be supposed to have suffered appallingly during those few minutes. It seems almost incredible that in the same city there were other husbands who brought about similar situations themselves, as if they meant to prove that in point of fact nothing is impossible in the sexual field.

Blind victim

Heller, copied by Wagner and Pauly, quotes the following evidence:

During some of my frequent punishments I was gagged even more tightly and had a bandage fastened over my eyes. I like being so utterly helpless. My husband likes showing his power over me to his closest friends. It makes me ashamed but also rather excites me. On these occasions I wear a short, closely-fitting dress of black silk, white bloomers and black stockings. It's particularly embarrassing for me, because generally I'm tied up in such a way that my bloomers show. The dress, too, is cut very low and I'm not allowed to wear a brassière. But my husband's friends seem to enjoy the show very much and it's always flattering to realize that I'm the centre of attention in my attractive helplessness.

The friends then approached her. She admitted that she took a special pleasure in being squeezed and tentatively caressed by them, because she was unable to resist. She considered that she need not be so very much ashamed, since, like a human ostrich, she had a bandage over her eyes. The husband imagined himself to be a *souteneur* and she took the part of the prostitute he was keeping. But it would be wrong to say of the pair that they might just as well strike up Villon's ballad about 'fat Margot' with its refrain celebrating the brothel in which they both live. The whole thing amounted to nothing but fantasy projection and it saved the marriage from disaster.

The cases in which marriages have been saved in this way, by mere chance, must be innumerable, for people usually keep their mouths shut when their sexual predilections are in question, or at any rate only open them on the psychologist's couch, when it is almost too late. Arnold Henrici refers in his regrettably concise but highly instructive study, *Forbidden Desires*, to one such curative accident, which may be cited here as representative of all the rest in a field where the unknown quantity may be assumed to be particularly large.

Forbidden desires

A young wife stated at a certain consultation:

One summer evening I began to undress, for some reason, by pulling my dress over my head. I did the same with my slip, then undid my brassière and in that state even stepped out of my knickers. Probably I intended my next move to be to the bathroom, as I still had my sandals on, though no stockings, but I just can't remember now. Anyhow, at that very moment, while I stood there naked except for my sandals, my husband came unexpectedly, not knowing I was there, into the bedroom. Naturally I had not yet drawn the curtains or removed the counterpane from the bed.

I still don't understand what came over him then. He looked so strange, all of a sudden, that I didn't recognize my own husband. I was aware of that somehow, though I didn't know what it meant and I couldn't understand my own feelings either. He took possession of me, just as we both were, as if I had been – well I don't know exactly what.

We said no more about it at the time and I thought at first it had been only one of those crazy fits that come over a man sometimes. But only about a week later he spoke about it giving me to understand that he would like me to keep something on again next time, though not necessarily shoes. Ever since then he keeps on making the same requests and I have to ring the changes, sometimes retaining my stockings, sometimes my brassière and once even my spectacles. Although he himself doesn't still wear his suit, as he did the first time. I can't help thinking it's all dreadfully indecent.

But the comments which Henrici, by adroit questioning, was able to elicit from the wife on this significant behaviour are even more interesting than the experience itself. They are most revealing. This admirable young woman, who knew her husband, was well aware that by giving in to his wishes she would be preserving him from the clutches of other women and she was also very pleased that this aspect of her marriage had suddenly acquired a new animation, with positive effects, moreover, on the general domestic atmosphere, the little attentions she expected and harmonious relations as a whole between the couple. And yet she felt the situation to be 'indecent' because of all the firmly and deeply rooted taboos she still retained, consisting of the prejudices and fears which after a few years of marriage dull its sexual pleasures through familiarity and the absence of fantasy-building. When disaster finally ensues and the first step has already been taken in the arms of another woman, who has rather different ideas about decency and indecency, it is usually too late to save the marriage, since a psychological estrangement, in addition to the physical one, has then to be healed.

What seems so indecent to many women and is dismissed by them under the vague description of 'perversity' very often creates for the first time the climate required for true sexual intimacy and it is very often, too, the husband who needs it more than the wife. A wonderfully effective example in this connection appears in the French film *Beyond the Rhine*. The actor Aznavour plays the part of a young French prisoner of war who during his captivity has a purely sentimental affair with a German girl. After the war he returns to his baker's shop, where he is harried and strictly supervised all day long. No one treats him with any consideration or addresses a friendly word to him. When at the end of one of these bleak and gloomy days his wife demands her conjugal rights he considers her coarse readiness for intercourse without preliminaries characteristic of a prostitute and goes back to his German girl. He was repelled by his wife's assumption, constantly made in all marriages and always in vain, that sexual satisfactions, like meals, can be served up at fixed points in the daily programme.

Every prostitute knows how trifling a husband's requirements may often be and what absurd predilections often drive him into her arms. Henrici cites the case of a man who only interrupted the course of an otherwise perfect marriage by visits to a call-girl whom he paid to attend on him for a whole evening like a waitress, except that she had to be nude. He demanded nothing more. The present author remembers the case of an enriched artisan who hardly dared to yawn in the presence of his well-bred wife and maintained a mistress with whom he was in the habit of playing cards, always the same game, for a whole evening in his shirt-sleeves, with his belt undone and wearing old slippers. It was not until the last hand was dealt that they played strip-poker. Meanwhile the girl had long since found out that it was not the subsequent act he looked forward to so much as the feeling of relaxation and the card-game. The man had only persuaded himself that his mistress interested him more than his wife in order not to have to admit that his marriage, perhaps even his rise in the social scale itself, had deprived him of a home.

The four H's

In many marriages chance or a frank exchange of views has led to a compromise. Again, a couple may find that they have certain preferences in common. The more peculiar these are, the closer are the ties formed between the pair. Oddly enough the truly emancipated women of the United States or Sweden often go further with such compromises than their fellow-sufferers in Central Europe. 'High heels, happy homes' has become a proverb in the States. For housewives there have realized that they ought at least to offer their husbands what a casual glance may reveal to them. Very many also, owing to the relative distance of their homes, which may be twelve miles or more from the centre of the city, have resigned themselves to putting up with excessive sociability. A letter written by an American lady who had been frankly describing her extravagant wardrobe after her second marriage ends complacently with the information '. . . and with it I wear gold glacé kid gloves reaching nearly to the shoulder. I know that my husband could never find so much of what he likes anywhere else and it's all for him only'. This passage is quoted by Heller, followed by Wagner and Pauly.

The prostitute's share

Even so, the prostitutes still have plenty to do, for only a proportion of all these predilections can be satisfied with a wife. Only harmless kinks are confessed, since to reveal perversions of a more exacting nature would usually be more dangerous to a marriage than to keep quiet about them and confine their gratification to the occasional services of a whore. There is hardly anything more distressing than the experiences of such couples as have lost the inner resilience which can give new energy to matrimonial intercourse. A wife's familiar figure is not rendered more attractive by the decorative underwear which the husband purchases with reluctance and tries out on her with a beating heart. She simply looks grotesque in it and the despair induced by such attempts is not lessened by the realization that each partner has been made to appear ridiculous in the eyes of the other. Many a husband, accordingly, rather than undertake such experiments, prefers to run a relatively slighter risk by resorting to a brothel.

If there appears to be absolutely no chance of solving problems of this kind within the bonds of matrimony, the husband usually and the wife occasionally becomes a member of the so-called sexual minorities and therefore in the overwhelming majority of cases enters the world of prostitution. In every large country these people can be reckoned by millions, thus constituting a serious social question. Consequently, many adversaries of Marthe Richard and her colleagues outside France have ventured to call attention to the plight of this part of the population. For those concerned can by no means all be stigmatized as deliberately immoral perverts. Very many had no choice in the matter. They include cripples, deaf-mutes, divorced men who for various reasons do not wish to marry again, widowers with growing children on whom they are unwilling to impose a stepmother, married couples deprived of sexual intercourse owing to the ill-health of one partner or the other, soldiers and sailors, labourers employed in remote districts on mining or road-building, etc.

Life in Montana

Some time ago [wrote the American physician and sociologist Harry Benjamin], my wife and I visited the extremely interesting mining community of Butte in the State of Montana. I asked one of the senior police officials there for his views on the problem of prostitution. He answered: 'We have to tolerate a red-light district here. Otherwise we should never be able to prevent assaults on women and children. Butte is full to overflowing of vigorous young miners, who are unmarried and can't do without females. Quite recently certain religious bodies persuaded us to close the district. But it didn't work. Too many offences against morality occurred and we had too few police to deal with them all. So we were obliged to ignore the prohibition and reopen the area. But juveniles are not allowed to enter it, no alcohol is sold there and the girls undergo regular medical examination. These conditions have proved satisfactory We are simply taking no further notice of our opponents and can only hope that they will now leave us alone.'

This testimony is only exceptional in its lucidity, not in its content. The large male labour forces often assembled at short notice, as in cases of dam construction, prospecting for oil, military manœuvres and similar undertakings, create on each occasion a problem which is exhaustively discussed in military and industrial circles, though hitherto little has been heard by the public of their deliberations.

A bold step towards publicity in this connection has been taken by one of the Scandinavian countries, which are nowadays regarded not only as admirably functioning democracies but also as communities with a considerable degree of feminine emancipation. In the effort to restore the situation undermined decades ago by the zeal of newly-appointed women deputies to parliament, the most important Danish feminist organization, the *Dansk Kvinde Samfund*, demanded in 1965 official reopening of the forbidden brothels and even their protection by the State, as well as the professional designation of their inmates as sexual welfare workers.

Modern white slave traffic

The Butte police commissioner and the Danish Women's League could be unreservedly applauded if the problem of prostitution had not been for years so closely and regularly associated with two genuine evils as to suggest that the connection is actually of an existential nature. These two phenomena are the practice of living on the earnings of prostitutes and the crime of engaging in 'white slave traffic'. Unfortunately Book IV of the present work, entitled *Lost Illusions*, cannot be allowed to end with the assertion that these two evils may now be dismissed as legends that have lost their point. It is true that the legends have departed with the illusions. The false realism of such a novelist as Claude Farrère, together with countless fanciful films and even such journalism as that of Albert Londres, have been discredited by a fresh set of circumstances. The Interpol network has come into extensive and successful operation. Even the larger international organizations, the League of Nations after the First World War and the United Nations after the Second, have shown surprising energy in concerning themselves with the traffic in women. They have attacked the legal and social problems involved and are in a position to provide the police with most important bases in law for intervention in hitherto inaccessible directions.

But in so far as criminals prove to be capable of dealing with a problem, its abolition can only be partial. Armand Mergen wrote in his brief but outstanding study of modern prostitution:

I have not been able to discover in practice any case in which a criminal has brought pressure to bear on any other individual, either by violence, by threats of grievous injury or by cunning, so as to force any such person into sexually immoral life abroad or with unspecified partners. Whores who travel about, either openly or in the guise of innocent women, with their keepers, who may also call themselves 'managers', and prostitutes who register at so-called 'employment agencies', are already hardened in their trade and no longer have to be forced into it by violence or trickery. The really guileless country girl who falls in with bad company and is seduced with the object of compelling her against her will to prostitute herself in a foreign country no longer exists, if indeed she ever did.

Legal protection for prostitutes

These considerations clarify the position for jurists. Even Sicot and other police officials take up a similar attitude. They call attention to the more efficient and widespread organization of the traffic in women today and agree with Mergen in emphasizing transport conditions and the evasion of immigration regulations more than the enslavement of innocent or unwilling persons. The latter undertaking would be pointless, uneconomic and moreover scarcely practicable in the face of modern forms of communication, so long as the use of aircraft is not voluntarily abandoned and one reverts to the romantic junks of M. Benoit. At the same time victims do continue to exist in the shape of girls already on their own confession quite familiar with the underworld and ready to adopt its ways. These young women are no more legally protected than any species of insect and yet depend more absolutely on the essentially criminal organization of their keepers than any factory hand on his employer. At an epoch in which any girl clerk will walk out of her office as the result of a trifling squabble and charwomen have to be handled with kid gloves, prostitutes too, who actually pay taxes in their latest incarnation, will not hesitate to claim protection while at work. It is already no longer a matter of indifference to them whether they are paid by boulevard loungers or North Africans, sailors or foreign labourers, transient or regular customers. No doubt their requests will be long ignored, since society has decided to outlaw them. But to the extent that Augustine's dictum is still recognized at the present time, when he declared: 'Take the harlot out of circulation and you will have chaos,' the authorities who accept the prostitute's mite of tax will also have to concern themselves more energetically than hitherto with the trade which brings it in.

The souteneur

A most ancient feature of her profession, in addition to the problems of its recruitment, is the presence of the *souteneur*. His peculiar protective function may be performed by a single individual or a corporate body with many ramifications. In either case the cost of maintaining such support is met exclusively by the earnings of the prostitute. The fact that the individual *souteneur* only very seldom supplies a customer proves that his appellation is a misnomer. Nor is it true, except in a sense now restricted to only a few countries and towns, that a whore needs any sort of protection at work. Yet it seems that *souteneurs* will survive the traffic in women for some time, owing to the obvious reluctance of the prostitute to dispense with their services, which always appear to an outsider the most cruel infliction she has to endure.

In no department of the wide sphere of clandestine and undisguised prostitution at all its levels are the views of competent authorities so strikingly at variance as in this very matter of the *souteneur*. The Freiburg jurist Wolf Middendorff declared that such persons are 'some of the most unmistakably culpable figures with which criminal law has to deal'. Marcel Sicot on the other hand has stated his belief that the typical apache *souteneur*, with his cloth cap, sweater, cigarette-end and red waist-band, is no longer nowadays anything but an item in the programme for the excited tourists who pack the 'Paris By Night' coaches. According to Sicot the former bosses in this line have long since turned to more remunerative trades, such as smuggling and other forms of fraud. 'The modern *souteneur*,' he adds, 'is a well-dressed businessman who frequents smart society, runs an export-import office and very often uses the charms of his female staff to promote his operations.'

Social and psychological problems

Armand Mergen and Harold Greenwald go far beyond such classifications, Mergen scenting a social problem and Greenwald a psychological one. Certainly the centuries-old addiction of the prostitute to so indefinite a profession remains inexplicable in any but psychological terms. Yet the attraction of such a life cannot be wholly accounted for in this way, for after all the trade is different from all others and its practitioners can hardly be psychologically normal.

At the present time no less than 159 countries throughout the world have prohibited brothels. Only a small minority of such states have gone back on their decision to the extent of permitting the concentration of prostitutes, once more, in certain streets and blocks of buildings. Consequently more individual whores are left to their own resources than has been the case since the age of Solon. Their need for permanent association with one particular male has therefore increased. In the mid-twentieth century such a person is no longer the sinister figure he used to be in the inter-war period, both in sensational fiction and in real life. But his conventional clothes and American car have not noticeably altered his social significance. The emancipated modern prostitute, who earns plenty of money and lives alone, requires a companion for both domestic and psychological reasons. Accordingly, the typical *souteneur* of today resembles an exceptionally well-paid assistant rather than a slave-driver.

A call-girl's life

It is of the utmost importance for a top-tanking harlot, known nowadays as a call-girl, to be always accessible. Even while she is actually 'at work' there must be someone reliable in her flat, who understands her trade, to answer the telephone, recognize the suitability or otherwise of a client and judge whether his application is likely to be lucrative or the reverse. An intelligent maid might of course be able to do so. But just as men often prefer women assistants, so as to guard against rivalry and intrigue by their own sex, so the call-girl would rather have a male secretary than another woman who might well prove detrimental to her principal's interests.

If it is further realized that a prostitute often has to begin by establishing friendly relations with her neighbours, that she must defend herself against attempts at blackmail by her landlord, keep competition within bounds and bribe the police – this last proceeding being of some importance across the Atlantic – the social function of the *souteneur* becomes fairly clear. At the same time his emotional relationship with the call-girl is complicated by the fact, substantiated by unanimous reports and first-hand information from every century, that whores are strongly drawn to Lesbianism whenever they are at leisure and wish to forget their profession for a while. Yet even so very many cases occur of a sexual association with the *souteneur*. For example, a high proportion of prostitutes are frigid, only taking genuine pleasure in consorting with their resident 'protectors'. This may also happen when a call-girl specializes in abnormal practices. For then of course ordinary congress with her regular companion constitutes a sort of revenge on clients who demand extravagant behaviour without considering the preferences of their partner or even inquiring about them.

The prostitute of today knows perfectly well that ninety per cent of her clients require special treatment and that in these cases 'one doesn't just simply lie down'. After greetings have been exchanged the stereotyped question has to be put: 'Well, what are we going to do?', though this question might strike a masculine novice as the most superfluous that could be asked. It is only in the United States, where men have always been used to feminine dictation, that a client who has ordered a call-girl to come to his hotel sometimes politely inquires how he can best entertain her, though an hour later he slips a hundred dollar bill into her handbag.

The sponger

In all civilized countries marriages in which the wife earns more than the husband are on the increase. In all capital cities cases are familiar in which the wife who has married a student bears their domestic expenses for a long period, until the husband has concluded his studies. In these altered circumstances even the *souteneur* can no longer be regarded as confined to the narrow sphere of a purely criminal existence nor are his ranks so often recruited, as formerly, from the underworld. Mergen found from a questionnaire addressed to a hundred and seventy *souteneurs* that only seventeen per cent had previous convictions and that even of this percentage none had committed offences against sexual morality. 'I was only able to deduce a marked disinclination for work, an anti-social disposition in the sense of an inability to accept existing social conventions, a high degree of acquisitiveness and a taste for gambling.' This is precisely the character so wonderfully well drawn by Pasolini in his novel, *The Sponger*.

The *souteneur* now very rarely plays the part of a pander and hardly ever obtains his personal staff by first making friends with a girl, then abducting her from her parents' house and eventually making her give up her employment and go on the streets. Such proceedings have of course not been entirely abandoned, but they are no longer the rule among *souteneurs*, since they had the disadvantage of offering the police too many chances to intervene. For ever since all non-Communist countries came to terms in some way or another with prostitution the *souteneur* has become the favourite target of official action. The intention is to reach the prostitute through him, when he is sentenced for this unacknowledged reason to terms of imprisonment and on his release, which has to come some time, he makes one more tough youngster at large in the prostitutes' quarter, a fellow who has tasted blood, been given tips and accumulated vengeful sentiments. He and his like are apt to develop into true gangsters, those who operate the big prostitute and call-girl rings, organize transport and form blackmailing syndicates.

Souteneurs *may be on the way out*

In dealing with the special problem of the *souteneur* the authorities, just as elsewhere in the world of prostitution, are confronted by long-standing arrangements too purposeful, massive and resolute to allow sheer coercion to achieve much. The prostitute will always need a *souteneur* so long as she remains defenceless and works independently. Only some of the whores confined to apartment-houses occupied exclusively by themselves are now beginning to do without *souteneurs* or else to live with them simply as other women do with a partner for life who performs no special function and takes no share in the woman's professional life. Strict checks on the entertainment industry, in which the owners of bars and *souteneurs* operating on a large scale very often come to a personal understanding, might be able to create further areas of neutrality, in other words a kind of no-man's-land where the women could practise their trade undisturbed either by police or gangsters and consequently would need no one to keep such obstacles out of their way. Measures of this kind, affecting both the main scene of action and living conditions, may probably be expected in the long run to be more successful in countering the activities of the *souteneur* than the pinpricks of judicial sentences, training schools, residential prohibitions and cancellations of driving-licences.

Increase of sexual interests in the mid-century

The present-day picture of prostitution is as complex as that of modern life itself. Probably no one now takes seriously the proposition that society will ever be able to hold its own without toleration of the manifold forms of mercenary sexual pleasure. It is an open secret that such pleasures are not only themselves easily sold but also help to sell other things, which is perhaps even more important. International traders are riding on the crest of a wave of sexual interests, remarkable for the absence of anything like a guilty conscience. Neither Americans nor British, neither French nor Italians, feel themselves to be sinning when they enjoy floor-shows, strip-tease and similar spectacles as a preliminary to more robust pleasures. Only in Central Europe is the epithet 'sinful' still required in order to create, in conjunction with violet lighting, a corrupt atmosphere.

In proportion to the rise of a preference for 'black' humour, and novels of a Utopian character, accompanied by more and more familiarity with the perils of nuclear fission, sexual activities are becoming progressively associated with gaiety. The old-style film with a moral is dying. The sex-wave initiated in Italy and France, faithful to the recommendations of psychoanalysis, persistently calls attention to the function, shared by both sexual pleasure and humour, of relief from tension. Only the Germans and Scandinavians lag behind in this respect. Although they cannot dispense with sex in their entertainments, they still remain overloaded with taboos. The sexual factor continues to operate, but delight in it slumbers on, since only freedom from bias could revive any such element.

Against this background no deliberate and comprehensive attack on prostitution can ever be undertaken in any of the free countries. Western society is alert and suspicious, less than ever inclined to allow its opportunities for enjoyment to be curtailed. It does not even intend to be deprived of such frivolities as the phenomenally successful magazine for 'Men Only', the restaurant with waitresses in the nude, the girl petrol-pump attendant in her 'Bunny' costume and the attractive lady secretary symbolizing managerial power. The same society is ready to allow the United Nations, even to call upon them, to campaign against the slave-markets of Jibuti and Aden, and to support the efforts of Interpol to obliterate the last traces of the 'white slave' traffic. But modern western society is not interested in the *souteneur* or the brothel, not even in prostitution as such. It is only interested in the acquisition, at all times and in all places and with the least possible risk to security, of a maximum of amenities, dominated by the very sex factor already stressed.

Simone de Beauvoir and Huxley on future morality

The shrewdest suggestion yet made for the removal of prostitution as a permanent feature of society and the only plan with at least a theoretical chance of execution in the distant future is accordingly the idea, which originated with Simone de Beauvoir, of a community in which love-affairs are unregulated. To such amoral human beings as are represented in Aldous Huxley's *Brave New World* the prostitute would seem as superfluous as she would under Simone de Beauvoir's dispensation of the rule of free love. In such circumstances, however, no one would be able to say whether society had suppressed prostitution or merely been, in the end, suppressed by it.

EPILOGUE

*

The Dubious Experiment

'The important part played by eroticism in modern
society can in my opinion be explained by the
protection it affords from fear.' –
BERNARD MULDWORF

When Queen Victoria's haughty phrase to the effect that the existence of prostitutes constituted an affront to Her Majesty was reported in Berlin, a registered whore named Christine Leichtfuss
remarked to her steady boy-friend, a dealer in musical instruments,
'I'd rather be the loose character I am than have Victoria's responsibility for the Boer War.' Twenty years later women had both
sexual freedom and political responsibility over a sixth of the
globe.

Personal record of a Berliner

Christine Leichtfuss underwent her first treatment for syphilis at
the age of fifteen, her second at sixteen. At seventeen she gave birth
to a seven months' child, which was born dead. She is unlikely to
have survived to see the new age. 'I shall go on being a waitress,' she
said, 'I'm fond of the trade. However long they put me inside I shall
go back to it.' Millions of other women lived to see the October
Revolution and hear the decree of 18 – 31 new style – December
1917 proclaiming equality of rights for women and the legality of
civil marriage. These measures substituted for middle-class matrimony the sexual partnership of working-class comrades. It was
characterized in the new Soviet fiction, which at that time was
pretty outspoken, by Alexey Yakovlev when he made one of his
heroines say: 'Esteemed comrade, I am going to give you pleasure

293

and you are going to do the same for me. But I may as well warn you, to begin with, that if I find it's your fault that I have to go to hospital afterwards, I'll do you in the first chance I get.'

These decrees, now half a century old, began the boldest and most promising experiment, consequent upon a deeply-based renovation of society, ever directed to the elimination of prostitution. Everything was abandoned which, according to Marx and Lenin, had repeatedly caused this institution to arise and last. No capitalist state or nation populated by a Christian majority will ever be able even to attempt to embark upon a similar adventure. Its course, however, and the results it achieved are of more than merely academic interest.

Sex legislation in the Soviet Union

One of the main preliminary conditions for the success of the experiment was the new legislation in the sexual field. Although at a later stage many of the pronouncements made by Communist theory in the first flush of its revolutionary enthusiasm were dropped, the measures passed in those early years aroused a certain amount of envy among European liberals. One of their first commentators declared: 'The sexual habits of citizens under capitalism are a subject of purely ethical interest to society. The State only intervenes in such matters when they adversely affect the personal or material rights of other citizens. The Workers' and Peasants' community, on the other hand, only takes steps against such so-called sexual crimes as constitute a real danger to the established forms of law.'

This situation therefore conferred impunity upon a number of actions which had always involved penalties, or for which penalties had again been introduced, in many countries where the standard of living substantially exceeded that of the Soviet Union. These offences included adultery, concubinage, male and female homosexuality and prostitution. The latter was however the object of special attack in Russia, since it had always been regarded by Marxists as the most striking example of the enslavement of women.

It is clear that a wholly new basis had here been provided for the struggle against the oldest profession, the present study of which is now drawing to a close. Such words as 'morality', used for two thousand years by the western world, though in vain, in its operations against prostitutes, do not appear in Soviet legal language. But it gives a very wide connotation to the idea of rape, so as to include indirect forms of compulsion, for example when the victim is materially dependent on the aggressor. With a view to the formation of a specifically Communist morality, the law could only take steps to protect work for that object and progress towards an entirely classless society. In a sense, therefore, sexual interests were subordinated to higher aims and renunciations of the most private possible nature were demanded, if the common task made such sacrifices appear necessary.

Roll-call for collective farming

It was very soon discovered that prostitution, whether forbidden or not, would be bound to come to an end owing to the inadequacy of the labour force available to perform the duties in principle re-required of it. Just as Hitler at a later date, in order to preserve his armies of millions from infection, was obliged to divert women from their former work to the brothels, so in the Russian totalitarian state not even the tiniest group of feminine servers of Venus could be exempted from service in industry and the collective farms. The table below shows in percentages the rise of active female participation in every sphere of Soviet life.

	1929	1940	1950	1957
Industry	28	41	45	45
Trade	16	38	52	65
Administration	19	35	45	51
Popular education	54	58	67	67
Public health	65	76	84	85

Today twice as many women are employed in the whole field of Russian economic activities as there were in 1929. In other words the numbers of male and female workers are equal, so that no circumstances can arise in which the male supplies only cash and the woman only her person. The ground is therefore cut away, so to speak, from under the trade of prostitution, owing of course to the complete disregard of all individual protests by the enormous pressure of a general social development. This was so much taken for granted, from the start, in every department of Russian life, that the inclusion in it of prostitution and the consequent decline of that institution became automatically, as it were, accompanying features of the Revolution. It was even necessary to take special, somewhat complicated steps in order to reserve, for prostitutes of all people, a certain limited area within the framework of socialism.

Roots of the evil

The campaign against illiteracy and venereal disease, against ignorance in the villages and the other degradations which serfdom had been inflicting upon Russian society for centuries relieved the bigger cities of the influx of naïve and easily corruptible femininity. The strict supervision of students, their accommodation to a great extent in hostels, the cult of sport and communal activities, all obstructed the rise of the more intelligent type of whore, the 'good time girl' and similar 'bohemian' individuals. The *Great Encyclopaedia of Medicine*, published in Moscow in 1962, complacently made, in its twenty-sixth volume, one of the few official announcements relating to this theme:

The systematic attack on such relics of prostitution as survived during the first years of the Soviet régime was not directed against the prostitutes themselves but against the actual institution and all the causes which compelled women to succumb to it.

The end of 1919 saw the inauguration at the Public Health Office of the Committee for the Suppression of Prostitution. It was followed by the appointment, in the Public Welfare Department, of the Inter-office Committee for the Suppression of Prostitution and the nomination of advisers to the Government on this subject, to act as local authorities. They were responsible to the USSR Public Health Office Central Council for the Suppression of Prostitution. This body was staffed by the People's Commissar for Public Health, the Director of the Venereal Department of the Public Health Office and representatives of the Home Office, the Central Council of the Trade Unions and the Women's Branch of the Central Committee of the Communist Party ... The People's Ministries of Labour, Social Welfare, Culture, Justice and Public Health carried out the following measures: requalification and direction to employment in the case of unemployed women with children under the age of one year, the provision of work for all inmates of the State orphanages, preferential provision of work for women discharged from protective nursing and labour homes, systematic extension of a network of public establishments for adult and juvenile re-education, the setting up of special accommodation for homeless women with guarantees of material assistance, intensification of the campaign against the professional maintenance of squalid taverns and other agencies for the encouragement and support of prostitution and finally the extension to further areas of protective nursing and labour institutes for homeless and unemployed, venereally-infected women.

This programme includes all the measures carried through during the years in question and at the same time outlines the new tactics required for intensifying the effort to do away with the surviving relics of prostitution.

The Social Welfare Office founded two labour colonies, that of Kalyaev at Sagorsk and that of Svirsk, some two hundred miles from Leningrad.

In 1937 the Ministry of Culture founded an institute for the technical training of homeless boys and girls under sixteen, where several hundred young people were re-educated and later transferred first to factories in Moscow and then to colleges and intermediate instructional centres for various trades.

The Public Health Office has created, since 1924, a closely interconnected system of protective nursing and labour institutes for women. Large establishments of this kind were built in Moscow, Leningrad, Gorki, Rostov on the Don, Kiev, Tiflis, Baku, Irkutsk, Tashkent and many other cities.

Tosika and her admirers

Nevertheless, the continued existence of prostitution in the Soviet Union is frequently mentioned in the national Press. For instance, an article in the *Literaturnaya Gazeta*, No. 42 of 14 March 1963, refers to a prostitute named Tosika without expressly indicating her profession. The headline runs:

'TOSIKA STILL LIVES, AS BEFORE, ON THE MONEY PROVIDED BY HER ADMIRERS.'

That hers was no exceptional case can be deduced from the decree ordering such women to be sent to Siberia. The article proceeds:

'It can hardly be supposed that such a "metropolitan flower" as Tosika will not instantly find "admirers" wherever she goes.'

It is further reported that the wives of miners address the following sort of plea to the authorities:

'Please don't expose Bodaibo* to people like Tosika.'

Her name was therefore already a catchword in Siberia and if wives were petitioning the authorities not to send any more females like her to that area, there must have been a whole lot of them there for some time.

The existence of prostitution was again implied by a contribution entitled *Five Citizens of Veretchino* which appeared in the official newspaper *Izvestia* for 3 April 1963.

'A mother and daughter named Pimenov, who had opened a drinking-den in their apartment, were publicly charged with this offence.'

Statements by officials provide further evidence of the availability of prostitutes. A. N. Burmistrov, for example, a member of the Department for the Preservation of Public Order in Moscow, declared in *The Young Communist* for 1963, No. 1:

A woman begins by taking to drink, then starts bringing men she hardly knows back home for the night. At last the police concerned with public order become interested in her licentious mode of life. They discover that the room in which the carousals and other so-called entertainments take place is also used to sleep in – or sometimes to keep awake in - by the woman's under-age daughter . . . After a few years it is found that a girl brought up in such conditions has been arrested in a hotel bedroom in the company of a man she had met in the street only a short time before . . . or else she is picked up drunk in the street . . . or again she is called to the police station on account of the mounting complaints received there of her reckless conduct.

It is alleged that legal penalties are only applicable to acts which promote prostitution, such as the professional maintenance of haunts of vice, pimping, forcing women to practise prostitution or the production and distribution of pornographic matter. This last proceeding is dealt with under Sections 226 and 228 of the Penal Code of the USSR for 1960.

Some inconsistencies

Nevertheless, it must be admitted that women who practise prostitution always were and still are prosecuted in the Soviet Union. In the earlier years of the régime they were dealt with administratively,

* A town on the River Vitim, some 250 m. N.E. of Lake Baikal. [J.C.]

but not as a matter of law, under Article 35 of the Penal Code of the USSR, as socially dangerous elements of the population. Since 1957 prostitution has been punished as 'a mode of life involving danger to society and parasitism', and also as the 'provision of means to live without working'. The law 'to intensify the suppression of elements involving danger to society and parasitism' envisages the prosecution of such offences. Women have been sentenced for having found means to support life without engaging in ordinary employment, for never having worked at all, or for only apparently doing so.

In view of these and other reports it looks today very much as though the painstaking Russian experiment is going to fail like all the other attempts to get rid of prostitution. Nor would such failure be due to collective agriculture, the subordination of the consumer goods industry to armaments or the incapacity of the average bureaucrat, but rather to the opposition of those young people of whom Lenin had said that they 'will live to see the coming society when it had been perfected and are called upon to assist in its creation'.

According to the investigations set on foot some five years after the passage of reforming legislation, sixty per cent of the female students questioned at the University of Sverdlovsk and thirty-four per cent of the males declared that the Revolution and the new social order had made no difference at all to their attitude in matters of sex. Seven years later further inquiries made among the young manual workers of Leningrad revealed that they considered the conduct of youth, including the Young Communists, to be in the main unwholesome, even corrupt, while sixty per cent of the girls admitted that they had undergone their first experience of sex while under the influence of alcohol.

Normal erotic appetites

It therefore proved impossible, even during the oppressive rule of Stalin, to restrain the normal erotic appetites which affect all human beings who pay any attention to their physical welfare and are not endangered in so doing. The conditions under which adults suffered, such as arbitrary laws, police tyranny, professional informers and lack of liberty, were taken for granted by young people who had never known anything else. They did not abandon for that reason the service of ideas to which even young people in the western world aspire in the course of nature after puberty.

The old Marxists, in their dealings with the young, acted and still act as teachers to whose lessons their pupils listen in the full consciousness that they will be allowed to forget them immediately after taking the examination for their leaving certificate, though that should be the very moment at which to remember them.

Consequently, the West today is inclined to regard the conceptual structure of Marxism, not only in its relation to modern art and literature, but also in its attitude to sexuality, as an imposing palace with walls of glass, the panes of which are shattered one after the other by the stone-throwing of real life. This process need not have been at all so surprising as is believed elsewhere, for the famous exchange of letters between Lenin and Klara Zetkin proves that at this early date the acute intelligence of the man from Simbirsk had already dropped the freakish notion that for a Soviet citizen the sexual act would be as casual and insignificant a performance as the drinking of a mouthful of water. He concluded that this view would be not only anti-Marxist but anti-social into the bargain. 'Our sexual life reveals not only natural propensity but also acquired characteristics, whether elevating or the reverse.'

After Lenin

This sentence was written on the eve of the Revolution. But its truth was not illustrated until the aftermath of the Second World War in the middle of the twentieth century. The influences at work on both sides of the Iron Curtain became clearer at that time than they had been, for instance, in 1925, when Russian literature was the most modern in the world and the Soviet Union still really afforded some hope to a progressive intelligence. But now full employment in the west as well as in the east of Europe, together with the emancipation of women and their political weight, exercised through their votes and organizations, have created a situation which has robbed the Marxist catchword of 'capitalist marriage'' of all meaning. It may be that even now there are rather more marriages of convenience on this side of the Elbe than on the other. But on the whole freedom of choice of partner is today so much the rule in all civilized countries that a starting point at any rate for satisfaction of the sexual impulse within the bonds of matrimony appears to have been secured.

Lenin's argument from acquired characteristics, especially in the form given it by modern Marxism, is more difficult to meet. The present theory runs somewhat as follows. It is true that human beings can live alone if they are obliged to and so long as they limit their requirements to food and clothing. But they need to associate with at least one individual of the other sex in order to gratify their erotic appetites. Such sexual activities therefore represent a cultural and social impulse in the direction of community of interests, as well as a natural instinct of outstanding importance which ought not to be allowed any kind of adulteration. The activities in question, however, have been intellectualized, poisoned and misdirected in the western world. Its voluptuaries have turned nature into a source of amusement, seasoning it with jests and stimulants of a cerebral character and thus perverting a process of vital significance. Western women accordingly, if not voluntarily joined in this behaviour, are degraded and forced into the condition of merchandise. Sexuality is distorted by being concentrated from time to time, as fashion dictates, upon various anatomical areas, incessantly changed. Meanwhile choice of partners is disturbed and controlled at a distance by endless visual presentations of popular idols of dubious worth on outsize posters, cinema and television screens and in illustrated magazines.

It does seem, however, that the personality cult covertly condemned by such arguments becomes very much more serious on the political plane than it is in the common run of western democratic constituencies, where a sceptical outlook is encouraged in any case.

The new opium

Russian teenagers themselves have shouted down the theoreticians of the Kremlin with unexpected emphasis during the visits of Yves Montand, Greco and certain jazz bands to the Soviet Union. The authorities have therefore been convinced that they have discovered in the alluring flow, actually sex-obsessed, of modern mass-media, a new opium of the people comparable with the Christianity so described by Marxists some decades ago. Religion had set up taboos and diverted natural impulses into a maze subsequently occupied by a motley crew of strident and bewildering guides. In this glistening hell the citizen has gone far astray from a choice of partner in the ordinary natural way and the efforts of each partner in common to produce a sound posterity.

Such considerations underlie the prohibition of prostitution in the Soviet Union, remarkable in the fact that it is also aimed at the client. The so-called 'womanizer', often regarded in the West as a victim, is not indeed actually penalized. But he is denounced by name, a proceeding which can be decidedly more disagreeable than the fines imposed upon him in the United States, for the duty of a Soviet citizen is to behave impeccably even after a celebration. The question arises whether the Russians are aware that in taking this step they are following the advice of the Archbishop of Canterbury, Dr Fisher, who once exclaimed in the House of Lords that 'the quickest way of restricting prostitution would be to confine attention to the man and punish him'.

In Russia prohibition succeeds as a whole because the general standard of living is low, there is little leisure and the authorities are all-powerful. The measures involved may therefore be justified in practice, though the population is hardly convinced that, as Muldorf put it, prostitution has turned relations between the sexes 'into a perpetual war with subterfuges, resort to violence and fraudulent manœuvres'.

Dreams and reality

It is scarcely possible to estimate the future chances of this experiment. Ever since Stalin's death western influence has been flowing into the Soviet Union and its satellites. More precisely, it is not exactly flowing, but being absorbed by all those young people who neither can nor mean to satisfy their hunger for experience in university lecture-rooms, spotless libraries and the Tretyakov Gallery.

Eliane Jacquet wrote:

Yesterday evening I visited Red Square in order to do my duty as a Frenchwoman. For three hours I scribbled my name on postcards presented to me with shining eyes by young men and girls of the Soviet Union . . . Meanwhile they kept asking me the same questions in half a dozen phrases always identically worded. Where did I learn Russian? Is Paris as big as Moscow? Is Yves Montand as popular in France as here? For years these young people have been deprived of any contact

302

with foreigners and countries abroad. Now the doors had suddenly been opened and they didn't know what to ask . . It's not easy to renounce one's dreams. But it's even more difficult to live with them after they have come true.

One does not have to be a prophet in order to foresee that the existing separation, so anxiously supervised, of the pleasures offered to tourists from the puritanical diversions available for proletarians at leisure will not remain effective for long. It was possible perhaps to preserve such an illusion in the East, so long as intercourse with foreigners was restricted to mercantile centres like Posen, Leipzig, Zagreb and Budapest, where even then the first establishments could be found and approached as the haunts of a discreet but attractive underworld. But this phase has passed, owing to the tourist invasion of the last few years, more rapidly than might have been anticipated. At the same time prostitution in East Europe is obstructed by a whole series of purely practical considerations, for example that of accommodation, since after all it is no part of the duties of Intourist to reserve hotel bedrooms by the hour.

Nocturnal drives in Moscow

But in this connection it is once more evident that no bureaucracy can deal effectively with the oldest profession and its talent for improvisation. The Moscow girls on the look-out near the Foreigners' Club get themselves escorted into these premises, which they cannot enter alone, and return the compliment later on in taxis or cars hired by the tourists, since detectives, invariably female, called *deshunaryas* ('orderlies'), keep close watch on all the corridors. At Bucharest the public gardens, on account of the mild climate, provide accommodation for brief sexual intercourse throughout the tourist season. At Prague and Budapest certain hotels took the initiative in catering for this subversive trade. As the porter was an official personality care was taken to avoid him by first entering the bar, from which a lift transported couples direct to the upper floors. Such is the procedure also at the Neva Hotel in East Berlin, at the International in Prague and also at the Yalta in the same city. That ancient stronghold of prostitutes, Budapest, which remained a favourite holiday resort for Viennese citizens up to the end of the

1930s, maintains the old royal and imperial traditions with its ladies in fox furs strolling round and round certain cafés on the banks of the Danube.

Danubian strip-tease

The extra-territorial rights accorded to the influx of foreigners also apply to the chief river of eastern Europe, the Danube, and a short stretch of the Adriatic coast between Trieste and Dubrovnik. Like the unlicensed gamblers' ships which lie at anchor off the coast of California, outside the three-mile limit, the steamers equipped as casinos and the floating bars on the Danube, with their roulette tables and strip-tease displays, are available for visitors who can be readily picked up on the footbridges. Natives of the country are so strictly excluded that aboard Tito's pleasure-craft, for instance, the *Barba Rude*, Rumanian girls undress for the debauchees, while in Rumania itself only Yugoslav beauties perform this service. The taboos of the medieval city fathers, who at least protected the young people of their own more limited abodes from this kind of exposure, are thus still in force within the very regions where middle-class pretensions have been officially abandoned.

The People's Democracies still hold a few trump cards in their contest with prostitution, notably the ease with which irregular sexual relationships can be formed, the immunity of abortions from prosecution and State provision for illegitimate children. But the seductive Serpent is active, offering gifts manufactured in the West which are regarded as luxuries by a materially worse off population and which break down, as luxuries always do, the capacity of girls to resist temptation on moral grounds. The tourist's mode of life and the influx of films, magazines and other illustrative material arouse the suspicion of the inhabitant of the Eastern Paradise that to be driven out of it would not constitute such a very severe punishment. Once this general impression gains ground the Fall of Man from the Soviet Eden can only be a question of time.

Neither monk nor Don Juan

This feeling of insecurity, too, had been vaguely forseen by Lenin when he told Klara Zetkin that the ideal Russian, the Communist of the future, would be neither a monk nor a Don Juan and of course not a German philistine either. Lenin did not, however, go on to explain what the character in question ought to be in other respects.

In any case it will be impossible to withhold from a nation of sportsmen and cosmonauts, continually broadening the basis of its intelligence and courage, that sense of inward independence which leads a man to take full advantage of the adventure of life and gives the modern young Russian woman, who has grown up in unquestioned possession of equality of rights with the other sex, full proof, at last, of her emancipation.

It is open to any dictatorship to label the prostitute and her profession as parasitic and coldly expel them from society. Hitler, by forcing prostitution underground in this way, acted in just the same fashion as the rulers of the Soviet Union. Probably all nations would acquiesce in such a treatment of the problem for a relatively prolonged period, if prostitution had been all that the dictators had forbidden. But isolated excommunications of the oldest profession have never succeeded in their object. Societies permitted free development have always contrived in one way or another to evade persecution of their need for sexual enjoyment. Prostitution will accordingly only submit to suppression in the Soviet Union for so long as the whole system, with all its regulations, continues to function. Any weakening or relaxation of it, indeed any reform or new generation, may alter the situation. No one can want hundreds of millions of people to go on living under the Communist régime merely for the sake of a temporary solution of the problem of prostitution. The young on both sides of the Iron Curtain, as they grow up and out of the era of the Cold War, are the greatest, perhaps the only, hope of surmounting that obstacle. With the achievement of greater freedom for the individual citizen of the Eastern block, demand for the arrangement by the individual of his own sex life will also rise.

Practical experience and methods in Russia

The results of the Russian campaign against prostitution are of only limited value for the nations of the free world. A state of emergency would have to be declared in the West and emergency regulations passed before unpopular handmaidens of Venus could be packed off to the Massif Central, the Hebrides or Lüneburg Heath and put to work on the land there. Even then one would be using artillery to shoot sparrows. The apparent impossibility of finding practicable solutions affords no ground for satisfaction. No doubt Western man would be very glad to apply the Communist principle of parasitism to prostitutes and their keepers. But unfortunately neither of these groups constitutes the only parasites on Western society and would moreover, as examples prove, be able to exploit legal expedients to the utmost, with a view to recognition as equal in status to any other group of citizens. Once the principle of equality before the law is accepted – and no one would wish it ignored – its application should not be rendered relative by making the value of the individual and his right to live dependent, as under Lenin or Hitler, on such criteria as productive labour, conformity and so forth.

The slow and painful rise of humanity from the promiscuity of the horde through slave-owning societies, serfdom, despotism and the age of enlightenment to modern forms of democracy is a circumstance that cannot be partially eliminated. The advanced industrial nations of the West are aiming at the realization of a set of ideals among which the life and personal development of the individual take the lead. Very real differences of opportunity and resources still prevail even among citizens of the same country. But on the whole they can be said to have been accorded, during the last few decades at any rate, equality in principle and impartial recognition of their claims to happiness and enjoyment.

Misuse of freedom

Among the many who continue to misuse the new liberties and opportunities must be reckoned prostitutes and those who procure and maintain them, as well as the entire subsidiary host of caterers for sexual pleasure, from the last of the white slavers to the first specialists in improvised teenage parties. Throughout the long history of social progress prostitution clung like a vampire to the shoulders of every community and could not be shaken off. During the slave-owning centuries the male had tasted blood. For a prolonged period women as slaves and booty constituted a prize of war intelligible to the most barbarous Scythian without a great deal of proclamation. In a society almost wholly unproductive, with neither industry nor an agriculture capable of exporting its crops, with trade at an extremely low level, women and boys schooled to act as the slaves of appetite were commercially exploitable objects of special importance, since they were all that the backward regions of central and northern Europe could barter for the weapons and other manufactured articles supplied by oriental merchants.

The inordinate sensual excitation caused by the view of women as mere commodities again set Europe alight, as though from a spark, after the decline of the slave economy, when the Crusaders came in contact with the civilization of the East. The lady of the manor in her castle, courted as she was by poets, minstrels and her masculine guests, remained a prisoner. The walls of the bower were just as thick as those of any harem. The male also ruled and the female served in every other interior, from the baths to the women's quarters on an estate or in a town. Any woman, moreover, who might venture to claim a measure of personal freedom would be doomed. Death by drowning or burial alive would unquestionably be her fate.

In the ever-present shadow of such capital sentences women had no standing. They traded their persons and their affections unprotected but also unpursued by the law, eventually coming to be regarded as essential for the health of society. Otherwise, the Christian Church, for so long all-powerful, would have exterminated them all, one after the other, at the stake. Even the popes, however, who administered their own city and before whom emperors often knelt, took no measures against prostitution, which flourished in Rome more exuberantly than anywhere else in the world.

Classless women

The conspicuous numbers, social success and impudence of prostitutes were first evident in the full radiance of the Renaissance, with its brilliant courts and festivities, only too popular with a dominant class living gaily on the proceeds of its conquests and the labours of its inherited serfs. The accident of legal immunity ensured asylum if some monarch had an attack of moral scruples. An austere Habsburger could always be exchanged for a particularly vivacious Valois. One could desert the court of a strict pope for such liberal seaports as Venice or Genoa. The oldest profession developed under dozens of rulers, in the course of centuries, an adaptability comparable only with that of those resourceful personages who financed the whole foreground splendour of more or less capable princes from a position in the background. With the help of a few eminently gifted prostitutes and their keepers like, for instance, Madame du Barry and her count, or some equally valuable team of adventurers on a grand scale, the already weakened resistance of the old-fashioned to these innovations was widely breached. Courtesans were ennobled, bastards usurped thrones, entire groups of morganatic offspring had to be provided for out of public funds and made their way into the corridors of power.

Even during the most radical upheaval in European history, that of the French Revolution, inextricable complications in this process had already set in, with 'secondary growths' all over the place.

Is it really too late

'Since the Revolution,' wrote Jean-Gabriel Mancini, 'there can no longer be any such thing as a history of prostitution, but only an account of the whole system of toleration in which prostitution is a mere item and for which not even a name has yet been found.' The trade in question profits from the indulgence which has at last been granted to it and thus reveals one of the strangest associations which has ever come to light, that between religion and sexuality. Freedom of thought and the now guaranteed impunity of attitudes which had formerly led to the stake and eternal damnation found natural expression in the struggle against sexual taboos, which proved to be remarkably tenacious. Although modern intellectuals belong, at least theoretically, to an actually pluralistic society in which a man's religion and personal philosophy have at last been declared his own affair, the sexual customs and opportunities open to mankind today are contained in a social community still only slowly acquiring a homogeneous character and marked as clearly as ever by class distinctions. What seems normal to a peasant appears heathenish and primitive to many townsmen, while what is commonplace to the city-dweller strikes a provincial citizen as aberrant and perverse. National differences, moreover, go even deeper than the social.

The army of prostitutes and their adherents, better equipped than ever, has forgotten nothing and learnt much. With unparalleled agility it has occupied all the positions which the democratically constituted Welfare State has had to surrender. An unprecedented intensity of influence brought to bear on the masses and their permanent exposure to the glitter of allurements of every kind have not yet indeed rendered the code of morality invisible. But it is becoming more and more difficult to distinguish the more often the dazzling lights alter. Nor, of course, should prostitutes and their adherents be regarded as the chief beneficiaries of the growing insecurity of society any more than their clients should be supposed the most imperilled by it. No community has ever been ruined by this marginal feature of it. But all communities have tried to make scapegoats, for the future, of those who are already in any case outlaws, burdening them with the responsibility for the society's own decline, senseless as it is to do so. The very ancient and deeply rooted dissatisfaction of the individual who has outgrown the horde and unexpectedly found himself living on a monogamous group, lends fuel to the fire to which prostitution in any age contributed little more than a slightly scented cloud of smoke.

BIBLIOGRAPHY

The theme of this book is so closely interwoven with the history of civilization and morals that it has not proved practicable to cite, even in an abridged form, all the works consulted. On the other hand, the titles of all the studies to which merely abbreviated reference is made in the text are given below, together with those of a few selected volumes from which the last chapter in particular, *Two World Wars*, could be supplemented. Items of international literature, especially those by ancient writers and the authors of well-known memoirs, are not expressly mentioned.

Adorno, Theodor W.: *Sexualtabus und Recht heute*. In: *Sexualität und Verbrechen*. Frankfurt Main 1963

Avé-Lallemant: *Das deutsche Gaunertum*. 2 Bde. München o.J.

Bauer, Willi: *Geschichte und Wesen der Prostitution*. Stuttgart 1956. 5. Aufl. 1965.

Beauvoir, Simone de: *Das andere Geschlecht*. Deutsche Ausgabe Hamburg 1960

Benjamin, Harry: *Prostitution and Morality*. Penthouse 3/65

Bermann, Moritz: *Alt- und Neu-Wien. Die Geschichte der Kaiserstadt und ihrer Umgebungen*. Wien und Pest 1880

Blei, Franz (Hrsg.): *Die Sitten des Rokoko*. München 1923

Breton, Guy: *Histoires d'amour de l'histoire de France*. Paris o.J. (bisher neun Bände)

Dieckmann, H.: *Hetären-Katalog*. Zürich 1962

Dufour, Pierre: *Geschichte der Prostitution*. 6 Tle. in 2 Bdn., Berlin-Lichterfelde o.J.

Dühren, Eugen: *Das Geschlechtsleben in England*. 2 Bde., Berlin 1920

Eldersch, Ludwig: *Der Tiefe Graben*. Jahresgabe des Verlags für Jugend und Volk, Wien 1964 (nicht im Handel)

Englisch, Paul: *Geschichte der erotischen Literatur*. Photomechan. Neudruck des Textteils Berlin 1963

Fels, Florent: *Voilà*. Paris 1957

Friedländer, Ludwig: *Darstellungen aus der Sittengeschichte Roms*. 3 Bde. 9. Auflage Leipzig 1919

Graeffer, Franz: *Alt-Wiener Memoiren und Dosenstücke*. 2 Bde., München o.J.

Greenwal, Harold: *Das Call-Girl*. Deutsche Ausgabe. Rüschlikon bei Zürich o.J.

Hammer, W.: *Zehn Lebensläufe Berliner Kontrollmädchen*. 15. Aufl. Berlin o.J.

Helbig, G. v.: *Russische Günstlinge*. München 1917

Heller–Wagner–Pauly: *Der Flagellantismus*. Hamburg 1959. Num. Privatdruck, nicht im Handel

Henrici, Arnold: *Die verbotenen Wünsche*. Hamburg 1964

Hirschfeld, Magnus (Hrsg.): *Sittengeschichte des Weltkriegs*, 2 Bde. *Sittengeschichte der Nachkriegszeit*, 2 Bde. Wien 1931
– und Spinner: *Geschlecht und Verbrechen*. Wien 1930

Hoyer, Erich: *Krieg dem Bürger*. In: *Sittengeschichte der Revolution*. Wien 1930

Jacquet, Eliane: *Mein russisches Tagebuch*. Deutsche Ausgabe Wien 1962

Jirgal, Ernst: *Die Wiederkehr des Weltkriegs in der Literatur*. Wien 1931

Lanoux, Armand: *Paris 1925*. Deutsche Ausgabe Köln 1959
– *Amours 1900*. Paris 1961

Lenotre, G.: *Die Göttin der Vernunft*. Deutsche Ausgabe München 1948

Lewandowsky, H.: *Sittengeschichte der Pariserin*. Stuttgart 1962

Löpelmann, Erwin: *Erinn*. Brünn o.J.

Mancini, J. G.: *Prostitution et Proxénétism*. Paris 1962

McPartland, J.: *Sex in our changing World*. London 1947

Mann, Heinrich: *Käufliche Dämonie*. In Thiess (Hrsg.): *Wiedergeburt der Liebe*. Wien 1931

Marie-Thérèse: *Histoire d'une Prostituée*. Paris 1964

Mergen, Armand: *Die Prostitution*. In: *Sexualität und Verbrechen*. Frankfurt/Main 1963

Middendorff, Wolf: *Soziologie des Verbrechens*. Köln 1959

Mommsen, Theodor: *Römisches Strafrecht*. Photomechan. Nachdruck der Ausgabe Leipzig 1899, Darmstadt o.J.

Monnier, Philipp: *Venedig im achtzehnten Jahrhundert*. München 1928

Muldorf, Bernard: *Le point de vue marxiste*. Janus 3/64

Ostwald, Wilhelm: *Kultur- und Sittengeschichte Berlins*. Berlin o.J.

Parent-Duchatelet: *Die Prostitution in Paris*. Deutsche Ausgabe Freiburg 1903

Ranke-Graves, Robert v.: *Greichische Mythologie*. 2 Bde., Hamburg 1960

Romi: *Maisons closes*. Im Selbstverlag des Verfassers, num. Privatdruck. Paris 1958

Roth, Joseph: *Radetzkymarsch*. Roman. Wien 1932

Sacotte, Marcel: *La prostitution – fait social*. Janus 3/64

Salva, Anne: *Je n'en rougis pas*. Paris 1948

Scheffer, Thassilo v.: *Die Kultur der Griechen*. Wien 1935

Schmähling, Eberhard: *Die Sittenaufsicht der Censoren. Ein Beitrag zur Sittengeschichte der römischen Republik*. Stuttgart 1938

Schreiber, Hermann (Hrsg.): *Reise durch das galante Jahrhundert*. Graz 1964

Scott-Fitzgerald, Francis: *Die besten Stories*. Deutsche Ausgabe Berlin 1954

Semerau, Alfred: *Die Kurtisanen der Renaissance*. Berlin o.J.

Sicot, Marcel: *La prostitution dans le monde*. Paris 1964 (deutsche Ausgabe in Vorbereitung)

Spinner, siehe Hirschfeld

Stern, Bernhard: *Geschichte der öffentlichen Sittlichkeit in Russland*. Berlin 1908

Uzanne, Octave (Hrsg.): *Les mœurs secrètes du dix-huitième siècle*. Paris 1883

Werfel, Franz, *Erzählungen aus zwei Welten*. Frankfurt/Main 1952

Zweig, Stefan: *Die Welt von gestern*. Wien 1946

A selection of works for further study on present problems of prostitution:

Benjamin, Harry: *Prostitution and Morality*. London 1965

Filhol, P.: *Le monde des particulières*. Paris 1959

Giese/Willy (Hrsg.): *Mensch, Geschlecht, Gesellschaft*. Frankfurt 1961

Mead, Margaret: *Mann und Weib*. Stuttgart 1955 (gekürzt: Ham-
    burg 1958)
Philippon, Odette: *Le trafic des femmes*. Paris 1960
Rolph, C. H. (Hrsg.): *Women of the street*. London 1955
Sacotte, Marcel: *Où en est la prostitution?* Paris 1959
Schelsky, Helmut: *Soziologie der Sexualität*. Hamburg 1955

CHRONOLOGY

2300 BC and later   Temple prostitution in the service of love-deities, spreading eventually from Mesopotamia throughout the Near East.

1200–800 BC   Resistance of ancient Israel to the erotic cults of neighbouring peoples.

640–560 (approximately)   The Greek statesman and lawgiver Solon establishes a State brothel in Athens staffed by female slaves.

c. 450   Super-prostitutes flourish at Athens (Aspasia, Phryne, Lais and others).

425   Temple prostitution at Corinth.

350   The Golden Age of the *hetairai* in Greece draws to a close as more and more female slaves become prostitutes.

100   Towards the end of the Roman Republic prostitution organized in many brothels adjacent to the Tiber.

62   Sacrilegious invasion of Caesar's house by Clodius Pulcher in order to spy on the erotic Mysteries celebrated by women.

50 and later   Centralization of Mediterranean prostitution at Alexandria with pleasure-resorts and brothels of all kinds.

18/17   Sumptuary Laws of the Emperor Augustus.

48 AD   Death of the dissolute Empress Messalina.

100   Census of 32,000 prostitutes in Rome under Trajan.

350   Christians score one of their first successes in opposition to prostitution by preventing the introduction of temple prostitution from the Orient to Rome.

532   The former nude dancer and prostitute Theodora, after becoming empress, saves Byzantium by suppressing the Nika insurrection.

801   The Capitularies (laws) of Charlemagne represent the first strict legislation on German soil against prostitutes and procurers.

1158   Severity of the Emperor Frederick I (Barbarossa) in dealing with prostitutes and unchastity in general.

1161   King Henry II of England orders the opening of the first of the duly regulated London bawdy-houses. Soon afterwards official brothels are established in Venice, Avignon and other cities.

1200   'Women's quarters' set up in even the smallest German towns.

1254   After vain attempts to suppress prostitution altogether St Louis permits the reopening of the French brothels.

1300   Guild-type organization of prostitutes in medieval towns. Visits to such women not regarded as adulterous. They take part in public entertainments and celebrations. Guests of honour accommodated in brothels.

1414–18   The Council of Constance attended in force by the underworld. Estimates of the number of prostitutes present vary between 800 and 2,000.

1490   6,800 prostitutes at Rome, a city with a relatively sparse population compared with that resident both in antiquity and in modern times. The figure does not include the concubines of the numerous clergy.

1530   The Emperor Charles V issues a police regulation prohibiting prostitution throughout the empire and soon afterwards provides in the *Carolina* legislation for the severe corporal punishment of procurers.

1560   Climax of the struggle against venereal disease in France. Heavy penalties for infected prostitutes.

1665   The so-called *Refuge* in the Faubourg Saint-Antoine, Paris, is made an asylum and re-education centre for prostitutes, constituting as such an example to other countries.

1687   Louis XIV issues a decree announcing the most severe punishments, corporal and financial, of convicted procurers and brothel-keepers. Their noses and ears, for instance, might be cut off.

1700   Berlin brothel by-laws repeal some of the earlier repressive regulations.

1780   One hundred minor brothels in Berlin. About a thousand registered prostitutes in that city for its population of some 150,000.

1790   Two thousand Palais Royal prostitutes complain of the brutal methods and language used by the Paris police.

1843   Regulation of prostitution in Paris, including compulsory registration and the prohibition of activities during the day and after 11 p.m.

1846   Brothels closed in Prussia.

1886   Abolitionist legislation in England. Norway follows suit in 1890, the Canton of Zürich in 1897, and Denmark in 1901. At the turn of the century the numbers of prostitutes are estimated at 60,000 in London, 50,000 in Berlin, 60,000 in Paris, 30,000 in New York and 25,000 in Vienna.

1906   Compulsory registration of prostitutes abolished in Denmark.

1908   French law forbidding minors to engage in prostitution.

1918   The newly-established Soviet Union prohibits prostitution and closes the brothels of that country.

1919   Registration of prostitutes abolished in Sweden, where there had never been any brothels.

1927   Victory of the abolitionists in Germany and prohibition of brothels in that country.

1929   The League of Nations declares brothels to be hot-beds of the white slave traffic and condemns all the countries which officially tolerate them.

1933   International agreement to proceed against white slave traffic even if its victims agree to being transferred to another country for the purpose of engaging in prostitution.

1939   Abolition by Hitler of the law prohibiting the accommodation of prostitutes together in one building.

1946   The 'Marthe Richard' legislation in France, involving the closure of Parisian and provincial brothels within a period of no more than six months.

1949   Conservative estimates by the Government of the German Federal Republic conclude that between 100,000 and 150,000 prostitutes are active in the territory, excluding women working for the forces of occupation.

1955   Legislation in Italy for the closure of some two hundred State-controlled brothels. Law only enforced after much delay.

1960   In July France accedes to the International Convention for
        the suppression of traffic in and exploitation of females. In De-
        cember the Paris prostitutes demonstrated outside the Palais
        Bourbon to protest against the supervision of hotels letting
        rooms by the hour.

1963   Publication by Armand Mergen of the results of an investi-
        gation indicating that of 500 prostitutes examined fifty-six per
        cent were found to be 'obviously feeble-minded'. Eighty-one per
        cent admitted frigidity'

NEL BESTSELLERS

Crime

F.2131	GIRL IN A SHROUD	*Carter Brown* 3/6
F.2179	LAMENT FOR A LOUSY LOVER	*Carter Brown* 3/6
F.2185	DANCE OF DEATH	*Carter Brown* 3/6
F.1200	FAST WORK	*Peter Cheyney* 3/6
F.1291	DRESSED TO KILL	*Peter Cheyney* 3/6
F.1317	THE ADVENTURES OF JULIA	*Peter Cheyney* 3/6
F.1874	THE MISTS OF FEAR	*John Creasey* 5/–
F.1879	A KIND OF PRISONER	*John Creasey* 3/6
F.1920	DRY SPELL	*John Creasey* 3/6
F.1250	SECRET ERRAND	*John Creasey* 3/6
F.2068	THE MOST WANTED MAN IN THE WORLD	*Ellery Queen* 3/6
F.2178	DEATH SCENE	*Ellery Queen* 3/6
F.2341	MURDER MUST ADVERTISE	*Dorothy L. Sayers* 6/–
F.2317	STRONG POISON	*Dorothy L. Sayers* 5/–
F.2342	IN THE TEETH OF THE EVIDENCE	*Dorothy L. Sayers* 5/–
F.2316	CLOUDS OF WITNESS	*Dorothy L. Sayers* 6/–
F.2343	THE DOCUMENTS IN THE CASE	*Dorothy L. Sayers* 5/–
F.1286	GAUDY NIGHT	*Dorothy L. Sayers* 5/–
F.2209	THE NINE TAILORS	*Dorothy L. Sayers* 5/–
F.2210	THE UNPLEASANTNESS AT THE BELLONA CLUB	*Dorothy L. Sayers* 5/–
F.2211	FIVE RED HERRINGS	*Dorothy L. Sayers* 5/–
F.2212	UNNATURAL DEATH	*Dorothy L. Sayers* 5/–

Fiction

F.1923	TO SIR, WITH LOVE	*E. R. Braithwaite* 5/–
F.2113	PAID SERVANT	*E. R. Braithwaite* 5/–
F.2289	THE SPANISH GARDENER	*A. J. Cronin* 5/–
F.1316	HATTER'S CASTLE	*A. J. Cronin* 7/6
F.1450	SHANNON'S WAY	*A. J. Cronin* 6/–
F.1521	A SONG OF SIXPENCE	*A. J. Cronin* 6/–
F.2261	THE CITADEL	*A. J. Cronin* 7/6
F.2318	THE KEYS OF THE KINGDOM	*A. J. Cronin* 7/6
F.1975	THE HARRAD EXPERIMENT	*Robert H. Rimmer* 5/–
F.2074	THE REBELLION OF YALE MARRATT	*Robert H. Rimmer* 5/–
F.1500	THE ADVENTURERS	*Harold Robbins* 10/6
F.1822	A STONE FOR DANNY FISHER	*Harold Robbins* 7/6
F.2493	79 PARK AVENUE	*Harold Robbins* 9/6
F.2414	NEVER LOVE A STRANGER	*Harold Robbins* 10/6
F.2466	THE DREAM MERCHANTS	*Harold Robbins* 10/6
F.2416	WHERE LOVE HAS GONE	*Harold Robbins* 8/6
F.2155	NEVER LEAVE ME	*Harold Robbins* 5/–
F.2327	THE SERPENT AND THE STAFF	*Frank Yerby* 7/6
F.1119	THE GARFIELD HONOUR	*Frank Yerby* 3/6
F.1256	GRIFFIN'S WAY	*Frank Yerby* 5/–
F.2326	BENTON'S ROW	*Frank Yerby* 7/6
F.1323	FLOODTIDE	*Frank Yerby* 5/–
F.1406	FAIROAKS	*Frank Yerby* 5/–
F.1992	GILLIAN	*Frank Yerby* 5/–
F.1993	JARRETT'S JADE	*Frank Yerby* 5/–
F.2098	CAPTAIN REBEL	*Frank Yerby* 5/–
F.2099	TREASURE OF PLEASANT VALLEY	*Frank Yerby* 5/–
F.2100	THE VIXENS	*Frank Yerby* 5/–
F.2143	A WOMAN CALLED FANCY	*Frank Yerby* 5/–
F.2223	THE OLD GODS LAUGH	*Frank Yerby* 5/–

Romance

F.2152	TWO LOVES	*Denise Robins* 3/6
F.2153	THE PRICE OF FOLLY	*Denise Robins* 3/6
F.2154	WHEN A WOMAN LOVES	*Denise Robins* 3/6
F.2181	JONQUIL	*Denise Robins* 3/6
F.2182	LOVERS OF JANINE	*Denise Robins* 3/6
F.2241	THIS IS LOVE	*Denise Robins* 3/6
F.968	THE DOCTOR'S BRIDE	*Elizabeth Seifert* 3/6
F.1355	DOCTOR OF MERCY	*Elizabeth Seifert* 3/6
F.1394	SURGEON IN CHARGE	*Elizabeth Seif rt* 3/6
F.1482	A DOCTOR IN THE FAMILY	*Elizabeth Seifert* 3/6

F.2373	THE DOCTOR DARES	Elizabeth Seifert 5/-
F.2231	THE NEW DOCTOR	Elizabeth Seifert 4/-
F.2159	HARRIET HUME	Rebecca West 5/-

Science Fiction

F.1233	THE OCTOBER COUNTRY	Ray Bradbury 3/6
F.1234	THE SMALL ASSASSIN	Ray Bradbury 3/6
F.1803	STARSHIP TROOPERS	Robert Heinlein 5/-
F.2124	STRANGER IN A STRANGE LAND	Robert Heinlein 7/6

War

F.2423	STRIKE FROM THE SKY—THE BATTLE OF BRITAIN STORY	
		Alexander McKee 6/-
F.1686	EASTERN APPROACHES	Fitzroy Maclean 7/6
F.1875	THE LONGEST DAY (illustrated)	Cornelius Ryan 7/6
F.2146	THE LAST BATTLE (illustrated)	Cornelius Ryan 12/6
F.1270	THE RED BERET	Hilary St. George Saunders 5/-
F.1943	REPORT FROM No. 24	Gunnar Sonsteby 5/-
F.1084	THE GUNS OF AUGUST—AUGUST 1914	Barbara W. Tuchman 5/-
F.1880	END QUIET WAR	Hedger Wallace 5/-

Western

F.2134	AMBUSH	Luke Short 3/6
F.2135	CORONER CREEK	Luke Short 3/6
F.2142	THE ALAMO	Lon Tinkle 3/6
F.2063	THE SHADOW SHOOTER	W. C. Tuttle 3/6
F.2132	THE TROUBLE TRAILER	W. C. Tuttle 3/6
F.2133	MISSION RIVER JUSTICE	W. C. Tuttle 3/6
F.2180	SILVER BUCKSHOT	W. C. Tuttle 3/6

General

F.2420	THE SECOND SEX	Simone De Beauvoir 8/6
F.2117	NATURE OF THE SECOND SEX	Simone De Beauvoir 5/-
F.2234	SEX MANNERS FOR MEN	Robert Chantham 5/-
F.2060	SEX AND THE ADOLESCENT	Maxine Davis 5/-
F.2136	WOMEN	John Philip Lundin 5/-
F.2333	MISTRESSES	John Philip Lundin 5/-
F.2382	SECRET AND FORBIDDEN	Paul Tabori 8/6
U.2366	AN ABZ OF LOVE	Inge and Sten Hegeler 10/6
F.2374	SEX WITHOUT GUILT	Albert Ellis Ph.D. 8/6
F.2358	CANDY	Southern and Hoffenberg 10/6
F.2511	SEXUALIS '95	Jacques Sternberg 5/-

Mad

S.2955	A MAD LOOK AT OLD MOVIES	3/6
S.3523	BOILING MAD	4/6
S.3496	THE MAD ADVENTURES OF CAPTAIN KLUTZ	4/6
S.3158	THE QUESTIONABLE MAD	3/6
S.2385	FIGHTING MAD	3/6
S.3268	HOWLING MAD	3/6
S.3413	INDIGESTIBLE MAD	3/6

———————————————————————

NEL P.O. BOX 11, FALMOUTH, CORNWALL

Please send cheque or postal order. Allow 9d. per book to cover postage and packing (Overseas 1/– per book).

Name...

Address..

....

Title ....
(MARCH)